RENDEZVOUS WITH DESTINY

RENDEZVOUS
WITH
DESTINY

A
SAILOR'S WAR

Theodore C. Mason

NAVAL INSTITUTE PRESS
Annapolis, Maryland

Library of Congress Cataloging-in-Publication Data

Mason, Theodore C., 1921–

    Rendezvous with destiny : a sailor's war / Theodore C. Mason.

    p.   cm.

    ISBN 1-55750-580-2 (alk. paper)

    1. Mason, Theodore C., 1921–   . 2. World War, 1939–1945—Naval operations,
American. 3. United States. Navy—Biography. 4. World War, 1939–1945—Personal
narratives, American. 5. Sailors—United States—Biography. I. Title.

D773.M357   1997

940.54'5973—dc20   96-44138

Printed in the United States of America on acid-free paper ⊗

97 98 99 00 01 02 03 04   9 8 7 6 5 4 3 2

First printing

For Rita Jeannette Mason (née Bolduc)

Avec tout mon amour

Contents

Foreword

In his first book, *Battleship Sailor*, Ted Mason recalled his experiences on board the USS *California* on December 7, 1941. In this, the third segment of his World War II trilogy, a kind of summary, he takes us once again back to that "date that will live in infamy," adding details gleaned from sources other than his personal recollections and reflecting on how certain persons reacted to the cataclysm that descended on Pearl Harbor that day. He also picks up threads from his second book, *"We Will Stand by You": Serving in the* Pawnee, *1942–1945*, and carries the story through to his discharge from the Navy after the war. Along the way, he lets the reader in on slices of wartime experience seldom revealed: the task of "the little ships" that don't make the headlines; the terror that very ordinary people experience when other people seem bent on snuffing out one's existence; the tedium that makes up most of wartime, especially for those not on "the front line"—and often even for them.

Many, many books have been written about the battles of the Pacific phase of World War II. Biographies of top commanders abound. A few leaders have published memoirs. But the necessary, unheroic, humdrum experiences of ordinary "white hats," the enlisted men whose work makes battle or who make battle possible, have gone almost unheralded except in very general fashion. As the fiftieth anniversary of the Pearl Harbor attack has arrived and passed, however, more of the experiences of enlisted men has come into print. Ted Mason has contributed significantly to the story that will, inevitably, soon fall beyond our grasp as the veterans of that war go to their final rest. One can only hope that before the tribute, "Sleep, sailor. Rest your oar," is rendered to those surviving veterans, they will put their recollections on paper or tell them to some oral history project. The "Jack Nasty-Faces" of WWII deserve their chronicles as well as the Nelsons.

While Ted was going through Hell in the Paradise of the Pacific, my family and I were several thousand miles to the east of "Pearl" enjoying a day at the beach. "Dad" was Chief Boatswain's Mate Frank J. Battick, stationed at the Naval Air Station, San Juan, Puerto Rico, as Chief Master at Arms—the naval equivalent of Chief of Police. The family consisted of Dad, my Mom, Dorothy Otto Battick, my nine-year-old self and my baby sister, not quite five months old. After church that Sunday morning, Dad packed us in his "car," a Navy pickup truck, with lunch, beverages, a beach blanket, towels, etc., and drove to a deserted stretch of beach on the eastern shore of the island. There we were joined by another chief petty officer and his wife and spent the day enjoying the last moments of peace we would know for almost five years.

My father had joined the Navy back in the twenties, serving on the light cruiser *Marblehead* and the destroyer *Reuben James* with interspersed stretches of shore duty before being assigned to the USS *Augusta,* flagship of the Asiatic Fleet, in 1938. Mom and I joined him in China the following year, one of the very rare enlisted man's families to have ventured to a duty station so far out of the U.S. But in early 1941, all nonessential U.S. citizens were ordered out of China as U.S.-Japanese relations worsened. Shortly after we sailed for the States, Dad was transferred to NAS San Juan, and in due course, we followed him there.

Late in the afternoon of December 7, the beach party broke up and we headed back to our housing on the base. But this day Dad decided to swing by the Naval Radio Station to "cum-shaw" some sandwiches for supper—good Navy-type sandwiches on thick, hand-sliced bread with slabs of cold-cuts. He parked at the curb and he and I walked into the station mess hall. I can't recall just what the atmosphere was like in the mess hall, but I do remember someone shouting to Dad that "The Japs bombed Pearl Harbor! We're at war!" The men then plunged into a discussion of what details had come through, so I ran back to the truck and blurted out, "Mom, Mom, we're at war!" Kids don't really understand war and its manifold implications for themselves and society, so I was very puzzled when my mother started to cry.

By the fall of 1944, when Dad was transferred to NAS Barbers Point, Hawaii, I had acquired some appreciation of what war meant: All my uncles (eight) save one were in uniform, rationing had become a way of life along with scrap drives, War Bond drives, flags in windows with blue stars for service men and the occasional gold star for a serviceman who would not come back, and a tempo of unity and combined effort that this country has not seemed to experience since.

In January of 1946, Mom and we kids moved yet again, to join Dad at NAS BP, where he had arranged quarters on the base—the first enlisted family so accommodated there in the wake of V-J Day. A Navy transport ship brought us from San Francisco to Pearl Harbor, where we caught only suggestions of the havoc wrought by the Japanese over four years earlier. We did see a row of surrendered Japanese submarines at the Sub Base piers, our own first contact with "the enemy." Our welcome to Barbers Point was facilitated by the commanding officer, Capt. Virgil Childers Griffin, under whom my Dad had served at San Juan and again at NATTC, Norman, Oklahoma, for most of the war. Months before, the captain had indicated to my father that if he wished, he might convert an unused Quonset hut behind the civilian employees' recreation building into dependents' quarters and bring his family out to Hawaii. The captain also loaned his Navy sedan to bring us from the ship at Pearl, Dad's official vehicle being a Jeep and hardly suited for family transport in this situation.

After we got to our new home Dad had to return the captain's car. He drove off and returned in his Jeep. Almost within minutes, Captain Griffin's car reappeared. The captain came in and personally welcomed our family to the base. Thereafter, when my sister and I went without our parents to the movies on the base and the captain was in attendance, he would sometimes invite the two of us to sit with him in the front row of the officers' section of the base theater.

V. C. Griffin was one of the earliest naval aviators, earning his Wings of Gold during World War I. He was a Virginian of the old school, gallant and genteel to the ladies, kind to children, and ever concerned about the well-being of the men he commanded. He would not have been out of place in the Army of Northern Virginia under Robert E. Lee. His relationship with my father was not unusual in "The Old Navy," that small cadre of professionals who had weathered the storms of severe budget reductions in the twenties and early thirties while carrying out the difficult and ambivalent policies of the U.S. government in the Caribbean and the Pacific. In that environment, there often developed associations of mutual respect and reliance between officers and senior enlisted men so that by the middle of the war it was practically an axiom that when

Captain Griffin was ordered to take some new command, Dad would shortly receive orders to the same base as Chief Master at Arms or some other responsible capacity. And so it was that we settled in at NAS Barbers Point.

As the first "enlisted kid" on the base, I had virtually the run of the place. Soon other dependents moved in, mostly the children of officers for whom base housing had been prepared even before hostilities had ceased in the Pacific. Initially, as the oldest of this gang of Navy brats (fourteen), I was assigned duty as bus monitor in the vehicle that took us to and from the Navy-run school at Pearl Harbor, about a half-hour drive away. It was then that I first encountered the Navy's caste system against which Ted Mason occasionally has raised his pen. After one incident in which I was carrying out my assigned duty of maintaining order on the bus, another boy challenged me with "Who said you could boss officers' kids around?" I was flummoxed—the idea that he and I were somehow different had never occurred to me before. The matter was settled the next day when the boy's father, the executive officer of the air station, summoned me to his home and delivered a lecture in my presence to his son about my responsibilities and his, the son's, duty to obey my orders.

Over the next couple of years, as the base settled into peacetime routine and social structure, things began to change. A club was organized for teenagers on the base and for a while a room in the Officers' Club was set aside for our meetings, recreation, and social functions. But as the number of dependents on the base grew, the room became inadequate to serve us all. Then, the children of enlisted personnel ceased to be invited to social functions at the club. Nor were we welcomed at the officer's recreational swimming pool—we were to use the enlisted men's pool and the other recreation facilities on the base, not those set aside for officers and their families.

It made little real difference, as far I was concerned. As one of the older kids on base, I had many close friends among the officers' teenage children and so, as their guest, I continued to frequent the officers' pool, though barred from most functions at "the club." Captains' and commanders' sons and daughters were my classmates at school. The bus monitor job was terminated, to become the collective responsibility of all of the older kids, subject to reports of misbehavior by the bus driver for which we were once in a while reprimanded. The "rank bar" was seldom invoked on a day-to-day basis.

A bit later, during the Korean War, I chose to avoid the draft by going on active duty in the Naval Reserve as a white hat. Following boot camp at San Diego I was ordered to the Submarine School at New London, Connecticut, and after that joined a "boat" undergoing conversion and recommissioning at the Electric Boat Company shipyard in Groton. After shakedown, we joined the Atlantic Submarine Force based in New London and engaged in many training routines, cruises to foreign ports, and exercises with our own and NATO forces. My earlier ambitions for a Navy career had by then been altered and I was content to remain a non-rated seaman, i.e., near the bottom of the ladder, until my active-duty commitment had been fulfilled, at which point I intended to go back to college.

From life-long contact, I had a pretty good understanding of the relationship of enlisted personnel and officers: obedience to orders, attention to duty, respect upwards, consideration downwards, and to leadership based on all of this. In the close confines of a submarine, a certain loosening of shipboard distinction was permitted: officers uncovered (took off their hats) when passing through the crew's mess in other than inspection circumstances, and enlisted men passed through the forward battery compartment ("officers' country") uncovered, without loitering, except if on official errands. But on-watch conversation across the lines of rank was not unusual. White hats did not normally initiate conversation with officers, but it was understood that some of the latter were more approachable than others. Yet there were occasions when "class distinction" did crop up.

I was once reprimanded for having made a suggestion while on watch. "You're not paid to think!" was the exact put-down. A few moments later, the validity of my suggestion was abundantly proven, but no apology for the reprimand was given nor was recognition that I had been correct ever forthcoming. The officer in question later rose to the rank of vice admiral. On another occasion I prevented another officer from being seriously injured, perhaps even washed overboard, during a particularly nasty North Atlantic blow. Later, after we were both on "civvie street," that officer, son of an admiral, tried to get me hired as his assistant at the industrial firm where he was in charge of production. But my scores on a standard test of personal preferences were not appropriate, and so the quest was not achieved.

What I am getting at in this roundabout fashion is that naval personnel, whether enlisted or commissioned, are only human beings.

Humans come in all shapes and sizes, personalities and capabilities. Some are "good" leaders or followers, some are not. And while consistency of behavior is a desideratum, we most of us have our "off days." What makes the military environment different—or at least it did in my days and those of my father—is that officers have power over their subordinates that civilian bosses don't have. A fractious employee can be fired; a disobedient white hat can be penalized over a wide range of disciplinary options. An employee who doesn't like doing what the job requires can quit; an enlisted man has no legal choice. Class distinctions in the military traditionally are based upon the need for discipline, for obedience, which, on board a naval vessel, can determine whether or not the ship and her company fulfill their mission and/or survive (no one knows this better than submarine sailors and officers). But it is in the thoughtless, reckless application of the rights of rank that conflict arises between the ranks. When the power implicit in an officer's commission is used to demean a man, when RHIP ("rank hath its privileges") is taken to imply that one man is "better" than another, then the bonds of disciplined obedience become strained.

Captain Griffin, as far as I know, never gave an order, never made a comment that would embarrass or demean—it was not in the man. He and my father respected each other as individuals charged with different and important responsibilities in pursuit of a common good. Yet toward another officer whose conduct made my father's job virtually impossible to carry out after Captain Griffin had retired, Dad yearned to reply (but didn't) that "the President of the United States may have made you an officer, but you'll never be a gentleman as far as I am concerned." As a result, Dad retired from active duty after over twenty-three years of meritorious service and earning five Good Conduct Medals, lest, in his own words, "I punch the SOB and blow it all."

In a review of his second book, "We Will Stand by You," Ted Mason was taken bitterly to task for "whinging," i.e., whining, by presuming to berate his superiors whose knowledge and abilities far outstripped his presumed limited intelligence and his petty understanding of "the Navy way." Based upon my own experiences in and about the Navy, that reprimand was unjustified. Ted deals with his superior officers in his writings as he found them, and they were a mixed bag, as we all are. I sometimes remind those Naval ROTC midshipmen who take my naval history course, "At times in your careers as naval officers you will encounter an enlisted person who is smarter than you are. Don't insult that person or his or her intelligence. If he or she is 'out of line,' there are ways of straightening out the situation without personal insult. Your people are your most important assets. Your career, your life, may depend upon that person. You earn respect by showing it."

—John F. Battick, Ph.D.
University of Maine

Preface

There is properly no history, only biography.

—Ralph Waldo Emerson

Rendezvous with Destiny completes a trilogy of memoirs that began with *Battleship Sailor*, an account of my experiences in the *California* through the attack on Pearl Harbor, and continued with *"We Will Stand by You": Serving in the* Pawnee, *1942–1945*. This range of assignments, even if planned, could hardly have afforded more vivid contrasts. The present volume is a summing up of the last year of peace and the four years of war that followed, as seen through the eyes of a young enlisted man who joined the Naval Communication Reserve in 1939 and volunteered for active service with the fleet a year later.

Such memoirs are hardly worth the writing, or the publishing, unless they meet at least two criteria. The history of his time must have involved the writer in notable events. And he must respond to these experiences with revelations and insights that are more than an echo of the accounts of others who have gone to war and survived to tell of it. If I have succeeded in meeting these criteria, it has been achieved, at least in part, by greatly reducing the use of the first-person singular pronoun.

In addition to the above standards, any true account of man's savage propensity to kill his fellow man—whether set in World War II, Korea, Vietnam, the Persian Gulf, or the former Yugoslavia—must have a timeless quality. To survive combat is to receive a passing mark in the test of valor, foolish and wasteful as it is, that war represents. In my three memoirs, I have been at pains to pay tribute to those who went beyond the call of duty, from Pearl Harbor to the Luzon Strait, while pondering the necessity for it.

My two previous memoirs were tightly organized. In this one, I have opted to include elements of the picaresque in descriptions of both officers and enlisted men. I am also sharing substantial sections of three chapters with two officers whose accomplishments would otherwise fail to receive the attention I think they deserve. Their vignettes and war journals, written with candor and a judicious use of irony, bring a special quality to my account of life in the South Pacific Theater. My special thanks to Arthur G. King, M.D., and to the memory of Capt. Flavius J. George, USNR (Ret.).

Several shipmates of the *California* contributed to my early chapters, which culminate in the sinking of the ship at Pearl Harbor. Notable among them is T. R. Liles, who as a corporal of marines was a member of the ship's radio gang, and who later retired as a captain. Others are John H. McGoran, Robert H. "Rebel" Boulton, and M. D. "Murray" Penhollow.

Three others who made substantial contributions to my account of the attack were Capt. Victor Delano, USN (Ret.); Jesse E. Pond, Jr., editor of the *Newsletter* of the Pearl Harbor History Associates and author of *The Square Peg: A Tight Fit in a Tin Can;* and Leonard Marsden, then a quartermaster in the *Nevada.*

My chapters on the South Pacific profited from the assistance of Ted Blahnik, editor-director of the *Echoes* of the Guadalcanal Campaign Veterans and a survivor of the sinking of the storied light cruiser *Helena;* Richard "Dick" Hansen, a crewman in the fast minelayer *Gamble,* now historian of the Naval Minewarfare Association; and a *Pawnee* shipmate, the late Mike Penovich, a gunner's mate who wrote a charming account of our mascot, the cat V-6. And I must not forget three other *Pawnee* shipmates of stout heart: William J. Miller, I. J. H. "John" Day, and Le Roy E. Zahn.

From the USS *Houston* Association, Cleo B. Isom (now president of the association); John J. Skarzenski, the long-time secretary; and Kermit A. Lamm deserve special thanks for their help with my chapter on "CripDiv 1."

The chapter on my return from the Western Pacific to "The Civilian Navy" posed special problems, for very little has been written about the radio materiel schools that made such a substantial contribution to our victories at sea. I turned to the Old-Timer Communicators of Southern California and received the generous help of five outstanding men, graduates of the schools, who went on to long and successful careers as radio engineers. I regret that I could only skim the surface of a subject that surely merits book treatment. My warmest thanks to Charles Dane, Eugene Hildeman, Earl Marshall, William Nameny, and Leroy Nelson.

Additional help with my manuscript came from an old and treasured friend, David H. Jackson; another friend, John L. Whitmeyer, a quartermaster in the *Canberra* during the now-famous rescue of that heavy cruiser and the *Houston;* and my cousins, Douglas Boyd and June Boyd Conrad.

Paul Wilderson, executive editor of the Naval Institute Press, deserves a special, heartfelt thank-you for his encouragement and support, from the earliest planning stages through publication. Bruce Guthrie was most helpful as manuscript editor, suggesting several revisions that improved the work.

The public libraries of our nation are indeed public treasures, and their librarians universally helpful. I am especially indebted to the Kerr Library of Oregon State University, Corvallis; my local library, Driftwood of Lincoln City; the Detroit Public Library; and a corporate resource, the Research Center of the Henry Ford Museum & Greenfield Village, Dearborn. I also received valuable help from the Naval Historical Center, and the National Archives.

This is the place for the standard disclaimer. While many contributed to this memoir, the opinions I express are my own, unless otherwise noted. I made diligent efforts to be accurate as to fact, with the same exception I gave for *"We Will Stand by You."* In setting down dialogue, I have removed that most popular, all-purpose expletive in a sailor's vocabulary. Judging by what I read nowadays, many writers have no such compunction; but I believe it is possible to recapture the reality without giving offense.

Looking back at the labors and the toll they inevitably exact, one asks: Was it really worth it? One answer is that many writers on nautical subjects would be delighted to exchange their toil for a contract with the Naval Institute Press. Or one can turn to the justly renowned Dr. Samuel Johnson, who wrote: "Whatever withdraws us from the power of our senses; whatever makes the past, the distant, or the future, predominate over the present, advances us in the dignity of thinking beings."

Finally, the reward is more personal. As Shakespeare observes with his customary brilliance of insight and phrasing: "Things won are done; joy lies in the doing."

RENDEZVOUS WITH DESTINY

Mason and his battleship colleagues had sensed that they had an unwritten contract with the Navy and their officers. In exchange for their obedience, loyalty, and second-class shipboard citizenship, subject to stern regulations and sometimes harsh discipline, they believed their more privileged seniors would take care of them.

—Capt. Hugh Nott, in the *Naval War College Review,* 1983

1

Christmas of 1940

O what is that sound which so thrills the ear
Down in the valley drumming, drumming?

—W. H. Auden

The distant sounds of that December of 1940 were of war on three continents, but I ignored them. Boarding the M.V. *Kalakala* in Bremerton on this particular Saturday, I was much more interested in weekend liberty in Seattle.* I had been invited to join my *California* shipmate M. G. Daley and his girlfriend, Mary Jane, at her room in the Morrison Hotel.

From the Colman Dock at Pier 52, it was a brisk ten-minute walk to the seven-story, red-brick hotel. M. G. had introduced me to Mary Jane the previous weekend during a dance at Craven Recreation Center in the Puget Sound Navy Yard. I envied his good fortune in meeting such an attractive and charming young lady.

Mary Jane's room was more or less typical of the times, with a few feminine flourishes added. The double bed was covered with a pink chenille spread; in place of the usual chest of drawers was a vanity with the walnut veneer finish, rounded front edges, and accompanying round mirror popular in the late 1930s. Two sparsely upholstered, straight-backed chairs and the inevitable small writing table, inevitably scarred with cigarette burns and stained with condensation rings from countless highball glasses, completed the furnishings. Near the door to the tiny, white-tiled bathroom, the coils of the steam heater hissed and

---

*I described the life and times of the *Kalakala* in "The 'Flying Bird' of Puget Sound" (U.S. Naval Institute *Proceedings*, January 1984, p. 62).

gurgled. For 1940 it was not a bad room. It even had a view, for just across Jefferson Street was a small, triangular park with shrubbery and a blue-tiled reflecting pool.

A table-model radio with a speedometer-type tuning dial and five push-buttons was playing "San Antonio Rose" (pronounced San An-*TONE*), a current hit by Bob Wills and his Texas Playboys. On the table was a bottle of Ten High bourbon, along with ginger ale and a dented metal ice bucket. After Daley made drinks all around, the conversation begun at the Craven Center dance resumed. He and I occupied the two chairs, with Mary Jane seated demurely but slightly above us on the bed, her legs tucked under her, her shining brown hair falling to her shoulders.

This was no typical sailor's girl. Her features were delicate and refined, her voice low and pleasant, with no discernible accent. She had recently moved from Kansas City and was working as a secretary in Seattle. I was a little surprised that she was living, even temporarily while she hunted for an apartment, at the Morrison. It was not a "flea-bag," but it was a long way from a first-class hotel and was not at all averse to taking a sailor's money should he appear at 1 A.M. with a woman who obviously was not his wife. In later years her residence would have run up the yellow and black Interrogatory flag in my mind, and I would have tried to find out, discreetly, why a young woman so pretty and ingratiating was alone so far from home and staying at such a hotel. But, in that last season of our innocence, the young and the naive did not even consider asking such questions.

Having yet to learn another lesson, the advantages of dissemblance, I was soon telling Mary Jane about my lost love who had married a rival following a quarrel. She seemed interested. Leaning forward, she asked many perceptive questions about practical matters of job, money, children, future. Finally she held her glass out to Daley for a refill and asked: "Did you love her, Ted?"

If a man has been in love but once, and that at seventeen, he is certain it was the grandest passion since *Romeo and Juliet*. "Oh, yes. Of course."

Her quizzical look was chased by a smile. "I believe you. Yes, I think you're capable of it. Unlike most men."

Perhaps she, too, had a lost love. At her request we drank a toast to "real, true love." We were solemn for a moment, but soon were laughing and singing along with "You Are My Sunshine" on the radio. It all seemed like perfectly good fun. But in the fashion of one lass with two lads, Mary Jane was directing most of her glances and smiles at one of us; and I was the one.

My friend was either unaware of these undercurrents or was unconcerned about them. So much so that he finished his drink and said he had some errands to run—a new supply of writer's and Western magazines to pick up at the G & G cigar store in the nearby Smith Tower—and would be back in an hour or so.

"Sit over here, Ted, where we can talk," Mary Jane directed, indicating Daley's vacated chair next to the bed. She was looking at me in a way that could be interpreted either as sisterly friendship or as subtle challenge.

"You know, you're very fortunate you didn't marry your little Dust Bowl refugee from Oklahoma," she continued, shifting to a more comfortable position. "She's the kind who will have children, lots of children. That will make her old, while you're still young and handsome.

"You mark my words. You'll go home some day and see her, and you'll think: 'My God!' Oh, Ted. Now you have the chance to meet other women, and to learn many things. I'm so happy for you—and you should be, too."

Mary Jane was the only woman I had met recently. Was she interested in being my adviser, or in teaching me some of those things I hadn't yet learned? I decided I had better find out.

"I would be happy, if I'd been as lucky as M. G. and met someone like you."

She smiled, a smile of infinite possibilities. "Maybe you have, Ted."

Now I knew, or thought I did. And I wrestled with my conscience, like Jacob with his angel. Women like Mary Jane, who were both desirable and available, were always in short supply in a Navy town. With such a teacher, a host of eager sailors would volunteer for instruction. Why not be the first?

For the best reason in the world, I reminded myself sternly. She was my buddy's girlfriend. Even if I thought he soon would be odd man out, I could not stay in the game.

I forced a smile. "Yes, I sure wish I had met you first." And turned the conversation to lighter subjects until Daley returned half an hour later.

I escaped the infinite possibilities of the red-brick Morrison Hotel and went looking for other members of the *California* radio gang, pursuing

Navy girls in some sailors' hangout on First or Second Avenue. Just in time, I had remembered how important shipmates are to a man-o-war's man.

Perhaps to any man.

Hard by the navy yard's main gate, at the corner of Washington Avenue and First Street, was the five-story Navy YMCA, built in 1919, enlarged in 1924, and now chock-full of young sailors from the expanding fleet and a growing number of shipyard workers. An express purpose of the "Y" was to offer wholesome alternatives to the enticements available at a price (sometimes a very high price) in sinful Bremerton and Seattle.

On the third through fifth floors the Y had sleeping accommodations for about eighty men in small, sparsely furnished single and double rooms. Most were reserved for sailors and the Shore Patrol; a few were rented by the week to properly accredited shipyard workers. There were no elevators; the heads were down the hall on each floor.

On the second floor were a gymnasium, a spacious "social room" with bandstand, meeting rooms, a locker club for stowing civilian clothes, and a dormitory where a cot could be rented for forty cents. All the cots were usually gone by early evening.

The lobby offered attractions that were commonplace then but are collector's items today: writing desks inset with real inkwells (the ballpoint pen being some years in the future); an upright piano, old even in 1940; one of the first coin-operated machine-gun devices; an apple machine that disgorged anywhere from zero to two Washington Delicious apples for a nickel.

Off the lobby were an eight-table pool room and a servicemen's lounge lined with well-worn armchairs, where a fire was usually crackling in a large fireplace and some musically gifted sailor might be softly playing a baby-grand piano. One flight down was the swimming pool, four lanes wide by twenty yards long, and workout rooms for weight-lifting and boxing.

Except for the sleeping accommodations and the locker club, most of these services were duplicated, if not exceeded, at Craven Recreation center, named for the friend of the enlisted man who had acquired and dedicated it in 1937, former Navy Yard Commandant T. T. "Tireless Tom" Craven. The fleet athletic field nearby offered a football gridiron, baseball and softball diamonds, and eight tennis courts. They were popular in summertime but largely unused while my ship was there; during the rainy Puget Sound winters, sane men confined themselves to indoor amusements.

But all these facilities were inside the navy yard, subject to service regulations and discipline, and the Y was outside, if only by a block. The latter made every effort to live up to its advertised slogan: "A home away from home for men of the Fleet visiting Bremerton." Many of these men were very young, some only a few weeks out of boot camp, and badly needed a zone of transition between their two worlds. At the Y, with only the occasional presence of the Shore Patrol a distraction, they could play pool or take a swim, write letters home, enter a checkers or chess tournament, meet a young lady (well-chaperoned, to be sure) at a square dance ("dancing teacher in attendance"), and, if so inclined (and a handful were), sing in a chorus or attend Bible class.

Generally speaking, seamen and firemen went to the YMCA. The petty officers preferred Craven Center, which had two enormous advantages: undress blues and beer. Their opinions of the letter-writers, pool players and square dancers can be summarized: "Goddam mama's boys—need someone to hold their hand!"

There was another reason why the "mama's boys" seldom stopped at Craven Center, except to attend the ships' dances, or ventured past Washington and First: a matter of economics. Their pay of $36 a month would finance few "beer busts" at the rec center, even at ten cents a bottle, and far fewer in Bremerton, where prices were double that or more.

While exploring the Navy YMCA on a research trip to Bremerton I uncovered, in a second-floor storage room, some primary source material which brought turbulent memories of that last full year of peace flittering back, ghosts of the unredeemable past. It was a five–by–eight-inch hardbound notebook with the title "The Log 2" inked across the cover.

It proved to be a handwritten journal kept by the YMCA desk clerks in late 1940 and early 1941 in the fashion of a quartermaster's rough log. Prosaically written half a dozen hands, "Log 2" paints a more intimate and revealing portrait of Bremerton as it was in those years than any amount of library research or dozens of letters and tape-recorded conversations with old sailors could capture. In the following excerpts I have provided nothing but the subject-matter headings and a brief introduction. My comments appear in brackets.

"Disturbances, Accidents or Other Calamities"

The lives of YMCA desk clerks had a good deal in common with the enlisted men they served. They were poorly paid, often overworked, and were subject to a great deal of harassment, particularly on their evening and midnight "watches." Their identification with the Navy is further revealed by their use of service slang.

11-3-40. The apple machine is out of order again. At times the machine gives two apples for one nickel. . . . The Machine Gun device needs repairing.

Sunday—Nov. 10-40. Reported for duty at 11:30 P.M., 11-9-40. . . . Lobby full and running over—40 to 50 men in lobby all night[,] 123 cots rented and of course all rooms taken early. I had to quell a near fight in lobby among the Sailors—we finally got them quieted down and dispersed with no damage.

11-30-40. Very busy day. Checkroom flooded with P. Coats[,] had to use T.S.L. for coat storage. Lobby crowded during movie. Lucky Strike & Camel cigarettes sold very well. Pool Room very busy but not very crowded late in evening. Sailors well satisfied with football score of Army & Navy Game. That is all. J.F.

[On 30 November, Navy defeated Army, 14-0, before 102,000 spectators at Municipal Stadium in Philadelphia.]

12-11-40. Started out with a bang. U.S.S. Tennessee had 1:00 liberty, . . . Lobby quite full, ping pong going strong. Wrapping table is being used quite a bit. We've had a couple of virtuosos playing the piano[,] there's one of them that's pretty good. . . .

Tuesday 12-31-40. . . . Some of the Arizona men over early with a 72 [72-hour liberty] over New Years. . . .

Monday Jan. 6-41. . . . No disturbances, accidents or other calamities to report. 9 men in Lobby all nite—no one allowed to sleep on floor or park on Pool tables which is strictly forbidden. . . .

Monday 1-31-41. *Another beautiful day.* . . . usual Mon. morning run of salesmen & new Navy Yard workmen looking for places to stay. . . .

1-31-41. Fairly busy evening—Probably be a good weekend, the California was paid today. . . .

[My ship returned to Puget Sound on 24 January. The ship's log, not untypically, makes no mention of paying the crew.]

Crime and Punishment

As always, there were a few civilians who visited the YMCA to prey on sleeping or intoxicated enlisted men. They were kept under close observation by the desk clerks, who did not hesitate to call the police. The solicitude of the Y employees for the welfare of their young guests (and their country) comes through quite clearly in these entries:

Sunday Dec. 15/40. . . . The Chief Shore Patrol Officers [sic] came in & made a clean up on all the service men in Main Lobby and sent them back to their ships altho they were all quiet—most of them fast asleep and none mis-behaving.

12-16-40. . . . Had an explanation about S.P.'s clearing lobby last night. The officers claim that the men are degraded to the level of bums when they don't buy a room but sleep on the floor instead. They also claim S.P. discipline is too lax so the S.P.'s are becoming stricter. We are requested to call them at the slightest disorder. . . .

[The reluctance of these men to return to their ships speaks volumes about the oppressive disciplinary atmosphere in some battleships, carriers, and cruisers of that time, as well as the poor heating and ventilation. Together, they provided the strong motivation that made men prefer a lobby chair or sofa to bunks in their own ships.]

12-17-40. . . . Two civilians were seen looting the pockets of sleeping sailors. Call[ed] police and had the two men picked up. Busy evening. . . .

1/12/41. . . . A fellow in the Army wrote his relatives in Switzerland a card this morning. He wrote in German telling them he was near Canadian border. . . .

[At this time Germany was master of Europe; many were expecting the fall of England. The alert desk clerk can be forgiven for being somewhat suspicious of a card written in German. No doubt he reported the incident to the police and the Shore Patrol.]

Friday Jan. 17-41. . . . 9 men in Lobby [including] 4 servicemen. Old faces conspicuous for their absence after the Police warning of pick-up. . . .

1-18-41. . . . Had to call S.P. headquarters this evening to have them pick up a sick sailor[;] he had just been let out of the hospital and was too weak to get around. . . . [In those days it was a good deal easier to get off the Sick List than on it.]

Scuttlebutt

In what was essentially still a peacetime Navy, sailors talked quite freely about the movements of their ships. The desk clerks noted any scuttlebutt that pertained to the operation of the Y, especially its financial well-being. Most of it was surprisingly accurate.

12-4-40. . . . Have information that the Maryland & West Virginia are leaving port the tenth of December. Pennsylvania is expected to leave the twenty-seventh of December. . . .

[At 0630 on 10 December *Maryland, West Virginia,* and *Colorado*—Battleship Division Four—departed the Navy Yard. On 27 December, *Pennsylvania* remained at Puget Sound, but *California* and *Tennessee* got under way for Long Beach at 0659 and 0715, respectively.]

12-6-40. . . . Three ships in today—so far. B.E.F.

[On 6 December *California, Tennessee* and *Enterprise* all stood into Puget Sound.]

12-6-40. With three ships arriving and all getting early liberty, we had a very busy afternoon[,] pool tables busy all the time. Apples both in machine and on counter. Machine sold out at 10:00. . . .

12-26-40. . . . Check outs today are: #205, #207, #413, #423, #501, #523 & #533—all of the USS California which is due to check out soon. . . .

[*California* and *Tennessee* "checked out" the following morning.]

12-27-40. Very quiet today. With 4,000 sailors gone the place is absolutely dead. Pool room and canteen very quiet. Still on first sheet of room register. Lots of kids wanting to play pool. Checkers, ping-pong and Acey-deucy checked out most of the day. . . .

12-29-40. . . . Enterprise leaves in morning[,] the town will be deader than ever. Sing-song and church party well attended considering the lack of men. . . .

2-3-41. . . . Fairly busy evening due to Saratoga payday.—Nevada gets paid tomorrow & Lexington is due to arrive in Yard. . . .

Saturday 2-15-41. Quite busy today—Lexington had 9 o'clock liberty. Incidentally, the scuttlebutt is that the Lex. will be leaving us very soon—perhaps next week.

[The *Lexington* departed Puget Sound on 20 February.]

Miscellaneous Intelligence

A reasonably astute observer can learn a good deal about the 1940–41 Navy and its times by a careful perusal of the desk-clerk entries:

Wednesday Nov. 20. . . . Mr. Jaksch of the West Virginia rented 205 for week. He drives for Admiral Pye and desk is requested to call him whenever phone call comes in. . . .

[At that time Vice Adm. W. S. Pye was Commander Battleships, Battle Force, with his three-starred flag in the *West Virginia*. Note that his enlisted driver rates a "Mister." Admiral Pye soon fleeted up to Commander Battle Force, with his flag in the *California*.]

Monday Nov. 25, 1940. . . . U.S.S. Colorado men came in 10 am to 11 am using swimming pool for qualifying men. 19 men in group. . . .

[Incredible as it seems today, many sailors of that era didn't know how to swim. The Navy was supposed to teach them in boot camp, but the program was honored as much in the breach as in the observance. These nineteen men from the *Colorado* probably represented only those of the ship's company who admitted they couldn't swim.]

1-20-41. . . . Quite a commotion in Washington D.C. this am. We had Inauguration Proceedings on the radio in Lobby. . . .

[President Franklin D. Roosevelt was inaugurated for a third term on 20 January 1941.]

Tuesday Jan 21-41.... In case of intoxication and a call is slated—don't forget to put a Dr. abbreviation for Drunk following the room number....

1-24-41. . . . Mr. Richmond in Room 525 checked out after being here only 2 days on perm. card. Charged him 75¢ per day.

[One wonders whether it was good fortune or ill that prompted Mr. Richmond to check out so soon after he had gone to the trouble of getting a permanent card. In any event, he paid the full daily rate rather than the lesser weekly or monthly one.]

Mon. 2-24-41. Shore Patrol men in 417 asking for lamp & writing desk— can do?————152 recruits in for [physical] exams. Taken care of in Social Room....

[The two Shore Patrol petty officers in Room 417 were from the *California*. They were still requesting a desk and lamp the next day. Such amenities were not to be taken for granted in a YMCA room. The physical examinations of incoming boots were primarily "short-arm" inspections to detect venereal disease. It seems singularly appropriate that they were conducted in the "Social Room."]

For the first time in more than a decade, the streets of Bremerton and Seattle were thronged with Christmas shoppers. President Roosevelt had been elected to an unprecedented third term the month before on a pledge of "no foreign wars"; nonetheless, the country's first peacetime draft had been passed by Congress, and our moribund heavy industry was retooling for war production, hiring three million new workers. At the Boeing Aircraft plant in Seattle, 7,500 men were working three shifts building B-17 "Flying Fortress" bombers. At the Puget Sound Navy Yard, employment had swollen to 10,000 workers.

The Christmas advertisements in the Seattle *Post-Intelligencer* of Sunday, 1 December 1940, reflected the new prosperity.

"A Lane Chest for *HER* Christmas," a full-page ad by Schoenfelds' Standard Furniture Company trumpeted. For $29.75 (only $1 a week), one could buy an "exquisite matched walnut-veneered chest . . . lined with aromatic red Tennessee cedar . . . to gladden her heart on Christmas morning."

For *his* Christmas, Klopfenstein's suggested "First Nighter Pajamas by Weldon." The copywriter made up for certain deficiencies in grammar and logic by the sheer exuberance he or she projected. "It [*sic*] has a crew neck pull-over of soft mercerized Balbriggan . . . slack trousers of dark broadcloth, pockets & all. Just the thing for snoozing, cruising, lounging & musing. $2.50."

Sears Roebuck and Co. suggested "A practical gift! . . . for the man who does things . . . working or sporting!" It was a double-breasted wool Mackinaw windbreaker for $4.98. "An actual $6.95 value!" Sears promised.

"Royal Purples!" another Sears headline proclaimed. These turned out to be "pure silk hosiery" in "new colors for winter" at 55¢ a pair, or two pairs for $1.00. "Limit, 4 pair to a customer!" the copy warned.

For those of a truly practical mind, a "Big Deluxe Frigidaire" was on special at Grunbaum Bros. for $139.95. A "perfectly rebuilt Electrolux (tank-type) vacuum cleaner" was only $18.95 at Sun Vacuum Stores.

A "4-Star 10-tube Deluxe Silvertone console" with five broadcast bands, nine push buttons, and an electric tuning eye could be picked up at Sears for $74.95 ($5 down). "Another windfall for homemakers!" announced by Sears was a three-piece bedroom set—five-drawer chest, vanity and mirror—for only $59.98. And a Kenmore Gold Seal Washer with a "turret-type tub, completely shrouded wringer with bar release . . . hand-high clutch and quick-emptying drain" was on special at any of the four Sears stores in Seattle and Bremerton for $59.95.

Newly affluent shipyard and aircraft workers, many of whom had to drive long distances because of a housing shortage that would soon get much worse, could buy a brand-new Pontiac Streamliner "Torpedo" Six sedan coupe for $923 ($25 more for an eight-cylinder engine).

Paddock-Belcourt, the Seattle Studebaker distributor with locations at 501 East Pike, 1703 Broadway, and 2100 Seventh Avenue, advertised some bargains in used cars: a '39 Plymouth DeLuxe "touring sedan" with radio and heater for $665; a '38 Studebaker Commander sedan with radio, heater, and overdrive, $695; and a '36 Ford touring sedan with radio for $365.

Where there are winners there are always losers. In the "Agony" column of the classified ads, a desperate owner placed this message:

EQUITY '34 Plymouth 4-door sedan,
Value $110. Trade, sell. ME 9350.

Under the "Help wanted—Men" category, an ad headed "AIRPLANE CONSTRUCTION" delineated the new opportunities in defense work:

1,000 men placed this year; over 400 men placed in Major Aircraft Factories in Sept. and Oct. Aviation means a permanent career and defense of our Country. Take your training where you will be placed in employment in 8 to 12 weeks if you have the qualifications; 60% of the Factories, the recognized Schools and expert instructions are located in Southern California. Part tuition paid after employment; work out board and room if necessary. When you can get expert recognized training, DO NOT accept anything else. Call or write Anderson Airplane Schools, Administration Bldg., Boeing Airport, Seattle. Open Sundays.

Turning to the main news section, prospective home buyers might have noticed this ad:

Open today—Brick, $3,850, in beautiful Jefferson Park, 5 rooms, large unfinished attic, thoroughly reconditioned, hardwood, mahogany, tile, fireplace, etc. See Classification 60, P.-I Want Ads.

Finally, a brief news item made it perfectly clear how draft dodgers were dealt with in 1940:

Not Mad at Nazis, Says Draft Evader

CHICAGO, Nov. 30—(AP)—Policeman Milton Bass said today that Thomas Reed had admitted that he failed to register for selective service because:
"I'm not mad at Germany."
Reed was turned over to the Federal bureau of investigation.

But all this evidence of rearmament prosperity meant little to me. After five months in the Navy I had lost any but nostalgic identification with the civilian world, but I was yet to be accepted in the Battleship Navy. I was looked down upon and often harassed by the Regulars as a "feather merchant" who hadn't earned the third-class crow (rating insignia) he was wearing. As I struggled with a recurring depression, I asked myself: What am I doing here in a battlewagon that's as noisy as a boiler factory by day and as cold as a tomb at night, with a sundowner Acting C.O. who seems to think war could break out at any moment?

The question was not difficult to answer. A child of divorce and subsequent adoption, I grew up near Placerville, California, in a tin-roofed shack with no electricity or running water and a "Chic Sale" privy in the back yard. I was graduated from El Dorado County High School in 1938 into a world that offered neither scholarships for college nor employment with any future. While working at a variety of jobs that called for considerable brawn but few brains, I joined the V-3 Naval Communication Reserve in June 1939. A year later my high-school pal Floyd C. "Bill" Fisher and I volunteered for a year's active duty with the fleet. Following abbreviated boot camp and radio school at San Diego Naval Training Station, we reported aboard the *California* at Pearl Harbor on 12 October 1940. Our ship was soon under way for Long Beach and then on to Bremerton for her annual yard overhaul at Puget Sound.

With the *California* moored at the navy yard's Berth 6-D, the main engines and boilers had been secured and we were receiving electricity, fresh water, and other essential services from dockside umbilical cords. But not even the disruption caused by the yardbirds (shipyard employees) was permitted to postpone a naval custom treasured by the senior officers, if not the enlisted men—the Saturday personnel inspection.

On the chill gray morning of 21 December 1940, the 1,200 men of the *California* were mustered on the quarterdeck. We were in dress blues and the rakish flat hats that still bore, a sign of peacetime, the ship's name on the ribbon across the brim.

But this inspection was different. It was being conducted by Comdr. Robert B. Carney rather than by the skipper, Capt. Harold M. Bemis.

"What gives?" we junior petty offices of the CD (radio) division asked each other as we stood at parade rest. "Since when does an exec conduct a captain's inspection?"

"This ain't no captain's inspection," a radioman first with hashmarks informed us. "If you ever read the plan of the day, you'd know it's a 'commanding officer's inspection.' Bemis is in the hospital. That makes the exec the acting C.O."

"Why is he so inspection happy? Can't he wait until the old man returns?"

"He won't be back. This inspection proves it. Carney wants all you boots and V-3s to know who's in charge now."

Carney soon emerged from the wardroom through the quarter-deck hatch, followed by the usual retinue of department and division officers, the chief master-at-arms, and a chief yeoman with his notebook. As the crew was called to attention, I muttered my usual prayer that the brass would pay me no heed.

In the presence of the hard-faced Carney, the prayer was more fervent than usual. The energy and ambition that were propelling him toward the naval heights as Chief of Naval Operations were well known to the crew, especially among the unfortunates who caught his baleful eye. Carney was an officer who did not look at enlisted men; he looked through them.

I had recently seen an example at a captain's inspection in Pearl Harbor. Captain Bemis and a visiting admiral paused before a third-class radioman of the V-3 Communication Reserve wearing white shorts which were a noticeable "tattletale gray." The man was put on report. Carney seemed enraged by the petty officer's failure to meet the flagship's standards of cleanliness and military bearing. Falling out of the inspection party, he stood eyeball to eyeball with the man and, red-faced, reamed him out in front of the entire ship's company. I had never heard one man so abuse another in a public humiliation the victim was powerless to prevent. The petty officer requested, and was speedily granted, a transfer to another ship.

Thereafter I viewed Carney, whom I saw occasionally as he made his ceaseless rounds of the ship, with trepidation. As I wrote in *Battleship Sailor:* "In my immature and dramatic fancy, Carney was a hot-eyed Calvin of execs, a burn-em-at-the-stake Savonarola, and only strict orthodoxy could save one from a possible inquisition." *

On Monday morning we learned that the senior first had been right. Bemis returned to the ship, but for only two hours. He was detached for duty as commandant of the Sixteenth Naval District at Cavite in the Philippines. What seemed a promotion was hardly that, I learned from a man who had been there. The Philippines were considered a place of slumbrous shore duty for overage and infirm officers awaiting retirement. This view was not shared by Adm. Thomas C. Hart, commander of the Asiatic Fleet—really a squadron comprised of the South China Patrol of nineteen destroyers, the Yangtze River Gunboat Flotilla, twelve submarines, and a few auxiliaries. With the exception of Hart's flagship, the heavy cruiser *Houston,* the ships were mostly as overage and infirm as the Sixteenth District officers. Bemis was soon returned to the States, where he served as assistant commandant of the Puget Sound Navy Yard through the war years, retiring as a rear admiral.

Later, when I could view the events on board the *California* that

---

* *Battleship Sailor* (Annapolis, Md.: Naval Institute Press, 1982), p. 111.

December morning more objectively, I saw that the change in command could be considered a metaphor. In late 1940 the Navy was undergoing a sea change, a transition from a peacetime service that had seen little action since World War I (and even the combat operations of the "Great War" were limited mostly to convoy duty) to one fleeting up for war. An officer aflame with ambition and preparing himself for the global conflict which lay ahead had replaced an ailing peacetime captain nearing retirement.

In a country struggling to recover from the most devastating depression in history—one which had left, as President Franklin D. Roosevelt said, "one-third of a nation ill-housed, ill-clad, ill-nourished"—the Navy's road to rearmament was slow and grudgingly funded. Of necessity, most Americans had been focusing on internal necessities of survival and jobs. They were reluctant to be drawn into the incessant quarrels of European countries that, with the exception of little Finland, had yet to repay us for the debts incurred during World War I. As for Asia, it was largely ignored, even after Japanese dive bombers sank the gunboat USS *Panay* on the Yangtze River near Nanking on 12 December 1937. The Roosevelt administration was looking across the Atlantic, not the Pacific, as it tried to mobilize public opinion toward saving England, the last beleaguered bastion of Western civilization, now in serious danger of falling to the Nazi war machine.

But the *California*'s course was west-southwest, to Pearl Harbor.

2

"Impregnable Pearl Harbor"

Ignorance is preferable to error; and he is less remote from the truth who believes nothing, than he who believes what is wrong.

—Thomas Jefferson

Opening his campaign against Republican Alf Landon at Franklin Field, Philadelphia, on 27 June 1936, President Roosevelt said:

"There is a mysterious cycle in human events. To some generations much is given. Of other generations much is expected. This generation has a rendezvous with destiny."

As the *California* departed San Francisco for Pearl Harbor in early April 1941, his words had an ominous ring for those few of us who remembered them, and the even fewer who understood them. When politicians deliver such ringing phrases, they usually spell trouble ahead for the citizenry. But most of us chose to leave the deep thinking to our leaders, civilian and military.

Of more immediate concern were recent changes in shipboard command. On the last day of 1940, our acting commanding officer was relieved by Capt. Joel W. Bunkley, a replacement for which we soon found no reason to thank Rear Adm. Chester W. Nimitz, Chief of the Bureau of Navigation (really the Naval Personnel Bureau), who was responsible for the assignments of all officers. Bunkley was a member of the "gun club" who had come to us from command of a naval ammunition depot. His command experience was limited to old four-piper destroyers; he hadn't served in a battleship since he was assistant gunnery officer of the since-demilitarized *Wyoming* in 1915. We quickly learned that his concepts of discipline went back much further than that: to William Bligh, commander of HMS *Bounty,* some of us thought.

16

His captain's masts soon filled the brig and kept the courts-martial boards busy.

For this transit to Pearl Harbor, we also had a new executive officer. In March Commander Carney had been ordered to Washington for duty with the Chief of Naval Operations; his replacement was Comdr. Earl E. Stone. And we had a civilian on board. He was Walter Davenport, writer and senior editor for *Collier's* magazine, who had been cleared by the Navy Department to write an article about Pearl Harbor.

I looked forward with great interest to Davenport's article, which appeared in the 14 June 1941 issue of the mass-circulation magazine. I bought a copy for five cents at the Ship's Service store and read the article with wonder and increasing astonishment. It was written in a kind of pseudo-tough-guy style, a potpourri of several schools of hard-boiled fiction, with a dash of Damon Runyun sprinkled in for seasoning. "Impregnable Pearl Harbor" was inaccurate as to fact, larded with exaggeration, reeking with coarse and offensive prejudice.

The distortions began with the description of our trip to Pearl Harbor. Except for a near collision with one of the President liners when, with a new navigator who apparently had trouble reading a chart, we steamed down the wrong side of the channel leaving San Francisco, the voyage was uneventful. Davenport did not find it so:

> We were westbound on an American battleship, two days out of Pearl Harbor. . . .
>
> A Jap—a tanker of perhaps six thousand tons— . . . appeared eastbound on the horizon, about fifteen miles dead ahead, directly on our course. And there she stopped, or slowed down to a crawl. . . .
>
> We'd have done the moving over and our dignity would have done a nose dive had the pig boat not arrived at that tense moment. . . . She was a Yankee—one of the new pig boats, a big black murderer. We could have kissed her—and her 21-inch torpedoes. That's how thump-thump we were.
>
> Being no sailor, we don't know what that Jap oilcan did in technical terms. But in our landsman eyes it literally spun on its narrow tail and got going. . . . Then [the submarine] submerged again, going east with the Jap.*

I was puzzled. If any such tense confrontation occurred, I would have heard the scuttlebutt. No one I talked to remembered any such incident.

*Walter Davenport, "Impregnable Pearl Harbor," *Collier's*, 14 June 1941, pp. 76–77.

An unarmed Japanese tanker making a battleship go "thump-thump"? That was good for a big laugh. To be sure, a couple of days out of San Francisco we had routinely answered the dip of a Japanese tanker that had passed close by on an opposite course. About the same time we sighted one of our subs, also on an eastward course. But there was nothing unusual about that; we were on one of the long-established West Coast-to-Oahu sea lanes. The consensus was that Davenport had invented a sea story for the Jap-haters back home.

Some years later I had an opportunity to check the ship's deck logs, looking for evidence of this encounter. What I found lacked any of the drama of Davenport's breathless account:

12 to 16: Steaming as before on course 245° T., 227° psc., standard speed fifteen (15) knots, steaming at sixteen (16) knots. 1208 cut #2 boiler in on the main steam line. 1217 changed speed to sixteen point five (16.5) knots. 1231 changed speed to seventeen (17) knots. 1245 sighted unidentified vessel, hull down, bearing 229° .5 T., distance estimated fifteen (15) miles on converging course. 1300 set condition of readiness Yoke in Group VIII . . . . 1330 Main and Secondary Batteries conducting director check . . . . 1355 sighted submarine bearing 265° .5 T., distance ten (10) miles on opposite course, passing well clear. Identified as U.S.S. ARGONAUT #166. 1423 answered dip to vessel previously reported bearing 229° .5 T., identified as Japanese Oil Tanker S.S. TATIRAMA MARU. 1437 shifted steering to main steering. 1452 shifted steering back to bridge. 1532 sounded secure from Condition Yoke in Group VIII. Completed director check Main and Secondary batteries.*

It was pure coincidence that we sighted an unidentified vessel shortly before Condition Yoke was set in one of the dozen or so readiness sections into which the ship was divided. Thirteen hundred hours was a normal time to commence one of these routine checks of the ship's water-tight integrity.

The director checks of the main and secondary batteries also were routine. The horizon was used for aligning directors in elevation, but a distant object was required to line up in train. If the directors hadn't been checked recently, they were often manned to take advantage of the presence of a passing ship. That apparently was what happened on this April afternoon.

Steering control would not have been shifted from the bridge to the main steering station had there been any concern about the Japanese

*Log of USS *California*, 14 April 1941.

tanker. Steering was shifted once a watch for drill. Since there was always a possibility that an electrical circuit would fail, leading to a steering crisis, this maneuver was not attempted if the ship was in any danger.

The presence of the *Argonaut*, too, may have been happenstance. More likely, she was using a chance encounter with the tanker to practice submerged torpedo approaches, a standard procedure then as now.

Obviously, Davenport had tried to fabricate a minor international incident from the scantiest of materials. He was just warming to his subject, describing a Honolulu and Oahu I could scarcely recognize:

We're sitting in Lousy Lui's on the two-bit end of the beach at Waikiki. We're drinking beer and talking Jap. Everybody in Honolulu talks Jap from the moment he opens his eyes upon Hawaii's jasmined morning until he turns in beneath the huge gloom of the semi-tropical night. . . .

Lousy Lui's is owned by a Jap. . . . Every civilian is suspect. He may be a spy, a stool, an intelligence officer, an espionage agent or counterespionage. . . . The enlisted men lump them all together and call them the Gestapo.*

In a blend of fact and fancy, Davenport notes that "Lui" was born in the Territory of Hawaii and is therefore an American citizen. But since his parents were born in Japan, he is a citizen of that country too and subject to Japanese law regarding traitors. Under the "they say" category, Davenport offers the scuttlebutt that Lui may be an officer in Japan's military intelligence. He states without qualification that people of all sorts and conditions—a rainbow of races and colors, from prostitutes through beachcombers and bartenders to Navy wives—are involved in the pervasive spying. In an excess of chauvinism, he describes the Chinese as "Chinks," the French as "Frogs," and the English as "Limeys." Natives of Brooklyn are treated rather more kindly, being labeled one and all as "Dodgers." This was long before the city lost its baseball team to Los Angeles.

The subhead to Davenport's article claimed that he had "talked with three admirals," as well as "boatloads of bosuns and their mates." This is how he interpreted what they told him:

Day and night, Navy and Army planes are droning down the warm skies in circles two hundred, five hundred, a thousand miles wide. . . . The defenses of Hawaii may not be impregnable. . . . But neither

---

*"Impregnable Pearl Harbor," pp. 11–12. There was, of course, no Lousy Lui's in Waikiki. He probably was referring to Lau Yee Chai's, a popular Chinese restaurant. Navy enlisted men parodied the name as "Lousy Chow's."

the Army nor the Navy believes that there is any power or combination of powers existing today that can prove it in the islands.*

The many misstatements in this inflammatory article would be devastatingly revealed six months later. If the military and political authorities thought they were warning off the Japanese by sanctioning Davenport's account of the state of readiness on Oahu and at Pearl Harbor, they were grievously wrong. The Japanese operated an efficient spy system from their consulate that kept them informed as to the actual state of readiness on the island. Davenport's article must have afforded the spymasters some amusement. As for the American public, it would soon learn that truth is not just the first casualty in war; it is often sacrificed in preparations for war.

The best short description of Pearl Harbor I heard in that summer of 1941 was supplied by a young leading seaman from the British dreadnought *Warspite:* "This bloody awful hole."

We had exchanged ship visits (described in *Battleship Sailor,* pp. 164–68) when *Warspite* paid a visit to the new home port of the Pacific Fleet in July. The gallant survivor of the epic Battle of Jutland in 1916 was en route from the Mediterranean to Puget Sound for repair of bomb damage inflicted by a Stuka dive bomber while opposing the German airborne invasion of Crete in May.

When the leading seaman and I parted on the quarterdeck of his ship, I wished him well.

"I'm going to be in your country," he said. "You're going to be out here, in this bloody awful hole, without half enough ack-ack. You're the one who needs the luck."

I shrugged off the Briton's prescient warning. It certainly seemed as if the fleet was aware of the tense international situation. The *California* had no sooner returned to Pearl Harbor when Adm. Husband E. Kimmel—who had replaced Adm. James O. Richardson, fired by Roosevelt for repeatedly urging the return of the fleet to West Coast ports—ordered an air raid drill that was joined by his opposite number, Lt. Gen. Walter Short of the Hawaiian Army Department. The harbor and Honolulu were blacked out, and sailors and soldiers were rousted from bars and bordellos and ordered back to their ships and bases.

The Pacific Fleet was reorganized into three task forces: the Battle Force, Task Force 1, under Vice Adm. William S. Pye in *California;* Air-

*Ibid., p. 75.

craft Battle Force, Task Force 2, Vice Adm. William F. Halsey in *Enterprise;* Scouting Force, Task Force 3, Vice Adm. Wilson Brown in *Indianapolis.* Each task force usually went to sea on training maneuvers for one week, then spent two weeks at Pearl Harbor. Occasionally, a simulated fleet engagement brought two or all three task forces to sea west and south of Hawaii, but Kimmel seldom flew his four-starred flag from the *Pennsylvania,* preferring the administration building at the submarine base.

I paid little attention to the increasingly tense international situation that summer of '41. I busied myself with copying the Fox schedule (fleetwide broadcast) in main radio, improving my skills on practice circuits and at the code machine, and making bibulous liberties in Honolulu with my close friends M. G. "Johnny" Johnson, "Red" Goff, Fisher, and other radio gang mates. (Daley had been transferred to the transport *Fuller* before we left Bremerton.) From the time I entered boot camp in the summer of 1940, the Navy had made it perfectly clear that it preferred to do my thinking for me, and I willingly agreed. Lacking the power of choice over my destiny, I elected stoicism.

In the summer of 1941, accordingly, I shrugged off the action of Harold R. Stark, then Chief of Naval Operations, when he reduced the strength of the Pacific Fleet by 20 percent. Alarmed by the success of the German U-boats against British shipping, and fearing a shooting war with the Nazis, he transferred the battleships *New Mexico, Idaho,* and *Mississippi,* along with the carrier *Yorktown,* four light cruisers, two destroyer squadrons, and miscellaneous auxiliaries, to the Atlantic Fleet. After all, wasn't one American fighting ship the equal of two or three of Nippon's? I couldn't have known that secret U.S.-British talks in Washington had produced a strategy of "Germany first" in case of our involvement in war. That policy would put and keep me in hazard for months mounting to years in the Pacific.

By means of WCX fast press, which was copied daily for the officers and men, and by short-wave radio, we followed with keen interest the engagement in the North Atlantic between the new German battleship *Bismarck* and the British battle cruiser *Hood* and new battleship *Prince of Wales.* When the Germans blew up the *Hood* with a few salvoes and bloodied the *Prince,* we wondered how our older battlewagons would fare against this super-dreadnought. That concern was removed when she was sunk by the combined efforts of the British Home Fleet, plus units of other commands.

I was not concerned on 22 June when Hitler unleashed an unbelievable 122 divisions against the Soviet Union along a 2,000-mile front. Now Hitler would do our work for us, the senior petty officers said, by destroying the Bolsheviks and their blood-stained leader, Joseph Stalin. I didn't permit myself to wonder what would happen if Hitler accomplished what Napoleon had failed to do in 1812 and then turned all his forces against the western democracies.

Nor did I pay much attention to other events that summer, with all their portents for the future. American forces landed in Iceland to relieve British troops for more important duties. Roosevelt and Churchill met on board the heavy cruiser *Augusta* in Argentia Bay, Newfoundland, where they formulated some glittering generalities they called the Atlantic Charter. And FDR issued "shoot-on-sight" orders against Axis vessels (in effect, the German navy) discovered in American waters. All of this was taking place in another hemisphere. Here we were facing a potential enemy that Roosevelt seemed to be ignoring: the Japanese.

There was one event I could not ignore. On 27 May, the same day the British sank the *Bismarck,* the president declared a state of "unlimited national emergency." For the growing number of reserves in the service, including myself and the four other V-3s in the radio gang, there would be no return to civilian life when our one year of active duty was completed. We were, as were all the regulars, in "for the duration" of the emergency.

In living compartment B-511-L on the starboard side of the third deck, at the gedunk (ice cream) stand, in the crew's library or recreation room, or idling topside in the cooling breezes from the Koolaus, I had one immediate concern: to avoid Bunkley at captain's mast. Men were put on report for the slightest infraction of the regulations; the brig was filled to capacity and running over, with prisoners-at-large restricted to the ship and awaiting their turn.

In addition to disciplining his own men, the captain often served as president of general courts-martial boards. When the forty-eight-starred Union Jack was run up and two-blocked at the starboard yardarm, the question was never of the guilt of the unfortunate sailor: that was foreordained. The only thing to be decided was whether he would first serve hard time at Portsmouth Naval Prison before receiving his dishonorable discharge.

One of Bunkley's eager allies in impressing our crew with the Navy way was a master-at-arms nicknamed "Boots the Boats." He slipped noiselessly around the ship wearing canvas leggings (the boots of boot camp) and gym shoes seeking someone to put on report. Since parties of twenty-five or thirty apprentice seamen from San Diego or Great Lakes Naval Training Station were reporting aboard all that summer, there was no shortage of "suspects." Those who failed to meet the standards of the proud Battle Force flagship met the captain at his main deck office for sentencing to brig time, courts-martial, or transfer to other ships (usually those that had no admiral on board, such as the *Oklahoma*).

Just as regularly, experienced seamen and petty officers were transferred off for school instruction, for new construction, and for duty in ships of the expanding Atlantic Fleet. It seemed obvious, according to the analysts in the petty officers' head, that Kimmel had been given two primary responsibilities: preparing the fleet for combat, and running a huge training program. They were mutually incompatible, and he seemed to be favoring training over preparation. When some pointed out that the men who were being transferred were badly needed on the North Atlantic Sea Frontier, where we were in an undeclared shooting war with the Nazi U-boats, they were hooted down. "To hell with the North Atlantic Sea Frontier; what about the Imperial Japanese Navy?"

There was no doubt about Captain Bunkley's efficiency at enforcing his concept of discipline; but his primary responsibility was to command his battleship in action against the enemy. From his first times out in the *California,* when he had turned over the conn to Robert Carney, his executive officer, I had wondered how well he was prepared for battle stations.

Before the summer was over, I had a chance to see him at the conn. I had been temporarily assigned to the bridge radio circuit. Near the end of a long gunnery exercise, I was sent to the armored conning tower with a message for the ship's communication officer, Lt. Comdr. H. E. Bernstein, Annapolis '26. A specialist in electronics, he was also the security officer.

The oval-shaped conning tower was dim, hot, and crowded, fitfully illuminated through slitted observation ports in the massive armor plate. The air was heavy with more than exhaled carbon dioxide; the tension was so thick I had the sudden irreverent thought that I might have to hack my way through it with a machete. Standing tensely behind the helmsman was the captain. At his right and one discreet step back was Bernstein, signal book in hand. On the other side were the navigator, officer of the deck, and a gaggle of junior officers and men, including Ens. Thomas P. McGrath, C-L Division officer. I had seen him a number of times before, noting that he had the Irish good looks of a young Gene Tunney; he was in fact the ship's boxing officer and referred at our smokers.

The captain's method of command was far removed from his authoritarian demeanor at captain's mast. It seemed to be the rasping of questions in a querulous voice: "What is our present course and speed? Why are we closing on the *Tennessee?* What does that signal mean?" The answers came with haste verging on frenzy from his officers. I prayed they would continue to be the right ones. From the perspective of a mere third-class radioman, making himself as small as possible against the steel bulkhead, I wondered if Bunkley knew what the hell he was doing.

The exercise was soon completed, and the captain gave permission to secure from general quarters. The ship had been buttoned up for many hours. When the announcement went out over the P.A. system, a spontaneous loud cheer echoed through the *California* from stem to stern.

The captain seemed bewildered by this unseemly display of emotion. "Why are the men making all that noise?" he demanded.

Gently and deferentially, Bernstein explained that they were happy because the long exercise was over and the ship was returning to port.

Not a glimmer of understanding crossed Bunkley's face. It was a long, well-structured face, but under a heavy tan his skin was weathered and blotchy. He was suffering from an ulcer, which some apologists said explained his irascible conduct. From observing him in the conning tower, it was obvious to me that the behavior patterns of these strange lower orders Bunkley had commanded for nearly thirty years were as much a mystery to him as if they had been a troop of African baboons.

The incident troubled me. What if there were a real crisis, not a training maneuver? At that point a captain must stop asking questions of his navigator and OOD and communication and signal officers and start issuing commands. Would they be the appropriate ones? Many an incompetent captain had got many a sailor killed; and I was a battleship sailor.

I mentioned my reservations to Johnny Johnson. As customary when moored to interrupted Quay F-3 at the head of the battle line in Pearl Harbor, we had escaped the airless confines of our compartment and carried our mattresses to the crown of No. 2 turret.

Johnson laughed, a short laugh. "He couldn't fight his way out of a peacoat."

"How does a guy like that get to be a four-striper commanding a battleship?"

"The way it's always been done in the peacetime Navy: the old kiss and kick. Kiss the ass of your superiors. Kick the ass of your inferiors. Don't forget to write lots of reports. Fire lots of salutes. Send lots of men to the brig. Then, with a little luck, you might make admiral, even if it's a tombstone promotion."

"How about Bunkley?"

He shook his head. "He's an old man with an ulcer and he's running out of time. . . ."

We could not have known just how little time Bunkley had left before his chance to prove himself a battleship commander. Nor how little time remained in the lives of many of his crewmen.

Much more adroit in his dealings with enlisted men was Admiral Pye. Although aloof and unapproachable, in the manner of admirals, he seemed of amiable disposition. He had a fine beaming smile that he bestowed like a benediction as he hurried past on his daily rounds between flag quarters at the aft end of the wardroom on the second deck and the flag bridge. I had a feeling that if only the admiral could be apprised of the latest injustice inflicted by the captain, all would be made well. I hadn't yet learned that men who have achieved eminence can well afford the impression of benevolence. They are, after all, shielded from the necessity of actually being benevolent. Pye knew what Bunkley never grasped: to the crew of a man-of-war, the appearance is often more important than the reality.

It is instructive to compare Bunkley's principles of leadership with those of a wartime battleship skipper, Capt. Ellis M. Zacharias, who took command of the *New Mexico* in September 1943. In *Secret Missions* he wrote:

This was my first battleship command, and those who know the Navy can well appreciate that it is an entirely different experience from command of smaller ships. The intimacy which characterizes the relationship between the commanding officer and his shipmates on destroyers, and to a certain extent even on cruisers, is completely lacking on a huge battleship with more than 1,700 men in the crew. It is virtually impossible to know all of them, and direct personal contact can be maintained with only a few on the ship. This made it impossible to exercise command by direct personal relations, which I had found so successful in the past. Even so, I decided to do what I could to weaken the barriers which usually exist between the commanding officer of a battleship and the men and officers under him.

One of my methods used previously had been to address the crew from time to time, explaining to them the over-all trends of war, thereby trying to create in them a feeling of actual participation in the great events of which they were a gallant and important part. It was also my custom to pass through the crew quarters as often as possible when the noon meal was being served, to show interest in their food and comforts. I made it a point to be critical of the quality, temperature, and manner in which it was served. Preoccupied as I was with the psychological problems of war, I fully realized that morale was one of the most important factors, especially on a battleship. I have always felt that food and the soda fountain were the basis of contentment, and contentment the basis of morale.*

If chow and the gedunk stand were necessities for crew "contentment," the men of the *California* had ample reason for their low morale. In addition to a martinet skipper from another era, we endured awful gedunks and even worse chow.

At the soda fountain we were served a thin, viscous concoction that tasted of dried milk solids and vanilla extract, slapped into a conical paper cup. It was necessary to add a nickel to the dime price to get a chocolate or strawberry topping, the latter as artificial as the vanilla extract.

Cpl. T. R. Liles was a marine radio operator assigned to the CD Division in 1940–41, as was the practice on battleships until shortly before the war. He lived, stood watches, and made liberties with the radio gang. As a result, he recalls, "I was generally detested by the Marine contingent as one of them special-duty-only SOBs."

"We had a pecking order at chow," he writes. "The senior man was table captain. We were seated in assigned places, and God help the guy who got in the wrong seat. The mess striker delivered up the chow to the table captain, who took his choice and passed the tureens on to the next senior man. The table captain was responsible for everybody getting a fair share.

"Two familiar dishes were shellacked (candied) beets, of which I never saw a bite eaten, and roast turkey. When you flicked the bone, the meat would fly off and the most God-awful stench would waft up from the bone. We generally agreed that the Navy had bought too many turkeys in World War I and was trying to get rid of them. I have stomach

---

*Capt. Ellis M. Zacharias, *Secret Missions: The Story of an Intelligence Officer* (New York: G. P. Putnam's Sons, 1946), p. 317.

trouble to this day, which I attribute to the horrible horsecock sand-wiches and black coffee we consumed on the mid-watches, and I can't stand powdered milk (KLIM)."

The dreadful chow, Liles remembers, often drove us to make navy yard liberties. "At the Marine barracks on the east side of the yard they sold ham sandwiches for 5¢ each. We would order a dollar's worth apiece, which was a stack about two feet high. We also went to the sub base at the north end of Pearl, where the two predominant features of interest were a library of about 2,000 sq. ft. with about ten sailors in it, and a slop chute [beer dispensary] of approximately 10 sq. ft. with what seemed like 2,000 sailors in it. The Navy was always fouled up in its priorities."*

On liberty in Honolulu, enlisted men soon discovered that they ranked at the very bottom of the island's social scale, even below the soldiers who were stationed at Hickam Field, Fort Shafter, or Schofield Barracks. Samuel Eliot Morison, the official Navy historian, was guilty only of understatement when he wrote:

Honolulu was and remained an unsatisfactory liberty port for blue-jackets. White women were few in number, and the shopkeepers gypped the men even more unmercifully than those of Norfolk, Virginia.†

A few intrepid enlisted men, believing their money was just as good as any officer's, went to one of the three Waikiki Beach hotels that catered to tourists and officers: the Moana, the Royal Hawaiian, and the Halekulani (where Admiral Pye and Captain Bunkley stayed when the ship was in port). While they would be served if they were sober, the seating and service left no doubt that they were intruders who didn't belong there.

T. R. Liles remembers "Rockape," a shipboard marine, veteran of the garrison at Tientsin, China, whose favorite line was: "No, daddy, I don't want to go to the circus. I want to go to the officer's club and watch the officers eat." There were few opportunities to observe officers at their leisure in Honolulu. Most of us, in any event, wanted to get as far away as possible from their inhibiting presence.

It is an ironic comment on the mores of Hawaii in those days that the only place a sailor was truly welcome (the many bars tolerating him

---

*Letter to author from Capt. Talmadge R. Liles, USMC (Ret.), 18 January 1984.

†History of United States Naval Operations in World War II (Boston: Little, Brown and Company, 1965), Vol. III, p. 46.

only for his money) was in one of the bordellos along Hotel, River, and North Beretania Streets that were sanctioned unofficially by the Navy and Army. These places were off-limits to civilians—and to non-white servicemen.

The girls, who were as all-white as their customers, were brought over from the States by the Matson Lines. The prudent ones who avoided the temptations of life as one of the despised demimonde could return as first-class passengers in the *Lurline* with a substantial amount of money. Scuttlebutt among the patrons invariably spoke of prostitutes who were supporting aged parents, were working their way through college, or who planned to buy businesses or marry unsuspecting pillars of the community on their return to the States. They were, after all, skilled at deceiving men.

Freedom to patronize a safe bordello where the girls were inspected weekly by Army and Navy doctors was one of the very few privileges enjoyed by enlisted men. It was a source of amusement to them that no officer would dare to climb the stairs and enter the reception room of the New Senator or one of the other establishments. (I was told later by more than one former officer that we were indeed envied for this freedom.) Inferiority, on some occasions, has its rewards.*

With the Pacific Fleet based at Pearl Harbor for the indefinite future, Admiral Kimmel began rotating the battlewagons and their screening vessels back to the West Coast for about a month (including travel time) of R & R. The *California's* turn came in early fall. After a five-day passage made tedious by our anxious anticipation of "strength through love," as Kimmel's "health cruises" were described with more style by the junior officers, we passed under the Golden Gate Bridge on 12 October, exactly one year after I had reported aboard. We entered the dry dock at Hunter's Point for an emergency repair of a discharge valve in the after engine room.

Fisher and I left the next day on leave and would rejoin the ship at San Pedro Bay, Port of Los Angeles. Knowing that it was easy to get a ride if you were in uniform, we hitchhiked home to Placerville.

The 150-mile trip was not the easy three-hour drive of today. We were not speeding along magnificent freeways or even divided high-

*I described a typical Honolulu brothel for servicemen in *Battleship Sailor*, pp. 17–19.

ways; they did not exist then, except for the just-completed Arroyo Seco Parkway between Pasadena and Los Angeles. Interstate Highways 40 and 50 were mostly one lane in either direction—a narrow and tortuous passage if any natural obstacles were encountered. The highway builders took the path of least resistance; they had neither the cash nor the cachet to chop into mountains, fill in stream beds, and flatten slopes with gigantic earth cuts.

Road shoulders usually were non-existent. If any guard barriers were provided, they were either flimsy white posts-and-rails that disintegrated on impact with careening steel, or they were exquisitely fitted and mortared granite (many constructed by WPA [Works Progress Administration] masons in the mid-1930s) that brushed off a speeding automobile as a mule dismisses a fly. Add the hazards of onrushing traffic, and danger existed on both sides. The tube-type tires not only were of uncertain quality but also were inflated to high pressures; blowouts were common. When two of the high-profiled, small-windowed, boxy products of Detroit ingenuity collided, the result was likely to be great bodily harm.

All these risks were taken for granted, much as present-day travelers accept flying on jetliners whose engines may fail on takeoff or which may smash into mountains. Fisher and I didn't give the danger a thought as we thumped along the concrete roadway, with its tarred expansion joints, at 55 miles per hour. We did notice several cautionary roadway signs by Burma Shave and read them with a chuckle:

> KEEP WELL
> TO THE RIGHT
> OF THE ONCOMING CAR
> GET YOUR CLOSE SHAVES
> FROM THE HALF-POUND JAR
> BURMA-SHAVE
>
> DON'T STICK
> YOUR ELBOW
> OUT SO FAR
> IT MIGHT GO HOME
> IN ANOTHER CAR
> BURMA-SHAVE
>
> HARDLY A DRIVER
> IS NOW ALIVE

WHO PASSED
ON HILLS
AT 75
BURMA-SHAVE*

Placerville seemed somnolent, continuing in its long decline from the glory days of the 1850s, when it was the "Hangtown" of gold-rush lore, but Fisher and I scarcely noticed. We were too busy renewing old acquaintances, hanging out at Mac's Jumbo Fountain, attending a country dance. Except for meals and sleeping, I spent little time in outlying Missouri Flat at the tin-roofed cottage of my foster-parents. The place still lacked running water, indoor plumbing, and electricity; and I lacked any meaningful communication with Clarence and Leila Mason. Since I could give only highly censored accounts of my Navy life and times, we talked mainly of neighborhood doings and the international situation.

With the German Wehrmacht racing toward Moscow, and with Roosevelt's "shoot-on-sight" orders to U.S. forces finding Axis (German) vessels in American waters, would we get involved in the European war? Japanese military forces were still threatening China and had recently taken over French Indochina (now Vietnam, Cambodia, and Laos) from the puppet government of Vichy France: Would we have to fight Japan, as well? Since I was serving in a capital ship, the Masons assumed that my leaders were keeping me informed of war developments. They didn't know that the Navy's policy was to tell enlisted men nothing. The little that I knew came from reading the ship's newspaper, which was copied in the radio shack from the WCX fast-press station and mimeographed for the crew. It was essentially a headline and lead-paragraph service, roughly equivalent to what is offered on radio and television today. Actually, my foster-parents were much better informed than I. They read the San Francisco *Chronicle* and Christian Science *Monitor* daily and listened to news programs and commentaries by such solemn pundits as Gabriel Heatter and Lowell Thomas on their battery-powered radio. Not wishing to acknowledge my ignorance, I assured them that Germany was too occupied with Russia to look past the British Isles, and that if the Japanese dared to attack us, we would deal with them as Adm. George Dewey had the Spanish fleet at Manila

---

*I recognized the inspiration for this sign. It was a patriotic poem by Henry Wadsworth Longfellow, "Paul Revere's Ride," which began: "Listen, my children, and you shall hear / Of the midnight ride of Paul Revere, / On the eighteenth of April, in Seventy-five; / Hardly a man is now alive / Who remembers that famous day and year."

Bay in 1898. I ignored the warning of the *Warspite* sailor about our deficiencies in A.A. defense. I was also forgetting the words of one of my favorite authors, Jack London. After serving as a war correspondent during the Russo-Japanese war of 1904–5, he had repeatedly warned about "the yellow peril."

That peril seemed very real to the Navy Department and to Admiral Kimmel in October 1941. When Fisher and I returned to the ship, anchored off the San Pedro breakwater, we learned that the crew had been mustered on the seventeenth and informed that relations with Japan were at a possibly critical phase. All leaves had been cancelled. No one from the ship had been able to get through to Fisher or me. For the first time, I blessed the limitations of the Masons' tinny, crackling ten-party-line telephone.

From the viewpoint of sailors who were henceforth restricted to two-hour recall when on liberty, it seemed an overreaction to events in Japan, similar to the Honolulu-Pearl Harbor alert of the past April. The cabinet had fallen, and the premiership had been seized by Gen. Hideki Tojo, leader of the war clique. A radio-gang mate who was an opera and classical-music lover told me that the posturing, shaven-headed Tojo reminded him of Pooh-Bah, the Lord High Everything Else, in the *Mikado,* the Gilbert and Sullivan comic opera.

Since the *California* was not scheduled to depart for Pearl Harbor until 1 November, I had another ten days to enjoy all-night liberties with M. G. Johnson, "Red" Goff, Fisher, several other shipmates, and three Navy girls who had come down from Seattle to San Francisco and then Long Beach to join us in the drinking, night-clubbing, and general merriment. (I described our times of "'Strength Through Love' in the States" in Chapter Ten of *Battleship Sailor.*)

I also made time for a more serious purpose. Children who have been adopted find themselves torn between two sets of families and loyalties. When they are old enough to consider such things, they discover the powerful attraction of blood. Always, they wonder why they have been so cruelly rejected; often, they imagine the responsibility lies in awful shortcomings of their own. Some adopted children do not know their parents and spend years as teenagers or young adults trying to trace them. Every person has a right to know the circumstances of his birth, no matter how unfavorable. If there is illegitimacy, it belongs to the parents.

In my case, I was six before I was adopted. I knew both parents, Bayard and Lilah Dale Bowman, and had been given conflicting reasons for the adoption of me and my two sisters by two different families following our parents' divorce. Consequently, I was inclined to believe little of what I heard. The truth, as always, was buried somewhere beneath the rationalizations.

When I rejoined the ship, I decided to call on my aunt and uncle, Norma and Hugh Boyd, who knew part of that truth. When I was five, I had lived with them in the Eagle Rock suburb of Los Angeles while my parents dealt with divorce, the chaotic effects of love that had turned to hatred. I called the Boyds from the fleet landing and was invited to visit.

They lived in a lovely Early California house with Spanish-style tiled roof and entrance on Panorama Terrace in the Silverlake-Los Feliz district. It overlooked John Marshall High School, where my uncle, a man short in stature but of iron-gray hair and distinguished appearance, was the admired and respected boys' vice principal.

I was greeted with a warm kiss from my Aunt Norma, my father's sister, large, red-haired, and matronly. Her demeanor always suggested she was well aware that she was a Bowman and a Bayard, and thereby kin to Christopher Bowman of London and Amsterdam, a Pilgrim deacon who died in 1619 en route to America, and Pierre du Terrail, the Chevalier de Bayard, a legendary French military hero.

Of my three cousins I was especially glad to see June, six months younger than I. We had developed a special bond when we played and attended kindergarten together; even then she treated me with a sort of maternal solicitude, sensing that I was a neglected child of divorce. Since she had red hair of a glorious copper hue and had grown up to bear more than a passing resemblance to the actress Claire Trevor, I had visions of her becoming a famous movie star. But, by 1941, she had turned down the offer of a screen test and married. With June, love always came first.

Blonde Cousin Lorna Lee, only twelve, was as reserved and well-mannered as she had been schooled to be. Cousin Doug, three years younger than I, was first string on the football team at John Marshall. He usually had his head under the hood of his chopped-top '34 Ford hot-rod coupe. Or he and his pals were holed up in his back bedroom, where the loud sounds announced they were playing swing music with an assortment of instruments that included saxophone, guitar, trumpet, cornet, a mandolin, drums, even a battered upright piano. Later I reflected that Doug and his classmates could have been the subjects of the Andy Hardy films had MGM been more dedicated to the truth about teenagers than to escapism. Of course, not even MGM's camera wizards could have made the shrimp-sized Mickey Rooney into a football player.

The evening of my visit my uncle had to make an appearance at some parent-teacher-student function, and he invited me along. The school, built in the early 1930s, was a classic example of Collegiate Gothic architecture, with an impressive castellated tower of red brick accented with wood and glass. Passing through a massive front entrance, we found ourselves in a wide hallway on floors of brown ceramic tile, with a border of decorative Spanish tile. Obviously, the school had been designed as a showplace.

As students greeted my uncle with deference, they eyed me, a sailor in dress-blue uniform, with some curiosity. When a mixed group approached, Uncle Hugh said: "Ah, there's Rosemary La Planche. She is Miss America of 1941, after being runner-up last year. Would you like to meet her?"

I stared, wondering why she would have any interest in meeting me, one of Samuel Eliot Morison's lowly "bluejackets." Still, I couldn't let such an opportunity pass. If John Marshall was a paradigm of high schools, it was only a fitting backdrop for Rosemary La Planche. She was both stunningly beautiful and wholesome-looking: the girl next door as every young man dreams she might be. Her hair was long and naturally blonde; her face was perfectly structured and without a blemish of any kind. Not even her casual school dress—sweater, pleated skirt, brown-and-white saddle shoes, and bobby sox—could conceal the striking figure of a Miss America. I had never seen such physical perfection at such close range.

When my uncle introduced me, she took my hand, held it, and told me, in a low, poised voice, how glad she was to meet me. My so-recently acquired worldliness as a battleship sailor in Kimmel's Pacific Fleet fell away, and I was back in school, blushing and stumbling over my words.

As she rejoined her entourage and passed down the hall, seeming to glide on air, my uncle said: "She is a lovely girl." It was, I thought at the time, a quite superfluous remark; but he was referring to more than surface appearances.

In a later conversation with Cousin Doug, I speculated that Miss La Planche had been nice to me because she was planning a career in show business, and being charming was only a rehearsal for her future. But he knew her well, having worked with her on the high-school yearbook, and quickly disagreed.

"She was not putting on or affecting any airs when she took your hand and seemed genuinely pleased to meet you," he explained. "She really is special and can sense people. That comes, I think, because she's from humble beginnings. She lives in a 1920s clapboard bungalow in the working-class area of Atwater. I've driven her home from school many times."

When people rise to prominence from blue-collar backgrounds, I have observed, many become arrogant and supercilious; only a few retain that special humanity that Rosemary La Planche had. Some Mustang naval officers I have met—Lt. (later Capt.) J. S. Lees of the *Pawnee* was a sterling example—become regulation- and promotion-driven martinets with no concern for the welfare of their men. To his kind I applied a line from Edgar Lee Masters's *Spoon River Anthology:* "Beware of the man who rises to power from one suspender." On the other hand, *Pawnee's* commissioning skipper, Lt. (later Lt. Comdr.) Frank C. Dilworth, who never finished high school, was a fine gentleman who was admired and even loved by his crew, as I pointed out in *"We Will Stand by You."*

But in the fall of 1941, shortly before Pearl Harbor and a war which brought many a man to power from one tattered suspender, I did not think on such things. I returned to the ship remembering the touch of Miss La Planche's hand and the sound of her voice. In the fifteen months I had been in the active Navy, I had had several remarkable experiences. At the San Diego Naval Training Station I had had dinner with Secretary of the Navy Frank Knox (Alfred M. Landon's vice-presidential running mate in the 1936 election); two rear admirals; a couple of captains; and Col. William F. "Wild Bill" Donovan, an assistant and adviser to Knox, later to head up the newly created Office of Strategic Services, predecessor to the CIA. At a Navy Relief Carnival in the same city, I had seen and heard film stars Robert Taylor and his wife, Barbara Stanwyck, close up to the stage. Now I had met a young lady so beautiful that she made most movie actresses look like wallflowers at a tea dance. Despite the previous five months of "Summer and Gunsmoke" around the Hawaiian Islands, being in the Navy sure as hell beat working at Beach's box factory or pumping gas at the crummy Signal service station on the outskirts of Placerville.

3

"Praise the Lord and Pass
the Ammunition"

"What a glorious thing must be a victory, sir."
"The greatest tragedy in the world, Madam, except a defeat."
—Arthur Wellesley, Duke of Wellington

Pride goeth before destruction, and an haughty spirit before a fall.
—Proverbs 16:18

At 0740 hours on Friday morning, 7 December 1990, I sat with Donald E. Magee, superintendent of the USS Arizona Memorial at Pearl Harbor. He was wearing the forest-green uniform of the National Park Service. I was wearing the standard garb of the Pearl Harbor Survivors Association: Hawaiian shirt, white pants and shoes, garrison cap with the PHSA emblem, my campaign ribbons and battle stars. Around my neck was a lei of red carnations.

Spread out before us at the Visitor Center, seated or standing, were some 2,500 people, for this was the forty-ninth anniversary of the Japanese attack on Pearl Harbor. Soon the invocation by Chaplain Joseph Morgan of the PHSA would be followed by a moment of reverent silence, the dramatic missing-man flyover by the Hawaiian Air National Guard, morning colors by a color guard representing all the military services, and the National Anthem by the Fleet Marine Force Band. After these impressive ceremonies, Don Magee would introduce me, and I would give the keynote address to an audience that included representatives of national and local TV, radio, and print media.

35

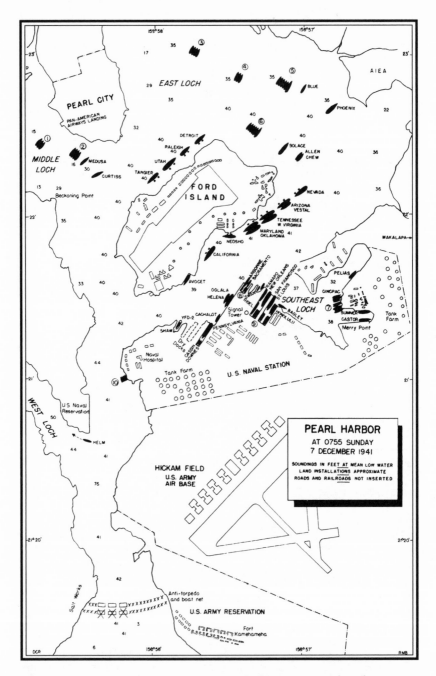

Ship positions at Pearl Harbor on morning of 7 December 1941. Several auxiliaries, tugs, and yard craft (including the only vessel still surviving from the attack, the yard tug *Hoga*) are not shown. (map by Robert M. Berish, courtesy of the Naval Historical Center)

I had been given a great honor, one that filled me with tumultuous emotions, and not only because I disliked public speaking and had never before addressed so many people. I looked to my right, toward Ford Island where the battle line had been moored that Sunday morning nearly five decades before. I had been there, an insignificant third-class radioman of the V-3 Communication Reserve, frozen on active duty by President Franklin D. Roosevelt's declaration of an "unlimited national emergency" on 27 May 1941. Considering my status as a former enlisted man who had committed no deeds of valor that day, only followed orders and did his duty, why was I here as a representative of all the men who had been on or around Oahu that morning?

For one thing, I had survived. As I had observed in the days following the attack, it is not the best men who run the world, only the survivors. Many men far more qualified than I, men who had won numerous medals and citations for valor, had not survived. Some of them were interred under plain or gold markers at the "Punchbowl," the National Memorial Cemetery of the Pacific, rather fittingly the crater of an extinct volcano. I had paid my respects to them on 6 December, driven there by a career enlisted man, Radioman First Class Don Till, who had taken a week's leave to be my companion, guide, and chauffeur through the nearly grid-locked streets of Honolulu. While there, I had reluctantly given an interview to a crew filming a documentary on the attack, agreeing only when the director promised to list the two naval memoirs I had written in the end credits. (The promise, typical of film and TV ethics, was not kept.)

Of the tens of thousands who had survived, all too many had lost their lives in the fierce naval battles and island invasions of the war. Most of the Pearl Harbor survivors soon were sent back to sea, for we represented part of that thin blue line of sailors who stood between the suddenly all-victorious Japanese and a possible invasion of the Hawaiian Islands, even the United States. After the war, the fortunate ones like myself returned home, mostly to the obscurity from which we came. Many were marked and scarred, emotionally if not physically, by our experiences. Readjustment to civilian life was slow and painful, sometimes never accomplished.

Previous years' keynote speakers were mostly professional naval officers of some stature who had a connection with the attack. One speaker was Walter Lord, author of the popular *Day of Infamy*. What were my qualifications?

Whether by destiny or pure chance, a battle-station assignment from my chief petty officer had placed me in the maintop of the *California,* where I had a precarious bird's-eye view of the entire attack. After V-J Day, I attended the University of Southern California on the GI Bill, where I majored in English, with minors in journalism and political science. After many years of going through "the newspaper and advertising career mills," as one book reviewer aptly described those humdrum decades, I wrote a long "Comment and Discussion" piece about the attack for the *Proceedings* of the U.S. Naval Institute. It led to a contract from the Institute's book-publishing division, the Naval Institute Press, for a memoir of my service in the *California,* which I titled *Battleship Sailor.* It was published to many favorable reviews in the fall of 1982.

While researching the book I had read a great deal, in the process learning more about the background and details of the attack than the majority of my fellow survivors knew. As I discovered with some dismay while conducting extensive interviews, many of them remained frozen in time, as if the trauma of the surprise air raid had stunted their psychic and intellectual development. Others became "professional survivors," feeding endlessly on the one event in their lives that gave it focus and meaning. A few became shrill defenders of their military leaders, particularly Admiral Kimmel and General Short, trumpeting dark conspiracy theories (all unproven and probably unprovable), with President Roosevelt as the arch-villain. In fact, an entire "cottage industry" has evolved around the events of 7 December 1941 as journalists and historians have rehashed the attack, sometimes with scant attention to truth and accuracy. One prominent "pop historian" who has written several books about Pearl Harbor had the entire battle line pointing in the wrong direction, away from the entrance channel.

There were reasons, then, for me to accept this invitation, and to prepare myself well for what would be the most important spoken remarks of my life. I felt that I knew a good deal about it all, and that my typed address, copies of which were handed to the media, expressed my true feelings. My two naval memoirs, *Battleship Sailor* and *"We Will Stand by You": Serving in the* Pawnee, *1942–1945,* had been written from the viewpoint of an enlisted man who often was critical of the Navy's rigid class and caste system. I resolved to maintain that perspective here at the Visitor Center, giving my audience something more substantial than the patriotic platitudes that seemed *de rigueur* on such occasions. This is what I said:

"Forty-nine years ago today, at this very hour, I was not far from here. I was over there, along Ford Island, at my battle station in the main top of the USS *California*. I can tell you that I am very glad to be back on this peaceful Hawaiian morning!

"Last year, on this day that is so special to Americans—and to Japanese, too—I was interviewed by a radio station in the Boston area. I said that I felt as if I had been living on borrowed time for nearly five decades—for I had survived the attack on Pearl Harbor, and three years of war in the Pacific. While I haven't always used this grace period wisely or well, it has been a gift. Many of my shipmates in the *California* and the other ships present that day were not so fortunate. I have paid my respects to them at the Punchbowl. I hope you will, too.

"When I visit the harbor today, I can still feel the presence of my fallen comrades. Their spirit seems to brood over the place; it is almost a tangible thing. For Pearl Harbor—*Wai Momi*, or Pearl Water, home of the shark god—has been visited by great violence and great tragedy. The ambience, or aura, of that violence, that tragedy, has not been dissipated by time. Perhaps it never will.

"Why is that true? During World War II, there were battles on a much grander scale than this one; death and injury on a much greater scale. Some of these battles are nearly forgotten, remembered only in the dry pages of history books and in the fading memories of the men who fought in them. But Pearl Harbor is different. It is not forgotten, and it never will be. The attack on this harbor was a hinge of destiny, a great watershed in the history of this century. Those of us who participated—like it or not, worthy or not—have thereby become part of that history.

"It was the surprise air raid on this place that brought the United States into the war. As Japanese Admiral Isoroku Yamamoto feared it might, it 'awakened a sleeping giant and filled him with a terrible resolve.' That national resolve, backed by our industrial might, saved Great Britain, France, Russia, and the other countries allied against the Axis nations. It ensured the defeat of Japan, Italy, and Germany. The attack was one of the great miscalculations of history. The winner here became the loser—but in the end we were all the poorer for it. There are no winners in war, only degrees of loss.

"Why were we here in 1941, strong units of the Navy and Marine Corps, the Army and its Air Corps? We were here because our leaders thought our presence would deter aggression by the Japanese militarists. That was a miscalculation, too. Our presence invited the very aggression we wanted to deter. Admiral Yamamoto was a good poker player. He knew we were trying to fill an inside straight; that we couldn't back up our bluff.

"Admiral James O. Richardson commanded what was then called the United States Fleet, but was really the Pacific Fleet, from 1940 to January 31, 1941. Following the annual fleet problem in April 1940, Washington ordered the fleet to remain in Hawaiian waters rather than to return to its West Coast ports. Richardson disputed the wisdom of this strategy with his Commander-in-Chief, President Franklin Roosevelt. He said that Pearl Harbor was 'a damn mouse trap.' The Washington politicians and diplomats didn't want to hear that. Richardson was relieved of his command. He was replaced by a man who would follow orders and make no waves. His name has become a metaphor for ignominious defeat—Husband E. Kimmel. Others share some responsibility for the debacle, but have largely escaped blame. Kimmel kept waiting for Washington to tell him what to do; but he was the top commander in the Pacific. He was supposed to *know* what to do.

"Richardson was right. Pearl Harbor *was* a mouse trap waiting to be sprung. We sailors of the Pacific Fleet agreed with him all along, but for different reasons. We knew nothing of geopolitics or grand strategies. We disliked the Hawaiian Islands, which we saw as "a paradise of the Pacific" only for the rich. We wanted to make our liberties in our home ports of San Pedro-Long Beach, San Diego, San Francisco, Bremerton-Seattle. We wanted to be near families and friends. We didn't think there was any great threat from an enemy we looked down upon as our inferiors in every way—and there we were wrong, too.

"What were we like, the enlisted men, the sailors of the Pacific Fleet? Mostly we came from the working-class poor of the farms, towns, and cities of America. Most of us had graduated from high school to face an uncertain future, for the Great Depression still depressed the country. There were few scholarships for college or trade schools. There were few jobs, and they were mostly low-paying and dead-end. The armed forces promised security: three meals a day, a place to live, job training, travel and adventure. In return, the military—especially the Navy, which had borrowed most of its customs, traditions, and disciplinary practices from the aristocratic British Royal Navy—demanded an un-questioning obedience. It was enforced by stern regulations and a fierce discipline that would not be tolerated today. In the Navy of the 1930s and 1940s, 'The Articles for the Government of the Navy' were known as 'Rocks and Shoals, or Death and Greater Punishments.'

"There were compensations, of course. We enlisted men shared many bonds of comradeship. We lived in a world within a world, a world of 'Us Versus Them'—'Them' usually being our officers and the civilians—where we looked out for our buddies. I made friendships that endure to this day, although many of those friendships can only be renewed at military cemeteries like the Punchbowl. One of my radio-gang shipmates in the *California* rests there under the gold marker of a Medal of Honor winner, the highest award our nation can give. Harry Truman said about this award: 'I would rather have *it* than be President.'

"In the *California* the radio compartment was located on the first plat-form deck below the third deck, on the port side, where the first tor-pedo struck. The room started to flood, and my chief radioman, Tho-mas J. Reeves, ordered an evacuation. From the third deck, Chief Reeves organized an ammunition-handling party. With all power out, the ammunition for our five-inch anti-aircraft guns had to be passed by hand up all the decks between the powder magazines and the gun deck. Chief Reeves remained at his volunteer post on the third deck until he was overcome by smoke and fire. He died there. During the war a new destroyer-escort, the USS *Reeves*, was named in his honor.

"Several other *California* shipmates sleep at the Punchbowl. These men were not necessarily the brightest—for many of them found ways to avoid places like Pearl Harbor—but they certainly were among the best our country has produced. They were loyal, steadfast, and brave. There was no drug problem among them, and very little crime. They had been brought up to believe in the symbols of patriotism, the pledge of allegiance to the flag, in duty to country.

"Of course, I must not present them as Boy Scouts. Their level of profanity exceeded that of today's Hollywood films, and with a good deal more imagination. The screenwriters only seem to know one word. The shipmates liked to drink, and sometimes to dismantle bars like Honolulu's Black Cat in brawls. They liked girls. Often they were bad girls, because those were the only kind a sailor could meet. In other words, they were very much as military men have always been. But they were more than that.

"They were members of a Navy they considered the best in the world, man for man, ship for ship, plane for plane. They were defending a country that, despite its flaws, they considered the best in the world. Oh, yes, they were chauvinistic! Their country had never lost a war, and they did not intend that it ever would.

"If they had a fault, I think it was that they put too much trust in their officers. Aboard ship they were second-class citizens, but in exchange they assumed—it was sort of an unwritten contract, as one reviewer of my battleship book pointed out in the Naval War College *Review*—that their leaders were competent and would look out for them. Sometimes they did, but sometimes—as was demonstrated here forty-nine years ago—they were not competent, and they did not look out for them.

"On a personal note, when I looked around at the carnage of Pearl Harbor on the afternoon of 7 December, I felt betrayed. After that, I could never fully trust any of my leaders, military or political, again. Over the past decades, that skepticism has proved a wise precaution.

"'Where ignorance is bliss, / 'Tis folly to be wise,' the poet Thomas Gray advised; but I could no longer agree. The blissful ignorance that preceded Pearl Harbor came at too high a price. I agree now with the poet Robert Browning: 'Ignorance is not innocence but sin.'

"Whatever the virtues and faults of these sailors—and I was one of them—we certainly had no inkling that we were marked by history. We stood our watches and inspections . . . griped about our officers in the time-honored American way . . . longed to return to 'the States,' for Hawaii was still only a territory . . . and made our bibulous liberties along the mean and narrow streets of Honolulu, which were so well described by James Jones in his now-classic novel, *From Here to Eternity.* During those liberties we sailors discovered that we ranked at the very bottom of the social scale in these islands. (After the attack, when I had temporary radar duty with the Army Signal Corps at Fort Shafter, I discovered to my surprise that the GIs received better treatment than sailors, who were here today and gone tomorrow. When I went into Honolulu with soldiers, I was invited into a Hawaiian home for the first time.)

"During all this time Clio, the muse of history—or was it Pele, the fiery goddess of the volcano?—was smiling down at our youth and ignorance. She was preparing a surprise. She was preparing to mark us with a special, if invisible, mark: Pearl Harbor survivor. It took us a long time to realize that we had been touched by destiny. We were too busy burying our dead, tending to our wounded, repairing our ships, taking the undamaged or lightly damaged ones to sea against an enemy who suddenly seemed invincible. We paid little attention to what the journalists and historians were saying. Later, when we should have, we were too busy going to college, getting married and having children, putting our lives together after the lightning bolts of war.

"For myself, I remembered Pearl Harbor as an awful humiliation, a stain on the national honor, and tried not to think about it. Except on December seventh of each year after I had returned to civilian life. On that date I would go alone into the bars of Los Angeles or Phoenix or Sacramento and drink too much while silently toasting my fallen comrades.

"It wasn't until a dozen years ago, when I was asked by the Naval Institute Press to write a book about my experiences in the battleship *California,* including her sinking in this harbor, that I had to come to grips with the subject. I began to read the many, often conflicting, accounts of the attack, and to get in touch with shipmates and other old sailors. My wife and I made a trip here for additional research. It was necessary to stand in the places I had stood to hear the distant echoes and remember the authentic sounds and voices of the past.

"The four chapters I devoted to the attack and its aftermath were painful to reconstruct. No matter how hard some naval authorities and some historians tried to justify what had happened, Pearl Harbor remained what it was: a shattering defeat. Americans don't like to lose at anything, and the search for scapegoats and conspiracies that might explain the defeat continues to this day. After I finished the book, I felt greatly relieved. I suppose it was a kind of catharsis, the purging of dammed-up emotions one is supposed to feel after watching a Greek tragedy like *Oedipus Rex,* or a performance of *Hamlet,* where the hero is brought low by his fatal flaw.

"What does one learn from such a defeat? During the war, not much. One is too busy hating, for hate is a defense against the fear which might make one weak and cowardly. After the war, some of us kept on hating. I must admit that I was one of them. I am glad to say that I am *not* one of them now.

"Some say that the lesson to be learned from Pearl Harbor is preparedness against any surprise attack in the future. In other words, to avert war by preparing for war. Well, men have been practicing preparedness for at least six thousand years. The success of that policy can be determined from a casual reading of history.

"I do not think preparedness is the answer. We have nearly spent ourselves into bankruptcy following that policy. To many, if not to our leaders, it is obvious that war is an obsolete institution. The technology of war has made it not only unwinnable but also unthinkable. I believe that we should try for closer relationships with our friends, and seek peaceful accords with our potential foes. That will make it possible to reduce our preparations for war. It will make it possible to stop the filling up of places like the Punchbowl.

"Some of what I learned about war is incorporated in my memoir about my years in the South and Western Pacific in the fleet salvage and rescue ship *Pawnee*. I summarized my theme in the closing eight words of *'We Will Stand by You': Serving in the* Pawnee, *1942–1945:*

"'It is better to save than to destroy.'

"The chapters of my battleship memoir that describe the two-hour-long attack on Pearl Harbor were purchased by the Japanese magazine *Maru* ('Ship'). Some time later I received a hand-written letter with a San Bernardino postmark. The letter had been written by a former sailor of the Imperial Japanese Navy and sent to a friend or relative in California for translation and forwarding to me. In the letter the writer praised my description of the attack, and closed with these words:

"'Please never let war come between the sacred countries of the United States and Japan again.'

"I certainly agree with Mr. Hashimoto!

"Thank you for inviting me here.

"Go with God."

The awful humiliation that was Pearl Harbor can be traced, at least in part, to national hubris, coupled with racial prejudice. Our concept of the typical Japanese male, I wrote in *Battleship Sailor* (page 16), "was that of an editorial cartoon from a Hearst newspaper: short, near-sighted, bowlegged, and buck-toothed, with a thirty-five millimeter camera hanging from his neck, smiling falsely and bowing obsequiously. . . . The idea that this pitiful island race would dare to challenge the mightiest nation in the world was ludicrous." This viewpoint was common, not only among the enlisted men but also among our leaders, military and civilian, who should have known better. We were thus victimized by our own propaganda.

To this arrogant underestimation of the potential enemy were added an astonishing series of miscalculations, errors of judgment, incompetence, and simple bad luck that left the Pacific Fleet vulnerable to attack in its supposedly secure harbor. With many senior officers ashore for the weekend, as if they had never heard of the war warnings from Washington, the command structure broke down completely. We were like a professional football team playing in the Super Bowl without a head coach or assistant coach, with a middle linebacker playing quarterback and the defensive and offensive lines and backfields filled with substitutes or men playing out of position.

From my vantage point in the "birdbath" of the maintop, I saw the admiral's barge come alongside the officer's accommodation ladder during the second phase of the attack. The short, blocky form of Admiral Pye, still in civilian clothes, hurried toward the bridge, followed by several of his flag officers. Some minutes later Captain Bunkley arrived in his gig. He was in uniform, but it made little difference now. His ship was burning and sinking from the effects of two torpedoes, a bomb hit amidships, and several near misses. A number of voids to the torpedo defensive system had been left open in preparation for an inspection on Monday, and water was flooding up and throughout the ship. As a result, the *California* had been as unprepared for combat as her captain was to command her. Of Pye's battle line, the *Oklahoma* had turned turtle, the *Arizona* had blown up, the *West Virginia* was sinking, and only the *Nevada*, although heavily damaged by a torpedo hit forward and several bombs, was preparing to get under way.

I cursed in rage, fear, and frustration. Behind all the pomp and circumstance with which my captain and admiral surrounded themselves, behind the privileges and prerogatives to which their "brass hats" entitled them, these had proven to be ordinary men indeed. Henceforth officers would command my obedience, for it was my duty to give that now that we were at war. But they would not merit, and would not receive, my respect until they had earned it.

Naval history records a number of famous battle cries, from Admiral Horatio, Viscount Nelson's understated, "England expects every man will do his duty" at the Battle of Trafalgar to the emotional reply of Capt. John Paul Jones of the *Bon Homme Richard* when the commodore of the *Serapis* asked if he wished to surrender: "I have not yet begun to fight!" There was Admiral George Dewey's laconic, "You may fire when you are ready, Gridley," at the Battle of Manila Bay, and Adm. David Farragut's impassioned orders when his flotilla was threatened by exploding mines at the Battle of Mobile Bay: "Damn the torpedoes! Captain Drayton, go ahead! Jouett, full speed!"

All these exhortations were made in winning causes. Probably, quotations even more stirring have been made by the losers, but rarely are they remembered: the winners write the histories. One which has passed down is the epitaph by the Greek poet Simonides for the three hundred Spartans and seven hundred other Greeks who fell to the last man in defending the narrow pass of Thermopylae during the Persian Wars: "Go tell the Spartans, thou who passest by, / That here, obedient to their laws, we lie." Another is the deeply eloquent surrender of the remarkable Chief Joseph of the Nez Perce to Col. (later Provost Major General) Nelson A. Miles when the men, women and children he had so brilliantly led were just thirty miles short of freedom in Canada: "Hear me, my chiefs. I am tired. My heart is sick and sad. From where the sun now stands, I will fight no more forever."

But these were magnificent lost causes, where Pearl Harbor's only claim to glory was in the many acts of individual heroism which the failure of the leaders engendered. One such act culminated in a battle cry which the nation sorely needed as it entered World War II with a series of crushing defeats at Pearl Harbor, Wake and Guam Islands, and in the Philippines.

Like so many other events of 7 December, the derivation of "Praise the Lord and Pass the Ammunition!" was cloaked in misrepresentation and controversy. One Navy chaplain, William A. Maguire, received the initial credit and national publicity for uttering the famous line during the height of the air attack. The real author, another Navy chaplain named Howell M. Forgy, went to sea and didn't return to correct the record until many months later. By that time the first chaplain, a *California* shipmate, had received a *Life* magazine cover, and the song inspired by the battle cry was blaring from every juke box in the nation.

Fleet Chaplain Maguire was perfectly typecast to be a Catholic priest: handsome, gray-haired, inspirational in voice and manner, as Irish as actor Pat O'Brien. For reasons known only to him, and doubtless to some alert press agent, Commander Maguire was given credit for the Pearl Harbor battle cry, and did little to disavow authorship.

The Protestant chaplain in the *California* was Raymond C. Hohenstein (shown on page 219 of *Battleship Sailor*), who was well acquainted with both Maguire and Forgy.

"Chaplain Maguire was detached as Fleet Chaplain from Pearl Harbor on 25 May, 1942," he wrote.* "When he left, he said to the rest of us [chaplains] with a smile, 'I guess I'll have to take the rap for "Praise, Etc."' At the time we all believed that the words were an editorial fantasy and that no one had really said them. He reported to the Commander of the Naval Training Station, San Diego, on 13 June 1942, and during the next four months he was given credit for 'Praise, etc.,' although to my knowledge he never claimed credit for it."

Meanwhile, Lieutenant Forgy was at sea in the heavy cruiser *New Orleans*, participating in the Battles of the Coral Sea and Midway, and several other actions. It wasn't until he returned to Pearl Harbor in the fall of 1942 that the true story was revealed.

"It must have been 29 or 30 October that Forgy showed up at the Waikiki cottage I shared with another chaplain," Hohenstein recalled. "It was during that evening visit that Forgy told us he had said, 'Praise the Lord and Pass the Ammunition!'" As soon as Chaplain Forgy's version was declared the official one at Admiral Nimitz's Pearl Harbor headquarters, the record was corrected by an article on 1 November in the Honolulu *Advertiser.*

In an interview with the Los Angeles *Times* on 7 December 1966, Forgy (then confined to a wheelchair and living in retirement in Glendora) gave the background of his famous exhortation:

When the *New Orleans* went to battle stations, he went topside, where he saw what remained the most shocking sight of his life: the battleship *Arizona* blowing up.

Forgy then heard a command over the P.A. system for the man with the keys to the 5-inch ammunition lockers to lay below. In a foul-up repeated with variations on other ships, including the *California,* he had gone ashore with the keys in his pocket. The chaplain helped crewmen break into the lockers with fire axes. But the ship was undergoing some steam-turbine repairs, and there was no power for the ammunition

---

*Letter to author of 24 June 1980 from the Rev. Dr. Hohenstein, Chaplain Corps, USN (Ret.) The first living Navy chaplain to receive the Purple Heart, he retired from the Navy in 1961 with the rank of captain.

hoists. Crewmen formed a line and began passing 5-inch anti-aircraft shells up to the gun deck by hand.

"It was hard work, and the boys were tiring," Forgy recalled. "It was then that I clapped one of the men on the back and said, 'Praise the Lord and pass the ammunition!'"

Nor is this the end of the story. *Life* magazine, never a publication to flinch in the face of cold facts, had already wheeled up its big propaganda guns. Appearing on the cover of the 2 November 1942 issue was a full-color portrait of not Forgy but William A. Maguire, accompanied by the famous cry. America needed live heroes and *Life* was pleased to oblige, although in somewhat weasel-worded prose on an inside page.

About the time *Life* appeared on the newsstands, on 31 October, the now-Captain Maguire held a news conference in New York City. With him was his superior, Bishop John F. O'Hara, head of the Military Ordinariate of the Catholic Church of America. With some equivocation, the renowned *California* chaplain disavowed the *Life* article and the sentiments expressed in the patriotic ballad. For a chaplain, a noncombatant, to encourage his men in an act of violence was a direct violation of the Geneva Convention.

Forgy later commented, in a column by Jack Smith (Los Angeles *Times*, 3 June 1982) that many people had capitalized on the phrase, but he had never earned anything from it.

Following the attack, fifteen Medals of Honor were awarded to naval personnel, an exceptional number. Seven went to officers, three to warrant officers, five to enlisted men. Ten of the awards were posthumous. Forty-eight Navy Crosses were also awarded.

A congressional act of 4 February 1919 established the criteria for the awards to naval personnel. The Medal of Honor was to be awarded to " . . . any person who, while in the naval service of the United States, shall, in action involving actual conflict with the enemy, distinguish himself conspicuously by gallantry and intrepidity at the risk of his life above and beyond the call of duty and without detriment to the mission of the command. . . ."

The Navy Cross was to be awarded to " . . . any person who, . . . has distinguished . . . himself by extraordinary heroism or distinguished service not being sufficient to justify the award of a medal of honor or a distinguished service medal." (The Distinguished Service Medal, known among enlisted men as the officer's medal, was to be awarded to

". . . any person who has distinguished, or who hereafter shall distinguish, himself by exceptionally meritorious service to the Government in a duty of great responsibility.")*

How well were these stringent criteria met by the officers involved in initiating, reviewing, and awarding the Medal of Honor? Let us consider the case of the *Arizona*.

When the attack began, both Rear Adm. Isaac C. Kidd, Commander Battleship Division One, and the captain, Franklin Van Valkenburgh, were on board. They immediately went to their battle stations on the signal and navigation bridges, respectively. Very early in the attack, before either one could initiate any significant action, the ship blew up with a stupendous explosion. Both men were killed, two of 1,177 *Arizona* officers and men who died. They were awarded the Medal of Honor. Only one other *Arizona* crewman, Lt. Comdr. Samuel G. Fuqua, USN, won *the* medal.

Admiral Kidd's citation reads:

For conspicuous devotion to duty, extraordinary courage and complete disregard of his own life, during the attack on the Fleet in Pearl Harbor, by Japanese forces on 7 December 1941. Rear Adm. Kidd immediately went to the bridge and, as Commander Battleship Division One, courageously discharged his duties as Senior Officer Present Afloat until the USS ARIZONA, his Flagship, blew up from magazine explosions and a direct bomb hit on the bridge which resulted in the loss of his life.†

Captain Van Valkenburgh's citation is similar.

For conspicuous devotion to duty, extraordinary courage and complete disregard of his own life, during the attack on the Fleet in Pearl Harbor, T.H., by Japanese forces on 7 December 1941. As commanding officer of the USS ARIZONA, Capt. Van Valkenburgh gallantly fought his ship until the USS ARIZONA blew up from magazine explosions and a direct bomb hit on the bridge which resulted in the loss of his life.‡

Lieutenant Commander Fuqua was one of the fortunate survivors of Battleship 39. As his Medal of Honor citation illustrates in graphic detail, survival was not his primary concern:

*Lt. Comdr. Michael W. Shelton, CEC, USN, "Who Are the Heroes?": U.S. Naval Institute *Proceedings*, Vol. 104/8/906, August 1978, p. 41.
†Donald K. and Helen C. Ross, *0755: The Heroes of Pearl Harbor* (Port Orchard, Wash.: Rokalu Press, 1988), p. 18.
‡Ibid., p. 25.

For distinguished conduct in action, outstanding heroism, and utter disregard of his own safety above and beyond the call of duty during the attack on the Fleet in Pearl Harbor, by Japanese forces on 7 December 1941. Upon the commencement of the attack, Lieutenant Commander Fuqua rushed to the quarterdeck of the USS ARIZONA to which he was attached, where he was stunned and knocked down by the explosion of a large bomb which hit the quarterdeck, penetrated several decks, and started a severe fire. Upon regaining consciousness, he began to direct the fighting of the fire and the rescue of wounded and injured personnel. Almost immediately there was a tremendous explosion forward, which made the ship appear to rise out of the water, shudder, and settle down by the bow rapidly. The whole forward part of the ship was enveloped in flames which spread rapidly, and wounded and burned men poured out of the ship to the quarterdeck. Despite these conditions, his harrowing experience, and severe enemy bombing and strafing at the time, LCDR Fuqua continued to direct fighting of fires in order to check them while wounded and burned could be taken from the ship and supervised the rescue of these men in such an amazingly calm and cool manner and with such excellent judgment that it inspired everyone who saw him and undoubtedly resulted in saving of many lives. After realizing the ship could not be saved and that he was the senior surviving officer aboard, he directed it to be abandoned, but continued to remain on the quarterdeck and directed abandoning ship and rescue of personnel until satisfied that all personnel that could be had been saved, after which he left the ship with the last boatload. The conduct of LCDR Fuqua was not only in keeping with the highest traditions of the naval service but characterizes him as an outstanding leader of men.*

Turn now to the *West Virginia,* which was hit by six or seven torpedoes and two bombs and sank at her mooring until the turn of the port bilge hit bottom. She lost two officers and 103 men dead and 52 wounded. There would have been many more casualties except for an "Away fire and rescue party" order from the officer of the deck. He saw the first Japanese bomb hit a hangar on Ford Island and thought it was an internal explosion in the *California,* which was in his line of sight.

Capt. Mervin S. Bennion was aboard and went to his battle station on the navigation bridge. Very early in the action a bomb detonated on the center gun of turret No. 2 in the *Tennessee,* which was moored

*Ibid., pp. 14–15.

inboard of the "WeeVee." Fragments of this bomb disemboweled Captain Bennion. Chief Pharmacist's Mate Leak administered a hypodermic, and Bennion was moved to another part of the ship, where he died. His Medal of Honor citation reads:

For conspicuous devotion to duty, extraordinary courage, and complete disregard of his own life, above and beyond the call of duty, during the attack on the Fleet in Pearl Harbor, by Japanese forces on 7 December 1941. As Commanding Officer of the USS WEST VIRGINIA, after being mortally wounded, Capt. Bennion evidenced apparent concern only in fighting and saving his ship, and strongly protested against being carried from the bridge.*

Although each of the three citations for the admiral and the two captains uses the same standard phrasing, "For conspicuous devotion to duty, extraordinary courage, and complete disregard of his own life" (adding "above and beyond the call of duty" for Bennion), no specific corroboration is offered, unlike the Fuqua citation. These three officers went to their battle stations, as was their duty, and were killed in action. So were 1,175 of their shipmates in the *Arizona* and 104 in the *West Virginia*. By the criteria applied to Admiral Kidd and Captains Van Valkenburgh and Bennion, all these men were eligible to receive the Medal of Honor.

The highest award our nation can bestow is depreciated when awarded by senior officers to senior officers who clearly do not meet the lofty standards of gallantry and intrepidity specified for this medal. Admiral Kidd and Captains Bennion and Van Valkenburgh were brave and honorable men. Had they lived, it is most likely that they would have refused their medals, insisting they be awarded to others who distinguished themselves that day, but to little or no recognition.

An additional factor in the case of the two commanding officers is that they lost their ships and nearly 1,300 men. Navy Regulations state: "The responsibility of the commanding officer for his command is absolute." Following World War I, there was such a furor over the awarding of medals that the Senate Subcommittee on Naval Affairs conducted a hearing. In its report to the Senate the subcommittee wrote that it could not ". . . too strongly condemn the practice of giving awards to commanding officers in the Navy who lost their ships unless in such

*Ibid., p. 9.

cases they shall have shown such marked heroism in spite of the loss of their ships." The report continued:

The subcommittee does not believe that because of the loss of their ships the commanding officers are necessarily ineligible for reward, but it does believe that in each such case these officers are on the defensive, and instead of the loss of their ships being taken as an opportunity where an award may be made, it is an obstacle, though not necessarily an insurmountable obstacle, in the way of an award.*

One wonders if those standards of "marked heroism" were applied when awarding the Medal of Honor to the commanding officers of the *Arizona* and the *West Virginia*.

Even where men deserved their medals, considerations beyond merit sometimes were a factor. Doris Miller, a mess attendant in the *West Virginia*, a sharecropper's son from Waco, Texas, became the first black to win a Navy Cross, the second-highest medal in the Navy pantheon of valor. His citation reads:

For devotion to duty, extraordinary courage and disregard for his own personal safety during the attack on Pearl Harbor by the Japanese, December 7, 1941. While at the side of his Captain on the bridge of the battleship USS WEST VIRGINIA, Mess Attendant Second Class Doris Miler, despite enemy bombing and strafing, and in the face of serious fire, assisted in moving his Captain, who had been mortally wounded, to a place of greater safety, and later manned and operated a machinegun until ordered to leave the bridge.†

Contrary to the citation, Miller was not at the side of his captain during the early phase of the attack, according to Walter Karig's *Battle Report: Pearl Harbor to Coral Sea*. Learning that Bennion had been badly wounded, Lt. Comdr. D. C. Johnson, the ship's communication officer, related: "I proceeded to the signal bridge where I found Captain Bennion lying on a cot in full uniform. I had brought a colored mess attendant with me, a very powerfully built individual [Doris Miller], having in mind that he might pick the Captain up and carry him below."‡

---

*"Who Are the Heroes?", pp. 44–45.
†Ross, *0755: Heroes of Pearl*, pp. 44–45.
‡Comdr. Walter Karig, USNR, and Lt. Welbourn Kelley, USNR, *Battle Report: Pearl Harbor to Coral Sea* (New York: Farrar & Rinehart, Inc., 1944), p. 73.

But Bennion's wound was mortal. "The Captain's abdomen was cut by a fragment of a bomb, about three or four inches, with part of his intestines protruding," according to Lt. (jg) F. H. White, USNR. "The Captain did not want to be moved, but he was carefully carried to shelter abaft the conning tower where Leak, Chief Pharmacist's Mate, administered first aid."

Meanwhile, Lieutenant White went to the .50-caliber machine gun on the port side, forward of the armored conning tower. According to Karig, another junior officer went with Miller to the starboard-side machine gun and showed him how to operate it. Miller fired the gun either until it ran out of ammunition or until he was ordered to leave the bridge.

"In the interest of a legend already in existence, it would be pleasant to report that Miller shot down one or more planes," Karig wrote. "A careful search of the records, including eyewitness reports of all those present, fails to bring forth either a contradiction or a substantiation in fact. Nevertheless, Doris Miller . . . merited to the fullest the Navy Cross which he so proudly wore."*

Karig's account of Miller's actions demonstrates that his *Battle Report,* written for a wartime audience, had other purposes than a strict adherence to fact. An eyewitness account by Victor Delano, then a junior officer in the *West Virginia,* brings immediacy and verity to Miller's role in the events of that morning.

Captain Bennion had been mortally wounded before Delano arrived on the bridge from his battle station in the Plotting Room, via Central Station through the wiring trunk to the conning tower.

"I decided to investigate two machine guns mounted forward of the conning tower," Delano wrote in his account of the action, handwritten on or about 9 December 1941, and expanded upon in a typed version compiled in January 1942.

I found that these guns were without cooling water but could be fired. One was slightly out of adjustment, but I readily repaired it and they were ready to be shot. I went to the conning tower, found an enlisted man, Lieut. (J.G.) White, and Miller, the mess boy, who in some inexplainable way had reached the bridge. Taking the three of them to the machine guns, I instructed them in their operation and then assigned the

*Ibid., p. 73.

Lieutenant to one gun, the enlisted man to the other gun, and Miller to keep the ammunition coming. As Miller was flying around in this capacity, after having one opportunity to fire the guns in which he became of more menace to us than to the enemy, he appeared happier than I had ever seen him before in his life. I had only seen him smile once before when, as the heavyweight boxing representative of the WEST VIRGINIA, he knocked out a much smaller white boy.*

Many years later, additional facts about Miller's award of the Navy Cross were revealed by Jesse Pond, editor of the *Newsletter* of the Pearl Harbor History Associates, Inc. Pond was present at Pearl Harbor on 7 December 1941 as a fire controlman in the destroyer *Chew* (DD-106).

"Fast forward now [from the attack] to July 10, 1974," he wrote in the Summer 1994 issue. "On that day I received a 'phone call from retired Rear Admiral Robert E. Cronin, a man whom I had come to know as fellow members of the Pearl Harbor Survivors Association. . . . [He] had been Engineering Officer in USS MARYLAND, the battleship moored inboard of the capsized OKLAHOMA."

The admiral was concerned, Pond's report continued, over remarks made by a black TV personality on a Washington, D.C., talk show. He claimed that Miller had grabbed a machine gun "when everybody else was splitting" and shot down twenty planes on 7 December 1941. Cronin wanted Pond, then national treasurer of the PHSA, to issue some corrective to such exaggerations, which denigrated all the people who were at Pearl Harbor on 7 December, especially those who gave their lives for their country.

"The gist of Cronin's 'phone call," Pond continued, "as recorded by me on a memo dated July 10, 1974, is that 'Doris Miller was awarded the Navy Cross in order to help recruiting of blacks into the Armed Services. The order came out from Washington to find a black man and give him a medal, and as Miller was the only black mentioned in any of the battle reports, he was selected. Recruiting was not going well at all and something was needed and this was it.'"†

The consensus among Pearl Harbor survivors with whom I have discussed the Miller affair, including Jesse Pond, is that Doris Miller earned the Navy Cross he was presented on 27 May 1942 at Pearl Harbor. One

---

*Letter to author of 25 January 1995 from Capt. Victor Delano, USN (Ret.), with copy of his typed action report of January 1942.

†Jesse Pond, "The Doris Miller Story": *Newsletter* of the Pearl Harbor History Association, Inc., No. 23, Summer 1994, pp. 1–2.

of a relative few afforded the chance to strike back during the awful defeat we were suffering, he give it his best effort. For his sake, it is regrettable that he was not returned to the States to help with the recruiting of blacks into the Navy. Instead, the detailers assigned him to the *Liscome Bay* (CVE-56), one of that class of small escort carriers dubbed "Kaiser Coffins" by the sailors. The epithet proved appallingly true of the *Liscome Bay*, torpedoed off Makin Island by Japanese submarine *I-175* on 24 November 1943. She disintegrated in a series of terrifying explosions, with the loss of Rear Adm. Henry M. Mullinix, Capt. I. D. Wiltsie, 51 other officers, and 591 enlisted men—including Doris Miller.

Of all the accounts of heroism which emerged from the attack, the most unsettling and essentially tragic was that of the *Nevada*'s chief quartermaster, Robert Sedberry. In a 1981 book review for the *Proceedings* of a novel titled *Battleship: Pearl Harbor, 1941*, by Wallace Louis Exum, I was pleased to remind naval readers of his nearly forgotten exploits. I wrote:

"The worthy protagonist of Exum's novel is the *Nevada*'s chief quartermaster, whom he calls Earl Toland and who in life was Robert Sedberry. It was Sedberry who [on 7 December 1941], nearly single-handedly, maneuvered his ship clear of Berth F-8 at the rear of the battle line without the aid of tugs; cleared the blazing hulk of the *Arizona* (BB-39) close aboard; took the *Nevada* past the other battleships to the cheers, prayerful curses, and even tears of topside sailors; squeezed her past a dredge that blocked half the channel and, under orders, beached her—first near Hospital Point and later, with the aid of tugs, on Waipio Peninsula.

"It was a superb feat of seamanship, performed with elan under desperate circumstances, and it earned Sedberry the admiration of this reviewer (who witnessed the entire sortie from the maintop of the *California* [BB-44]) and of every other officer and enlisted man present.

"With the captain and exec of the *Nevada* ashore, the acting CO was Lieutenant Commander Francis J. Thomas, U.S. Naval Reserve, the ship's first lieutenant and damage control officer.* Thomas coolly gave

---

*An Annapolis graduate, Thomas was recalled to active duty in February 1941. His actual title in the *Nevada* was assistant damage control officer under the ship's first lieutenant and damage control officer, Lt. Comdr. George C. Miller, who was ashore that morning.

the order to get under way, and later got most of the official credit; but all the sailors knew who the real hero was." *

Since then, conflicting reports of the *Nevada's* gallant sortie that tend to diminish Sedberry's role have appeared in *Naval History, Shipmate,* and the *Proceedings.* The mere suggestion that a chief quartermaster, an enlisted man, might have conned a battleship is anathema to some. The identity of the men who conned her has become the subject of renewed controversy.

The official account, in the ship's deck log, is unequivocal. For the 8 to 12 watch on 7 December 1941: "0840 Underway on various courses at various speeds, conforming to channel to stand out of harbor, Lieut-Comdr. F. J. Thomas, USNR, at conn, Lieutenant L. E. Ruff, USN, acting navigator, in conning tower." The log was written by officers involved in the action and signed off by the captain, Francis W. Scanland, who hadn't reported on board until the ship was beached at Hospital Point.

"Scanland's action report cites the same two officers and compliments Sedberry for his calm and effective handling of the wheel and his foresight in ordering the engine room to make preparations for getting under way."†

In *At Dawn We Slept,* Gordon Prange has a different (and rather clumsily worded) version:

> Although severely damaged, *Nevada* was still very much afloat and full of fight when Lieutenant Ruff scrambled up her side from *Solace's* [hospital ship, AH-5] motor launch. He knew that, with the captain and other senior officers ashore, unusually heavy responsibilities would fall to him and to Thomas, who was belowdecks at his battle station. When Ruff got close enough to communicate, he suggested that Thomas run the ship's activities below while he, Ruff, would manage topside.‡

The version favored by most former enlisted men was given by Capt. Donald K. Ross, USN (Ret.), Sedberry's shipmate and author with his wife, Helen, of the previously cited *0755: The Heroes of Pearl Harbor.* In a letter to Commander Bruce, he wrote:

---

*U.S. Naval Institute *Proceedings,* September 1981, p. 106.

†Comdr. Jack D. Bruce, USN (Ret.), "The Enigma of Battleship *Nevada,*" *Naval History,* Winter 1991, p. 52.

‡*At Dawn We Slept: The Untold Story of Pearl Harbor* (New York: McGraw-Hill, 1981), p. 515.

"I talked with him [Sedberry] many times prior to his passing away. . . . Admiral Ruff was our Com [Communications] Officer and was back from the *Solace* in plenty of time before we moved out at 0832; *at that time* he was not qualified for underway O.O.D. in *Nevada*. I have his report. Lt. Ruff told CQM Bob Sedberry to conn the ship, which he did."*

In a rebuttal to Bruce's article, and in an article in the Naval Academy Alumni Association's *Shipmate* magazine (September 1987 issue), Francis J. Thomas, who retired as a rear admiral, supports the official version of events, except for the grounding of *Nevada* at Hospital Point. He claims he was trying to anchor the ship when a bomb hit wiped out the forecastle anchoring detail (including Chief Boatswain Edwin J. Hill, who won the second Medal of Honor awarded to *Nevada* crewmen) and she inadvertently ran aground.

As the senior officer on board with the command duty, I manned my battle station in the below-decks central station. . . . From there I could communicate with all important stations. . . . The torpedo hit (port side, forward) came almost immediately, and we counter-flooded the aft starboard blister tanks to correct the consequent list.

The order for "all ships [to] get under way and stand out of the harbor" came soon afterward, and I notified the engine room to get up steam as soon as possible. . . .

Lieutenant Ruff soon informed me that all was ready, and I made my way up the steel tube to the conning tower, where Lieutenant Ruff, Chief Sedberry, and four or five other sailors were waiting anxiously to get the ship under way. I checked with the engine room and was told they were ready to "answer bells."

With Chief Sedberry at the wheel, the *Nevada* got under way. I had both engines backed one-third to give us room to swing past the USS *Arizona* (BB-39), then went ahead on the starboard engine in order to turn the bow to port. When the opening to the port of the *Arizona*'s stern appeared large enough, I ordered ahead one-third on the port engine. With the *Arizona* cleared, the *Nevada* headed for the channel—and the open sea.

---

*Bruce, "The Enigma of Battleship *Nevada*," p. 53. As a warrant machinist, the late Captain Ross won the Medal of Honor for "extraordinary courage and disregard of his own life" in the forward and after dynamo rooms of the *Nevada* during the attack. I treasure the inscription in my copy of Ross's book: "For Ted Mason, who fell in love with the Prune Barge, the Show Boat of the Battle Force. I'm glad I had the Cheer-Up Ship, no flag staff to screw up the works."

We were not far down the channel when we received a disheartening message—not mentioned in Commander Bruce's article: "*Nevada*, do not—repeat—do not leave the harbor." My first idea was to round the seaward end of Ford Island and head back up the other side, but Chief Sedberry said that the ship could not make such a sharp turn. I decided to turn to port and anchor near Hospital Point, thus clearing the channel.*

Admiral Thomas's version is disputed by three quartermasters and a yeoman who were present in the conning tower.

Leonard Marsden, a quartermaster second class, writes:

I was the first one in the conn. I put on the IJV headpiece and was in touch with a fireman in the engine room. I told him what was happening and that Oklahoma was listing to port. I said that I sure had no authority, but it would be a good idea to get steam up. For many years I thought I had gained us a couple of minutes, but when I met Don Ross at a reunion, he deflated my balloon by saying he had been ordering extra pressure for a while. I don't know how Sedberry ever got that credit, but he shouldn't have.

The conn filled up with people. I seem to remember Lt. Cmdr. Thomas in the starboard side of the conn, but not much more. Lt. Ruff arrived, still in civvies and it was he who took the conn. I don't know what conversation he had with Thomas. As lines were cast off, we had to back down to clear the burning *Arizona*. There was pipeline on piles astern of us running from Ford Island into the harbor. I forgot the engine commands even though I was standing just behind Sedberry and Ruff. However, Ruff gave the order "hard left rudder" when while backing should have been the opposite so as to swing the bow to port. Sedberry said "Did you say hard RIGHT rudder, sir." Ruff responded by giving the correct order and then said "Thank you Chief." I have never forgotten that under the stress of the moment that was a class statement. Roy Johnson QM3c [*sic*] also remembers this exchange. Sedberry didn't "take" the conn. He steered as told. "Go down the middle." He certainly performed well but no enlisted man would be the conn with an officer on the scene.†

Don Landry, a quartermaster first class, told Bruce that when the general alarm was sounded he passed through central station and climbed the sixty rungs of the emergency tube to the conning tower. "Lt. Ruff, Communications Officer, was senior officer in the conning tower. . . . I personally saw Lcdr. Thomas in Central Station when I

*"In Contact," *Naval History*, Fall 1992, p. 2.
†Letter to author, 18 July 1995.

climbed the tube to the Conning Tower. I didn't see him again that day." *

Roy Johnson, a quartermaster second class, arrived on the bridge for his battle station, but the bridge was a shambles from bomb hits, and Sedberry moved him to the adjacent conning tower. In a letter to Bruce, Johnson stated:

At 0815 the Arizona blew up and then we got a message from the Arizona (before she blew) to prepare to get underway. So we did. LCDR Thomas was the senior officer aboard and went to *his* battle station—Central Station—to handle the damage control duties. Lt. Ruff appeared about 0830 in the Conning Tower and became the O.O.D. and Conning Officer. . . . We received a visual signal from the 'Tower'—Do not proceed out of the channel as there were subs (small 2-man jobs) in the channel. We were badly damaged and couldn't make the hard right turn to go around Ford Island again [sic], so Ruff and Sedberry decided to go aground at Hospital Point.

In response to a query from Commander Bruce, Johnson replied: "No. Thomas was in Central Station (Damage Control) all the time—to my knowledge. [The decision to run aground rested] solely with Ruff and Sedberry. [They] had no time or way to communicate with anyone to make such a snap decision."†

James L. Snyder, a first-class yeoman, was Captain Scanland's writer. At general quarters he was the captain's talker on the JA phone circuit. He stated in a letter to Bruce:

"He [Thomas] was also the Ship's Damage Control Officer and as a result of the hits and hull damage he was urgently required in that area and only reached the Conn after ship was under way."‡

What was Admiral Thomas's response to these statements? In his "In Contact" rebuttal, he said only:

The people quoted by Commander Bruce undoubtedly gave their versions many years after the event. The ship's log—signed by Captain Scanland—was prepared for him by Ensign Charles W. Jenkins, officer of the deck during the attack, and Lieutenant Commander W. L. Freseman, the ship's navigator. They spent two or three days painstakingly preparing the log to ensure its accuracy.

*Bruce "The Enigma of Battleship *Nevada*," p. 53.
†Ibid., p. 53.
‡Ibid.

After the return of Captain Scanland, I turned to my damage control duties, which kept me very busy. Whatever information obtained about my activities during the under way period came from people who had observed them—not from me.*

Despite this rather disingenuous defense of the accuracy of the log, the question remains: Who was conning the *Nevada* when she was maneuvered away from Berth F-8 and made her unforgettable passage down channel past Battleship Row? It was a sortie that failed, on orders from above, but it remains, as I wrote in *Battleship Sailor,* "the most magnificent, heart-stopping failure I have ever seen." Was it Thomas at the conn? Ruff (who also made his stars)? Or was it Sedberry?

Thomas, although only assistant damage control officer, was senior officer on board, with the command duty. But if he was in central station, as the enlisted men and Captain Ross believe, he could hardly have been conning (defined as "directing the steering by orders to the steersman" in Knight's *Modern Seamanship*) the ship.

Was it Ruff? Don Ross, Medal of Honor winner that morning as a warrant machinist, says flatly that Ruff was not qualified as an underway O.O.D. at that time. Which leaves Sedberry, a career enlisted man. Regardless of what the log says, it is very likely that he became, de facto, the man with the conn.

While Admiral Thomas emphatically does not agree, he does praise Sedberry: "[I]f anyone deserved a medal, he did. Possibly Captain Scanland didn't recommend him for one because he was not present during the action and, therefore, believed he was not the one to do so. A board of officers was convened on board, I have been told, to select those who would be cited. I have wondered why I was awarded a medal—possibly being in command during enemy action was enough."†

Commander Bruce was more emphatic about the injustice done to Sedberry. "He received no recognition for his travail other than a 'well done' from his commanding officer. He deserved more. He should have been given a medal. *Sedberry probably could not have been recommended for a medal without bringing into question the identity of the conning crew* [emphasis added]. I hope some day this wrong will be righted, for in every sense of the word Sedberry played a hero's role that day."‡

*Thomas, "In Contact," pp. 2–3.
†Ibid., p. 3. Thomas was awarded the Navy Cross.
‡Bruce, "The Enigma of Battleship *Nevada*," p. 54.

Less than a year after Pearl Harbor, Sedberry died at the navy yard hospital in Bremerton of tuberculosis. In a sense, his eulogy was written by John McGoran, my shipmate in the *California*, following the attack: "Never before had I witnessed so much admiration, such great pride in one enlisted man. It was a valorous feat, one that brought pride to all of us in the enlisted service."*

Recently, John added a postscript:

It is interesting to note that history gives Chief Quartermaster R. Sedberry only a passing comment. Full credit went to Lieutenant Commander Francis J. Thomas, who was acting Commanding Officer during the greater part of the attack.

Today, when I asked *Nevada*'s Pearl Harbor Survivors their thoughts on the accuracy of the official report, I am met with a deep bitterness.†

---

*"And Where Were You When They Bombed Pearl Harbor?" Excerpts from McGoran's recollections were published under the title "I Remember It Well" in U.S.Naval Institute *Proceedings,* December 1979, p. 64.

†Letter to author, 23 November 1994.

4

Market Street Commandos

In nature there are neither rewards nor punishments—there are consequences.

—Robert G. Ingersoll

"Pier Fifteen, buddy, and step on it!" I told the Yellow Cab driver. I had just left Li Po's cocktail lounge in San Francisco's Chinatown with a young lady named Dolores, and my liberty expired in ten minutes.

"Don't worry, sailor," the cabby said with a grin. "I'll get you back to the 'Pennsy' on time. How you get your girlfriend aboard is your problem." He accelerated past the pagoda roofs of narrow Grant Avenue, made a right turn on Broadway, and sped toward the Embarcadero.

Until recently, Broadway had been nearly as garish with flashing neon above nightclub, restaurant, and theater as the Great White Way in New York. Now all the lights had been dimmed by Army proclamation; even the street lamps had been painted black on the top and seaward sides. It was early April, 1942.

I scarcely noticed the dimout, the clanging trolley cars, or the medley of uniforms on the sidewalks. Having just returned from Pearl Harbor, I was enjoying the company of an American girl for the first time in six months. This one had black hair that tumbled past her shoulders. Her eyes were brown, and her smile was an invitation.

I had also rediscovered one of the hazards of picking up a girl in a port city that was being flooded with servicemen destined for duty in the Pacific. The soldier who had followed us from the Cathay House to Li Po's was only a lonesome GI who wanted to date her, Dolores had told me. I didn't blame him, but he had brought along four of his pals.

"That's my girl you're with, swabby," the private said as the five of them made a tight semicircle around our table. Usually I was accompanied by buddies like the formidable Red Goff and Jim Baker, but tonight I was alone. Obviously, quick thinking was called for.

"I'm sorry, soldier," I said. "No one told me about that."

"Well, I'm telling you now. Go find someone else to impress with your goddam campaign ribbons." The five crowded a little closer. "Or else . . ."

"Wait a minute, men," I said, holding up both hands to show peaceable intentions. "You haven't asked Dolores. How about letting her decide? If she prefers to be with you, I'll shove off. If she wants to stay here, you guys leave. Fair enough?"

They consulted briefly and grudgingly agreed. All eyes were now on Dolores.

She was enjoying this encounter much more than I was. There was not another sailor in the place.

"I never made you any promises," she finally told the private. "I'm going to stay here with Ted."

Now, as we approached the Embarcadero, I cursed the midnight curfew in effect every other liberty. But things would be different next time, I was sure. The cabby stopped by a sandbagged barricade near the Mission-style facade of Pier Fifteen. Dolores and I parted with steamy embraces that drew envious snickers and wolf whistles from the sailors and marines guarding the pier. I reported on board the battleship *Pennsylvania* at 2358 hours.

In one of the more bizarre involutions of war, the Embarcadero had become the Navy's new "battleship row." The finger piers running north from the Moorish tower of the Ferry Building now sheltered the seven surviving dreadnoughts of a once-mighty force. The *Pennsylvania*, *Maryland*, and *Tennessee* had escaped the Japanese attack on Pearl Harbor with relatively minor damage. They had been repaired at West Coast navy yards and assembled here about 1 April. The *New Mexico*, *Idaho*, and *Mississippi* had been rushed from the Atlantic Fleet to join them. From Puget Sound came the *Colorado*, which had been under yard overhaul when the Japanese struck at Oahu. Behind us in the mud and blood of Pearl Harbor we had left the sunken battleships *Arizona*, *Oklahoma*, *West Virginia*, and *California* and the beached and badly damaged *Nevada*.

The crews of the Embarcadero battleships didn't have to be military strategists to understand what had happened. In 1940 the battle force had been shifted to Pearl Harbor from its home port of San Pedro to deter Japanese aggression. That policy had failed miserably. Now the surviving capital ships had been pulled back to the West Coast to prevent their annihilation by enemy land- and carrier-based aircraft. The one-time queen of battles had been reduced to a desperate last line of defense should the Japanese break through our Hawaii-Midway-Alaska perimeter, which was thinly defended by our once-despised flattops.

In the Indian Ocean and the South China Sea, the situation was even more critical. Early in the war the Allies had lost Guam, Wake, Hong Kong, and the important oil fields of Borneo. By February the Japanese had taken the Malay Peninsula and poured onto the island of Singapore, capturing 70,000 prisoners. In the four-day Battle of the Java Sea (27 February–1 March) they had destroyed the entire "ABDA" force (Australian-British-Dutch-American) of cruisers and destroyers, including the famous heavy cruiser *Houston*. The U.S. Asiatic Fleet was no more. Within a few days the invaders overran Batavia, capital of the Netherlands East Indies. On 10 March the Allied troops on Java surrendered unconditionally.

In the Philippines, the American and Filipino forces had fallen back to a crumbling defense line across the Bataan Peninsula. On 11 March, Commander-in-Chief Douglas MacArthur left his headquarters in the Malinta Tunnel of Corregidor and fled by motor torpedo boat and B-17 bomber to Darwin, Australia. President Roosevelt had ordered his withdrawal, but that meant little to servicemen everywhere; they called him "Dugout Doug" and accused him of cowardice (and a good many other things). He was the man, some remembered, who had routed the "Bonus Army" of World War I veterans on orders from the equally detested President Herbert Hoover. When they heard of MacArthur's vainglorious pronouncement, "I shall return," the soldiers and sailors hooted and jeered.

"You goddam right he wants to return," said one of my fellow radiomen. "He owns half of Manila!"

In San Francisco the civilians read their newspapers and listened to their radios, so they were even more aware of the dimensions of our unbroken succession of defeats than were the enlisted men. Many still feared an invasion of the West Coast by the all-conquering enemy. Wailing air-raid alarms and accompanying blackouts were common in the weeks following Pearl Harbor. The paranoiac statements of Lt. Gen. John L. DeWitt, chief of the Army's Western Defense Command, fueled the public anxiety. "This is war," he declared. "Death and destruction may come from the skies at any moment."

Once he claimed that thirty enemy warplanes had flown over San Francisco. Reminded that no bombs had been dropped, the general nonetheless refused to admit the flight had been a phantom one. "It might have been better if some bombs had dropped to awaken this city," he riposted.

Reckless actions seem logical, even inevitable, in such an atmosphere. Consequently, San Franciscans were cheered in February when President Roosevelt authorized the evacuation of 127,000 Japanese-Americans, two-thirds of whom were native-born citizens, to inland internment camps.

"A Jap's a Jap!" said General DeWitt. "It makes no difference whether he's an American or not."* In the city by the Golden Gate, the normally cosmopolitan residents agreed. They had been told that the internees, even those who held American citizenship, owed allegiance to Tokyo by Japanese law. And they remembered Pearl Harbor.

Their morale received another boost when the great battleships in their somber wartime gray arrived. San Francisco was a child of the sea, and sailors had always been welcome there. Perhaps, in an obscure way, that was why 19-year-old Dolores had preferred me to a private from the midlands.

The reminders of the city's maritime heritage were everywhere. The fishing fleet still set out each morning with the tide and returned in midafternoon (accompanied now by a "spitkit" naval escort). Daily, the freighters and oilers and troop transports stood down the channel and passed under the Golden Gate Bridge. Dominating Union Square was the victory monument commemorating Admiral Dewey's destruction of the Spanish fleet at Manila Bay. In Portsmouth Square, the center of the city in pioneer days, Robert Louis Stevenson was remembered with a fountain surmounted by the *Treasure Island* galleon *Hispaniola* in bronze. At Powell and Market the cable cars still pivoted on their turntable, with grinning sailors lending the conductors and gripmen a hand. The food was marvelous, the drinks strong, the girls attractive and often

*Ronald H. Bailey, *The Home Front: U.S.A.* (Alexandria, Va.: Time-Life Books, 1977), pp. 10, 12, 30.

willing. Although in transition during those early war months, San Francisco had not yet been overwhelmed by military men of all services and nations. It was still one of the great liberty ports of the world.

From any hill the residents could see the battleships snubbed to their piers. Bristling with 14- and 16-inch main batteries and other weaponry, they were a reassuring sight. But the civilians knew nothing about the combat-readiness of the dreadnoughts that had long been America's first line of defense. Neither, for that matter, did most of the sailors who manned them. The ships assembled at San Francisco were commanded by men who had been badly shaken by the overwhelming defeats their Navy had suffered at Pearl Harbor and in the Java Sea. In true service fashion, they closed ranks and became even more tight-lipped and secretive than they had been in peacetime.

Nevertheless, some perceptive enlisted men correctly evaluated the situation. They pointed out that the customary train of supply vessels was now based at Pearl Harbor. When we went to sea—which, scuttlebutt indicated, would be very soon—we would have to take along all the food, fuel and ammunition we would need for an extended period.

Once at sea, our only protection against prowling submarines would be one squadron of eight destroyers. Our only air cover would be the slow, lightly armed observation seaplanes we carried. The carriers had more important business to the south and west; we would be strictly on our own.

After Pearl Harbor few could doubt that the antiaircraft defenses of the battleships were totally inadequate. When the *Pennsylvania*'s bomb, fire, and fragmentation damage had been repaired at Mare Island, she had received new 20-millimeter machine guns and 1.1-inch "pom-poms" for close-in air defense. But she was still relying on the outmoded 5-inch, 25-caliber dual-purpose guns and Mark 28 fire-control directors against medium- and high-altitude attack. The 5-inch 25s had brought down few planes at Pearl.

Finally, what was left of the battle force (now known as Task Force One) was still commanded by Vice Adm. William S. Pye, who had been the top seagoing commander in the Pacific in 1941. On 7 December he had been forced to abandon his sinking, burning flagship, the *California*, and take refuge at the submarine base, where the Commander-in-Chief, Pacific Fleet (CinCPac), had his headquarters. When Adm. Husband E. Kimmel was summarily relieved of his command on 17 December, Pye had been named CinCPac *pro-tem*, pending the arrival of Adm.

Chester W. Nimitz. Here Pye's principal accomplishment had been to call back the Wake Island Relief Expedition organized by Kimmel. Wake Island had fallen. It was not a record that gave me and other members of his flag radio complement any cause for optimism.

I remembered 29 March, the day the flag allowance had left Pearl Harbor in the heavy cruiser *Louisville*, bound for San Francisco. From the cruiser's hangar deck I looked across the channel to battleship row. Four ships were still there; a fifth, the *Nevada*, was beached downstream at Waipio Point. At the rear was the *Arizona*, blown apart by bombs on 7 December, her fire-blackened bridge and foremast tilting forward at a twisted angle. More than 1,100 men were entombed in her broken hull. At the next quay forward was the *West Virginia*, mired deep in the mud of the harbor bottom, oily water washing over her boat deck. Next was the *Oklahoma*, in the same upside-down position she had assumed before my horrified eyes that Sunday morning. Only her keel, part of her flat bottom and the starboard screw were above water. At the head of the line was my old ship, the *California*. She had been refloated and would soon be moved to Dry Dock No. Two. I wondered if the months of salvage work had been worth the cost. With most of her guns removed and her mainmast chopped down, she looked more like a huge, oil-soaked crane-ship than a dreadnought. I wondered, too, how many bodies of shipmates remained belowdecks. The stench of blood still hung over Pearl Harbor.

When the *Louisville* arrived in San Francisco on 3 April, the two dozen flag radiomen reported to the battleship *New Mexico*. Although nearly as old as the *Pennsylvania*, she had been completely rebuilt in the early 1930s. Her crew spaces were freshly painted and, by battleship standards, were roomy and well-ventilated. The chow was good and the morale was high, for the *New Mexico* had not suffered the anguish of defeat at Pearl Harbor. We quickly decided we were going to like duty in Battleship No. 40. Almost as quickly, we were ordered to relash our bags and hammocks and reported to the *Pennsylvania*. Not knowing that our admiral was already on board the latter, we attributed the move to his irresolution.

One radioman had a more charitable explanation. "The 'Pennsy' has a more comfortable crapper in the admiral's head," he theorized.

Whatever the reasons, we shouldered our gear and marched down the Embarcadero to Pier Seven, where our flagship was moored bow-in to the south side. Our senior firsts took what some of us regarded as a malicious pleasure in telling us all about the *Pennsylvania*. Authorized in 1912 and commissioned four years later at Norfolk Navy Yard, she had served as the flagship of the U.S. Fleet through one world war and two decades of peace to the brink of an even wider war. Many a four-star admiral had trod her quarterdeck and, directly or indirectly, made life difficult for generations of enlisted men. When the fleet was reorganized in January 1941, the *Pennsylvania* became the official flagship of Admiral Kimmel, the new CinCPac (even though he seldom went to sea in her). She was the very epitome of Battleship Navy discipline and regimentation, and that was unlikely to change with the three-star flag of Vice Admiral Pye flying from her main. I felt depressed.

"Here's something else you hotshots may not have thought about," a radioman first concluded. "We had four old battlewagons with tripod masts in the Pacific Fleet. There was the *Arizona*, the *Oklahoma*, the *Nevada*, and. . . . " He paused for dramatic punctuation. "Welcome aboard!"

Our spirits sank even lower when we were led to our quarters, a smallish compartment on the third deck sandwiched between the No. 2 turret barbette and the boiler uptakes from the forward firerooms. The bulkheads were thick with many coats of once-white but now yellow paint. Soon there would be no paint at all, for a working party of seamen was attacking the quarter-century accumulation with chipping hammers. The deck had been stripped of its battleship linoleum and all furniture as well. The air had the familiar smell of sweat, fuel oil, and gunpowder. Gloomily I claimed a middle bunk in one of the three-high tiers and stowed my gear in a battered locker.

"By God, we've found it, men," Red Goff announced with a cynical grin. "This has got to be the original Black Hole of Calcutta."

Not surprisingly, the very petty officers who had been telling the sea stories about the "Pennsy" did the least grumbling about our accommodations. Careerists with long prewar service and highly developed communications skills, they stoically accepted living cheek by jowl in this watertight iron box. They knew the war was their passport for rapid promotion to chief, warrant radio electrician, or even a commission. Duty with the flag in the *Pennsylvania* was the price of the better quarters, pay, and privileges to come. It was only necessary to perform one's duties well, obey regulations, and keep one's nose clean. And, of course, survive.

My depression didn't lift until I visited main radio, one deck down on the starboard side of the first platform. The rust-red linoleum had not been taken up here; the bulkheads were painted in the officer's country color, a soothing pale green. Around three sides of the large, rectangular compartment were some fifteen operator's positions equipped with the Models RBA-RBB-RBC receivers, as the *California's* radio room had been. I knew the RBA series, which together covered the frequency band from 10 kilocycles to 30 megacycles, were superb receivers that could withstand even the shock of main battery fire.

The watch supervisor overlooked his domain from a large desk near the after bulkhead. This radio command post was equipped with sound-powered phones to the bridges and Radio 2 (transmitter room), a telegraph sounder for alternative communication with Radio 2 or emergency radio, pneumatic tubes to the bridges and coding room, and a patch panel for passing control of "hot" transmitters to any operator's position. Behind the supervisor's chair, a sliding glass window opened onto the communication office, which usually was staffed by the watch officer, yeomen, strikers, and a Marine messenger.

In this radiomen's enclave, the mind-numbing routine of a battleship receded to occasional shrill trebles of bosun's calls and terse announcements over the P.A. system. Here I was with my own kind, where the responsibilities of my specialized rating took precedence over my military duties as a petty officer, and where I enjoyed semi-privileged status as a member of the flag radio complement.

The other flag radiomen were comrades I knew and trusted, for they had served with me in the *California.* Ordered to abandon ship on 7 December, we had shared the hardships of those early war days in the emergency radio dugout on Ford Island and at the sub base. Some were close friends: Goff, Jim Baker, J. K. "Jawbones" Madden, Floyd C. "Bill" Fisher, my high-school pal from Placerville, Tom Moore, Al Raphalowitz. Others, while not so close, were more than acquaintances and always would be: Joe Goveia, Jack Mazeau, E. O. Smith, L. M. Ellison, J. F. Tillery, A. B. Montagne. Even Flag Chief "Pappy" Reinhardt had stopped calling me and the other young radiomen "a bunch of goddam gedunk sailors" and honored us with an invitation to his San Francisco apartment for drinks.

With Radio 1 as a refuge, that bare cell of a living compartment could be used only for sleeping and mustering on stations. In port, less than half the operating positions were manned by watchstanders on the Fox (fleetwide broadcast) schedule and the task-force commander's and ship-to-shore emergency circuits. Idlers could gather at the other receivers to write letters (on the special radio typewriters that made only capital letters), read, study, or hold bull sessions over coffee from a large electric percolator that was never allowed to run dry. Here were the thinkers, drinkers, strategists, poets, philosophers, lovers, and occasional brawlers who comprised any large radio gang.

On 7 April a pilot came aboard and the ship was shifted to the north side of Pier Fifteen. Each pier, I noticed, was protected by a torpedo net. Similar prudence at Pearl Harbor would have prevented the capsizing of the *Oklahoma* and target ship *Utah*, the sinking of the *California* and *West Virginia*, and the beaching of the *Nevada*, as well as the near-sinking of the cruisers *Helena* and *Raleigh*. Undoubtedly, far more than a thousand lives would have been saved. In fact, the attack might never have been launched had the Japanese learned, through their efficient spy system, that the battleships were so protected. But our admirals thought the waters of Pearl Harbor were too shallow for successful torpedo runs. (They were half right. The waters were too shallow for successful runs of *our* torpedoes, but not the Japanese.)

Waiting beside Pier Fifteen were several freight cars filled with provisions and supplies. Seaman labor gangs muscled the stores across the two brows rigged between the ship and the pier. The torpedo net was opened, and Standard Oil barges came alongside and pumped 46,964 gallons of fuel oil aboard. The magazines already were filled with ammunition taken on while the *Pennsylvania* was at Mare Island.

Imperceptibly, the ship began settling in the water. When fueling and provisioning were completed, the water line was above the armor belt. A flag quartermaster reported that the draft forward was 35 feet—more than 6 feet deeper than her designed normal draft of 28 feet, 10 inches.

"What that means," he said sourly, "is that the Pennsy has lost her reserve buoyancy and stability. If we take one fish, she'll either capsize like the *Oklahoma* did—or she'll go straight down like a chunk of goddam pig iron."

Jawbones Madden and I looked at each other. We were remembering the sailors who had died in flooding, burning, or fume-filled lower-deck compartments at Pearl.

"Buddy," he said, "I think it's time we made a tour of the ship. With one thing in mind. How do we get off this pig-iron son of a bitch?"

We began mapping out escape routes from the various radio compartments. Main radio offered a prayer of salvation if, as Madden said, "The Good Lord looks down upon a couple of poor sinners and takes mercy." Central station, the ship's fire-control nerve center, was just inboard. From there a wiring and escape tube five feet in diameter led up to the armored conning tower on the flag-bridge level. But most of the narrow passageways from Radio 2 and Radio 3 on the third deck ended at sealed vent trunks or hatches.

We emerged from our tour somewhat shaken. The opinion of a veteran storekeeper in the GSK issuing room just forward of emergency radio did not help. "You got as much chance of gettin' off this decrepit admiral's barge," he said, "as I got of scorin' with Rita Hayworth."

Whether or not the quartermaster and the storekeeper were right, Madden and I agreed that the *Pennsylvania* was held together largely with spit and polish. Considering the effective life of a battleship to be twenty years, she was already six years past retirement. She had been designed and built before the Battle of Jutland. Despite a reconstruction between 1929 and 1931, her torpedo defenses and protection against bombs and plunging shellfire were markedly inferior to those of the later battleships of the *Maryland, California,* and *New Mexico* classes.

Once past the spaces where the officers lived and worked—the wardroom, quarterdeck, charthouse and emergency cabins, and flag and navigation bridges—the Pennsy looked worn and weary. She had swung around the hook in too many Atlantic and Pacific ports, strained her old rivets against the shock of too many beam seas and practice firings of her main battery.

I thought about the *Warspite,* a gallant veteran of Jutland I had visited the past summer at Pearl Harbor. She, too, had shown her years. But there was something sturdy and indomitable yet about this thirty-year-old dreadnought. She had reminded me of an old ex-heavyweight champion, well past his prime but still able to deliver—and receive—a mighty punch.

The *Pennsylvania,* on the other hand, had never been tested in combat. There was no doubt about her ability to throw a fearsome punch—but did she have a glass jaw? She was a sister ship of the *Arizona,* which had blown up at Pearl in the very early stages of the Japanese attack. Some said a large bomb down the stack was responsible; others that a bomb must have touched off the forward powder magazines. Either way, Madden and I conjectured, the sisters had a fatal design flaw like the British battle-cruiser *Hood*. A few salvoes from the German battle-ship *Bismarck* had destroyed the 48,000-ton *Hood* in May 1941. The *Pennsylvania*, we figured, would last about ten minutes in combat.

For a vivid moment I was back in the maintop of the *California* at about 0815 on 7 December. I heard a mighty thunderclap of sound, felt the concussive waves, saw a red fireball shoot up from the forepart of the *Arizona*. The 32,500-ton battleship had broken in two as if she were a child's plastic toy. Within a few heartbeats, eleven hundred men had died. That vision would stay with me for the rest of my life. If I went into battle in the *Pennsylvania*, it was not likely to be a very long one, I feared.

That apprehension lent a special urgency to my date with Dolores. We met at Li Po's and sat long over drinks at a cozy rear table. From the piano bar Hazel played and sang favorites old and new—"Deep Purple," "Green Eyes," "Night and Day," "Smoke Gets in Your Eyes," "White Christmas." A brunette with long straight hair and an international face which could have been Mediterranean or Arabian or even half-Oriental, Hazel was very popular with the servicemen who nightly crowded around her piano.

I could not tell Dolores anything about my frail battleship or my fears for the future. Quite aside from the necessity for military secrecy, I considered that enlisting a woman's sympathy for purposes of seduction was a cowardly act. I talked instead about growing up in Placerville, and the hard, futureless jobs that had made me decide to join the Navy after finishing high school.

She understood. She had been raised in Hayward in the East Bay area, where her father operated a small dairy that kept him working from before dawn to well past dusk seven days a week. There was no future there, either; she had come to "the City," where jobs were plentiful and life was exciting. I got the impression she was rebelling against a stern upbringing and was anxious for new experiences. That made it unanimous.

On the other side of Grant Avenue we saw a small hotel above a long flight of wooden stairs. Behind a desk in the tiny lobby was a middle-aged Chinese clerk dressed in a Western business suit. He looked us over carefully and asked for our marriage license in only slightly accented English. I could see that it would do no good to lie. We didn't have one, I told him.

He smiled apologetically. It was against the hotel's rules to rent to unmarried couples, he said. He seemed genuinely sorry.

"You should go to one of the hotels on Eddy or Ellis Streets in the district called the Tenderloin. They will rent you a room." Bowing slightly, he wished us a good evening.

The clerk had handled an embarrassing incident with a civility and aplomb I appreciated. We went to a hotel in the sleazy Tenderloin and had no trouble getting a room for two dollars, payable in advance. I thought the Caucasian clerk sneered faintly as he glanced at the "Mr. and Mrs." registration and slid the room key across the counter.

The wake-up call came at 0630 hours. I dressed hastily and scribbled a note on the hotel stationery: "*Mil gracias, amiga mia, para la noche del amor. Hasta la vista!*" Since she spoke Portuguese, she would understand my high-school Spanish.

As I was crossing the lobby, the same clerk hailed me. "One moment, Mr. Mason. Your, uh, wife wants to see you."

Back in the room, Dolores smiled sleepily. She was holding my note against her breast. "You left your money on the dresser, *querido*."

I explained that I thought she might need cab fare home.

"Oh, no," she said. "That wouldn't be right. I couldn't take any money, not from the Navy!" She had made a gift of love, and there was no obligation.

My next couple of liberties had to be devoted to family. I was not close to my parents or foster-parents and regretted the fact. While I could not blame myself for the divorce and subsequent adoption which had darkened my childhood years, I felt vaguely guilty for what I could not feel. The least I could do was let them see for themselves that I had escaped Pearl Harbor relatively unscathed.

I spent an evening with my father, his second wife Carol, and my half-brother and -sister Richard and Joan, who lived in an old Victorian house on the flanks of Twin Peaks in the city. At 43, Bayard "Bev" Bowman was a figure a son could be proud of: 6 feet, 2 inches tall, 215 pounds, with features rugged rather than handsome, and not a trace of gray in his sandy-red hair. He was a master mechanic who had once built (and driven) racing cars and now was co-owner of a machine shop. A light-heavyweight boxer in his World War I days in the Army, he was a dedicated outdoorsman and a deadly rifle shot who always bagged his limit of deer.

Despite these virtues, he was a cold and rather forbidding man who had seen me but rarely while I was growing up. That distance lay between us now as I gave him a detailed account of the debacle at Pearl.

He already believed that our top military commanders had been privy to a conspiracy devised by President Roosevelt with the aim of drawing us into the war. My description of the locked ammunition boxes in the ships, the Navy's failure to take action after the *Ward*'s attack on a submarine near the harbor entrance early on 7 December, and the Army's rejection of the radar report on a large incoming flight of planes seemed to offer tangible evidence of his theory. But I did not accept the widespread rumors of a plot engineered by my admired Commander-in-Chief. That was only a convenient way of excusing the Army-Navy failure to be alert in the Pacific despite repeated war warnings. I blamed our defeat on stupidity, not design.

My father and I agreed to disagree. When I left, he tucked some large bills into the pocket of my jumper.

"Sailors like girls," he said in a conspiratorial whisper, "and girls cost money. Go out and have a good time, while you can."

In view of our imminent departure for sea, I had to choose between Santa Cruz and my mother, or Placerville and my foster-parents. I chose the latter, although it was 140 miles away and presented a problem in logistics. Unless a family emergency arose, it was impossible to get a 48-hour liberty. That the Navy had falsely reported me missing in action at Pearl Harbor, causing the Masons great anxiety, did not now constitute an emergency. The best I could do was an early liberty, which expired at 0730 the next morning. I went to the Bay Bridge approach and hitchhiked to Sacramento and on to Placerville. A cab took me the last five miles to Missouri Flat.

After an early supper, I repeated my Pearl Harbor report for my foster-parents, foster-uncle, and natural sisters, Beverly and Constance.

Dad Mason remembered that the Hearst press and author Jack London had long warned of the "yellow peril." Roosevelt and his military leaders should have known that the Japanese were given to cowardly sneak attacks. That is what they had done to the Russians at Port Arthur, Manchuria, in 1904. Still, he thought, victory was only a year or two away. I disagreed but said nothing. No need to alarm my family.

Mrs. Mason, a devout Christian Scientist, believed I had had divine protection in the maintop of the *California*. She was "working" (the Christian Science term for goal-directed prayer) to ensure that protection would continue. I rubbed the shrapnel scar on my left knee and remembered how I had escaped death or maiming by inches. Who was to say she was wrong?

My little sisters stared at me in awestruck wonder, as if I had just come back from the dead. As usual my bachelor Uncle Horace, who had been the only adult in whom I could confide as a teenager, said little. He got me outside and gave me a "snort" of whiskey.

No buses ran from Placerville until the following morning. I had to engage a cab for the 50-mile run down the narrow, twisting Lincoln Highway (later Highway 50) to Sacramento. The fare was fifteen dollars, a substantial sum for 1942. I was not sure my father would approve of the way I was spending the money he had given me.

The Greyhound bus I boarded near Capitol Park was crowded, airless, and none too clean. All through the early morning hours it labored toward San Francisco, stopping to discharge and load passengers at every city and town. I arrived at 0715 and dashed to find a cab. Urged on by prepayment and a generous tip, the cabby lead-footed it down Market Street. Being even one minute AOL would draw a captain's mast in the *Pennsylvania*.

I jumped out of the cab at Pier Fifteen, ran through the cavernous spaces of the warehouse, pelted across the enlisted men's brow, and reported my return aboard somewhat breathlessly.

The JOOW looked at his watch. It read 0729:30. "That's shaving it rather fine, sailor," he observed. "Was she worth it?"

I certainly didn't want to disappoint him. "Yes, sir!" I said with an enigmatic smile.

"Quo vadis, O great Admiral Pye?"

One of the ship's radiomen, a keen fellow with a fondness for Latin phrases acquired in a Catholic seminary, addressed this rhetorical question toward the flag bridge. He and I were standing on the boat deck, having just secured from general quarters and Condition Zed. It was high noon on 14 April 1942.

A few miles astern was the hazy outline of the Golden Gate Bridge, looking as delicate as spun glass at this range. Off the *Pennsylvania*'s starboard bow were the marooned rocks of the Farallon Islands. All around us, six battleships and a squadron of destroyers were taking cruising dispositions in obedience to our flag hoists and flashing signal lights. Task Force One was on the move, its destination known to only a very few of its 15,000 enlisted men.

Soon we had formed into two lines of division guides. From the van in the right division were the *Maryland, Colorado, Tennessee,* and *Pennsyl-*

vania. At a 6,000-yard interval was the left division, composed of the *New Mexico, Idaho,* and *Mississippi.* The eight screening destroyers of DesRon 10* were deployed around us in an anti-sub shield. Our course was 270° true, standard speed 14 knots.

Several flag radiomen joined us, and we compared scuttlebutt. The consensus was that the Japanese were planning a move far to the south, possibly threatening Australia and New Zealand. Probably, we would act as a distant covering force for our carriers, two of which were already in the Southwest Pacific. If they stopped the enemy offensive, we had nothing to fear but patrolling submarines. But if they were defeated, the result might well be an uneven contest of battleships with no air cover versus fast carriers supported by strong surface forces. Then the battleships of Task Force One and all their crews would be sacrificed to the national interest. Our leaders would consider the loss of so many ships and men most regrettable, but it would be done. We had no illusions about that.

The *Pennsylvania* was so heavily overloaded that she slid through even moderate seas with a peculiar, disjointed motion, as if the armor belt were working against the hull. When she fell into a trough with a shuddering crash, she seemed intent on plunging straight to the bottom. Slowly and reluctantly she leveled off under great geysers of spray and foam. Green water three feet deep rolled down her forecastle, broke against No. 1 turret, and fell back into the sea as the ship's protruding, bulbous bow fought its way to the surface.

Her struggles against a running sea seemed almost a metaphor for our mission. But this was no time for defeatism, I told myself sternly. Only a few days before, the Bataan Peninsula had fallen to the enemy, and Lt. Gen. Jonathan Wainwright had retreated to Corregidor for a last-ditch stand. Some 12,000 Americans and 60,000 Filipinos were now prisoners of war. Their fate at the hands of these Eastern barbarians, whose Bushido code was contemptuous of men who surrendered rather than perishing in battle, was not pleasant to contemplate. Once again, as I had on Ford Island on the night of 7 December 1941, I vowed I would never be taken alive. Better to die in honorable, if unequal, combat than that.

As we headed southwest, we conducted frequent firing exercises

---

*According to the *Pennsylvania* deck logs, the ships were the *Cushing, Dale, Drayton, Dunlap, Fanning, Porter, Preston,* and *Worden.*

with all our weapons: 14-inch main battery; 5-inch, 51-caliber secondary battery; 5-inch, 25-caliber A.A. battery; and 20-millimeter, 1.1-inch, and 50-caliber machine guns. Every morning we went to dawn G.Q. Twice daily we launched our observation seaplanes for reconnaissance. There were the inevitable casualties. Three men received broken bones, fractured ribs and multiple contusions during aircraft recovery in heavy weather. An emergency appendectomy was performed on Seaman J. B. Cummings. And Chief Electrician's Mate B. Q. Moorhouse died of a coronary thrombosis.

To the dismay of most of the radiomen, the flag communication officer, H. O. Hansen, had come along with Pye from the *California*. There his specialty had been browbeating the radiomen and signalmen on the flag bridge. Gaining half a stripe to full commander had not improved the disposition of HOH/30, as he was known throughout the radio gang. The commander apparently wanted everyone to remember that he was a graduate of the U.S. Naval Academy, Class of 1930.

During her battle-damage repairs at Mare Island, the *Pennsylvania* had received one of the new TBS (talk between ships) voice transceivers. It had been installed on the flag bridge, so that the admiral could direct his forces by day or night without relying on flag hoists, semaphore or blinker guns. The range of the very-high-frequency TBS extended no farther than the horizon under most circumstances.

Only second-class radiomen with good speaking voices and clear diction were assigned to this circuit. They soon had reason to regret that they didn't mumble, stutter, or lisp, for every watch brought them under the boundless tyranny of HOH/30. Hansen stalked back and forth behind the TBS operator's position shouting out messages, criticisms, and insults in roughly equal numbers. It was not unusual for a radioman to be ordered off the bridge in disgrace, to be replaced by another summoned from his meal, letter-writing, or bunk.

While still in the *California* I had sworn I would refuse an assignment to the flag bridge, even if it meant brig time. Now I might have to exercise that option. Hansen had banned so many radiomen from the TBS circuit that only a few of the junior seconds were left to choose from. My call to insult could come at any time. I went to Lt. Proctor A. Sugg, the flag radio officer, who had arranged my promotion to second class without an examination after Pearl Harbor. He got me assigned to a vital emergency circuit in main radio, where I could escape Hansen's attention, at least for a while. HOH/30 never visited the place.

On and off watch we exchanged snippets of scuttlebutt leaked from the coding room or overheard in the comm offices or on the bridge. We surmised that Task Force One had been ordered by Nimitz to rendezvous with Task Force Eleven, the group built around the carrier *Saratoga*, near Christmas Island just north of the equator. When we remained well east of the line islands, however, it was clear that the order had been changed. In late April we began a leisurely withdrawal to the northeast, interrupted by repeated battle exercises in which the *New Mexico, Idaho,* and *Mississippi* played the role of the enemy. At the same time, an increase in radio traffic of urgent priority indicated that a real engagement was imminent, probably in the Coral Sea area off Australia. Obviously, Nimitz did not intend to use his battleships: they were too slow to keep up with the carriers, even if he could have spared the oilers needed to fuel them. We would be called upon only if the situation was desperate.

In the Philippines the last defenses crumbled on 6 May. We got the news by WCX fast-press service, which we copied and distributed daily to the wardroom and crew. Wainwright had surrendered Corregidor to Lt. Gen. Masaharu Homma. The myth of Caucasian superiority had been shattered. The Japanese had destroyed our air forces, sunk our ships, and killed or captured our soldiers. They had done all this with ease. It was a humbling thought.

"Sic transit gloria mundi," said the Latin-loving radioman. "We've been running Asia on bluff and bluster for a long time. Well, the Sons of Heaven called our bluff."

The next day I joined a group clustered around the Fox sked operator. He was copying an urgent dispatch from the oiler *Neosho* in plain language. The desperation of a ship in its death throes was evident:

UNDER AIR ATTACK MANY DIVE BOMBERS 16 25 S 157 31 E X SINKING X REQUEST IMMEDIATE ASSISTANCE

The battle had been joined in the Coral Sea, and *Neosho* apparently was our first casualty.* I remembered her well. She was the first ship I

---

*When *Neosho* sent her distress message, the escorting destroyer *Sims* had already gone down with all but fifteen of her crew. The position given by the oiler's navigator was in error; the actual position was Lat. 16° 09' S., Long. 158° 03' E. Hit by seven bombs and a suicide plane, *Neosho* drifted west for four days before she was located. Only 123 of her crew of 278 were taken off before she was scuttled. Many were lost at sea because a premature abandon ship by part of the crew was compounded by the navigation error.

had gone to sea in, nineteen months before.* At Pearl Harbor she had been moored to the gasoline dock just astern of the *California*. The crew had cut her lines with axes during the attack, and she had escaped into Southeast Loch. There would be no escape this time. I grieved for *Neosho* and her crew.

All that day and the next the battle raged, but the messages from CinCPac to Rear Adm. Frank Jack Fletcher's Task Force Seventeen were encoded and we learned little. On the ninth, WCX informed us that we had scored a great victory and the remnants of the enemy fleet were in full retreat. Radio Tokyo, at the same time, reported that the Imperial Japanese Navy had sunk the carriers *Lexington* and *Yorktown*, as well as *California*- and *Warspite*-class battleships. Since we were steaming in the wake of *California*'s sister ship, *Tennessee*, and the *Warspite* was under repair at Puget Sound Navy Yard for battle damage, we enjoyed a tension-breaking laugh over the battleship claim.†

At 0630 on 10 May the National Ensign was broken from the gaff. Nearly four weeks of watches, drills and exercises with no action had made the crew restless and bored. Now there was general jubilation.

After breakfast, a seaman came rushing up to me at my lookout position on the forecastle.

"Hey, Mac," he said, "what port we coming into?"

I pointed to the smudged shape of a small island off the starboard bow. "Looks like San Nicholas," I guessed. "That means Los Angeles Harbor."

His face lighted up. "Hot damn! Liberty in Hollywood! Think there'll be any movie stars waitin' for us at the dock?"

I grinned at his naiveté. "Not unless they can swim like Johnny Weismuller," I explained. "We'll have to anchor or moor to a buoy out in the stream."

We passed San Clemente and Santa Catalina Islands, set Condition Zed, manned air- and torpedo-defense quarters, and followed *Colorado* into Los Angeles Harbor. At the fleet landings in San Pedro and Long

---

*See *Battleship Sailor*, pp. 52–63.

†TF 17 sank the light carrier *Shoho* and badly damaged the carrier *Shokaku*. In an earlier raid on Japanese-occupied Tulagi Harbor on 4 May, the destroyer *Kikutsuki* and a few small ships were sunk or damaged. We lost the veteran carrier *Lexington*, as well as the *Neosho* and *Sims*. The enemy won a tactical victory, but the strategic victory was ours; the transport force headed for an invasion of Port Moresby, New Guinea, was turned back.

Beach, no movie stars were waiting to greet us somewhat less than con-quering heroes. Waiting instead were many members of the Shore Patrol.

Despite the boatswain's mate ratings on their right arms, these SPs wore their uniforms like boots and did not walk with the typical rolling gait of the sailor. They looked, in fact, like ex-cops masquerading as sailors—and that in fact was what most of them were. With the fleet long gone from San Pedro Bay, the pool of qualified petty officers had dried up. The Navy had begun to recruit special SP detachments from the law-enforcement agencies. To the enlisted men of Task Force One, they were landlubbers. Worse, they had brought with them all the mean-spirited attitudes of their civilian occupation. By midnight of our first lib-erty they had begun to arrest the battleship sailors, particularly young seamen celebrating too exuberantly, and to return them to the ship.

San Pedro had once been the home port of the battle force. Then, when the battleships anchored in the lee of the breakwater, *"The fleet's in!"* had meant something. Now the battle force steamed fruitlessly in the Eastern Pacific while the sailors of the "brown-shoe Navy" fought the battles. Now there was not even a fleet train waiting to fuel and supply us; only an oddball collection of small barges, harbor tugs, and even private yachts and cabin cruisers. This motley force labored day and night for the seventy-two hours we were in port. Lurking at the landings and on the streets were the Shore Patrol civilians, who wore their shapeless white hats straight across their eyes like recruits and had never set foot in a Navy ship. *Sic transit gloria mundi* indeed!

Since Long Beach and San Pedro were no longer real Navy towns, being given over to oil drilling, shipbuilding, transport, and profiteer-ing, we were glad to return to San Francisco. By 15 May we were again moored starboard side to Pier Fifteen, safe behind our torpedo net. But many sailors were still paying for their misadventures in Southern California. Eight men had missed the ship. The brig on the third deck forward was full. Prisoners-at-large awaiting Navy justice numbered several dozen. One deserter was returned from the San Francisco Receiving Ship; he was not the first deserter from the Pennsy by any means. Our skipper—an officer with the aristocratic-sounding name of Thomas Starr King II—seemed to spend half his time holding captain's mast and passing out punishments of excessive severity.

On my first liberty I looked for Dolores in Chinatown. The bartender at Li Po's told me he hadn't seen her for a couple of weeks. Yes, she had been with a sailor. Well, I told shipmates Madden, Moore, and Baker with a wry smile, at least she was being faithful to the Navy. If she was looking for adventure, romance, even marriage, San Francisco was certainly the place to find them.

We went to the Streets of Paris, on Mason just off Market. The basement decor of this sailor's nightclub was vaguely French: red-checked tablecloths, fake French windows, and trellises with fake flowers. A busty young lady dressed like a French maid sold cigarettes for 50 cents a pack (they were 60 cents a carton in the ship). Another, equally busty, took souvenir photographs (one dollar a print). Judging by their décolletages, the young ladies were real. "Still the lousiest show in town" was the club's claim to fame, and that was no misrepresentation, either. The emcee, I told my buddies, should have had his mouth scrubbed out with soap when he was a nasty little kid. We soon took a cab to the Music Box, another popular Navy bistro on O'Farrell.

Here the furnishings were art-deco, the dance floor was crowded with sailors and their dates swinging to a passable band, and the stags were two-deep at the bar. Soon a blonde striptease artist who would hardly have felt inferior at the Streets of Paris would do her second show of the evening.

"See that first-class cook over there by the bandstand?" the cocktail waitress asked. We could just make out an uncovered head in the middle of a crowd. The head was thrown back in laughter. It was a round, jolly, well-nourished head.

"He seems to be having one helluva time," Jim Baker observed.

"He should be," she said. "He got out of the Philippines just ahead of the Japs. He's got seven thousand dollars in back pay and shipping-over money—and he's spending it all here."

That was far more money than any of us had ever seen. *"Seven thousand dollars? All here?"*

"All here," she said firmly. "He's already gone through two, three grand. Wait a little while. He'll probably buy drinks for the house."

"You gotta be kidding."

"No way." She sighed. "Oh, how I'd like to help him spend that *do, re, mi!* But our cheap little stripper got there first."

What could one say about a man who was squandering what must be his life savings on three or four gaudy weeks in a San Francisco nightclub? Baker, himself a reckless man with a dollar who was always prepared for a frolic or a fight, though he had the right idea. To Madden and Moore, he was a perfect example of a typical wartime attitude: live for today, for tomorrow you die. I thought what I could do with $7,000. I could buy a home for my foster-parents and still put aside a nest egg for college. While admiring his élan, I considered the waste of so much money almost sinful. How many friends would he have when it was gone?

The waitress came by with four drinks. "The Navy is buying," she said. "I told you so."

I guessed there were at least 150 people in the Music Box. The ship's cook had just spent half a month's pay for a first-class petty officer with hashmarks. Everyone in the place raised his or her glass and gave him a cheer. There was no doubt about one thing. He was spending his leave in classic Navy style.

As strangers in a large, urbane city, the battleship sailors were excluded from most social circles. To meet women, they had to rely on chance encounters in the bars and nightspots. There, in an atmosphere always commercial and often tawdry, the odds were very much against them.

"Sure, I can find chippies and whores," one radioman complained. "What I can't find is a real American girl. Hell, I wouldn't even put the make on her. I'd just like to spend the whole evening holding her hand and talking."

I was more fortunate than most. My foster-aunt Daisy had been a San Franciscan for many years. Over cracked crab at Fishermen's Wharf she introduced me to Helen Hazelton, a green-eyed brunette of twenty-two whose mother and Daisy were old friends.

Helen was pretty, gracious, and charming, the "real American girl" my radio-gang mate had despaired of finding. I learned to my great surprise that she had been working in Hawaii as a civilian employee of the Army when the Japanese attacked. Repatriated to the West Coast in the *Lurline*, she was now a secretary in a San Francisco office. In a sense, we had shared the century's most dramatic and stunning event. That alone made her special.

With Madden and another flag radioman, I visited Helen at her home, a modest bungalow in East Oakland not far from the famous Mills College for Women. Her mother, kid brother George, and a blonde girlfriend were present, along with Aunt Daisy. It was all most middle-class and proper, a 180-degree shift from the Streets of Paris and the Music Box.

We played ping-pong and Chinese checkers, took a ride in George's fifteen-year-old jalopy, ate finger sandwiches accompanied by no beverage stronger than Coca-Cola, and posed for snapshots in the back yard.

We sailors thought of our own hometowns and appreciated this reminder that American families were carrying on much as they had before the war. That, essentially, was what we were defending. The other shipmate gravitated toward the blonde, but my buddy Madden immediately fell in love with Helen.

"You lucky dog, Mason," he told me later with his customary volatile good humor. "It's obvious she prefers you. I ain't got a prayer. It's just like the movies, dammit. The leading man gets the girl, and his best friend has to smooch his horse!"

On 26 May, amid rumors of another big Japanese offensive aimed, possibly, at the Hawaiian Islands, the *Pennsylvania* and *Tennessee* slipped away for a couple of days of gunnery practice off Pigeon Point. When we returned on the twenty-ninth, all liberties expired at midnight.

Two days later we watched *Maryland, Colorado,* and three destroyers stand out, ostensibly for gunnery exercises. For once, the radiomen breached the flag officers' tight security. The task force had gone out, we learned, to search for an enemy light carrier reported some 600 miles northwest of San Francisco. Admiral Pye feared she might be planning an air strike on the city.

The next few days were tense ones in the five battleships still moored at the Embarcadero. Although the radio traffic gave few clues, it was common knowledge that our carriers would soon engage the enemy somewhere in the Central or North Pacific. Midway seemed a good bet; it was our westernmost naval base after the loss of Wake and Guam Islands. If Admiral Isoroku Yamamoto were to make good his alleged boast that he would dictate the peace terms in the White House, he would first have to take Midway and Oahu.

At 0530 each morning we went to general quarters and set Condition Zed. In the late afternoons air defense and Zed were sounded. Armed security patrols were sent across the brow to secure the dock area, while other patrols began prowling the ship.

Our first news of the developing battle came from NPM Fox shortly after 0800 on 3 June. An urgent message in the clear from the radio station at Dutch Harbor on the Aleutian island of Unalaska announced an air raid by nine carrier-based bombers and three fighters. The next afternoon the Japanese struck again with eleven dive bombers, six high-level bombers, and fifteen fighters. Was this a feint, or was the enemy preparing to land in force on the Aleutians?

Shortly after noon on 5 June the five battleships got under way and were joined outside the Golden Gate by our five screening destroyers. Steaming up with the "tin cans" was the strangest-looking ship most of us had ever seen. That she was some kind of aircraft carrier was obvious from the planes clustered at one end of a short flight deck, but the usual island structure and stack were missing. The ship was navigated and conned from a pod that protruded from the starboard side; exhaust gases were discharged from vents on both sides.

"My God," someone said. "They just chopped off the midships and after houses of a cargo ship and jerry-rigged a flight deck on top. She's a seagoing abortion!"

"Yeah," a twenty-year man agreed. "She looks like the original 'covered wagon'—the old *Langley*." (The Navy's first aircraft carrier, converted from the collier *Jupiter* in 1922, had been sunk south of Java by enemy bombers the past February.)

We were looking at the Navy's first escort carrier, the *Long Island* (AVG-1), which had started life in 1940 as the *Mormacmail*. Despite her unnautical appearance, she was a welcome addition to Task Force One, we decided. She carried about twenty fighter planes. If her green pilots knew how to fly them, our chances of beating off a determined air attack had improved from hopeless to marginal.

After steaming due west all night under a pale last-quarter moon, we sighted the *Maryland, Colorado,* and their three destroyers, formed into a cruising disposition, and began zigzagging in a northwesterly direction. Not until then did we learn from WCX and our short-wave receivers that a fierce carrier battle had been under way near Midway Island since the morning of 4 June. A 108-plane air raid on Midway had been repulsed with minimum damage and few casualties. Our carriers had destroyed two or three enemy flattops and badly damaged one or two others. Yamamoto's Midway invasion forces were retiring in defeat, and we were in hot pursuit.

The news unleashed cheers and excited conversation in the radio shack. The carriers *Enterprise, Hornet,* and *Yorktown* and their air groups apparently had scored a magnificent victory against overwhelming odds. The Hawaiian Islands had been saved, and the West Coast was now secure.

"Tokyo Rose" had a different story. Many U.S. ships, including two aircraft carriers, had been sunk and at least 135 planes had been shot down. Against these figures she admitted the loss of only one carrier, one cruiser, and thirty-five planes. Even though we knew she was lying, we wondered what our actual losses had been.*

The Japanese Combined Fleet, we heard, had included twelve battleships. They had been forced to reverse course without firing a shot because our carriers, brilliantly commanded by Admirals Raymond A. Spruance and Frank Jack Fletcher, had destroyed their air umbrella.

"Thank God for our flattops," one radioman said with some fervency. "Suppose they'd been sunk and we'd been thrown in against twelve or fourteen Jap battlewagons?"

"*Sicut Patribus, sit Deus nobis,*" said our erudite radioman. "Which roughly translated, gentlemen, means that by now we would have joined our ancestors, hopefully in heaven."

Since Pearl Harbor I had had little doubt that the ugly, utilitarian carrier was now the queen of battles. Midway erased any lingering hope that the battleship, somehow, would redeem herself. From now on, I knew, she would play no more than a secondary role in the engagements to come. I was very glad that Admiral Chester Nimitz, himself a former battleship sailor, had understood that and refused to commit his capital ships in the Coral Sea and at Midway.

By 10 June our task force was several hundred miles off the Northern California coast, steaming at 14 knots on a base course of 335° true. At 0600 the battleships began launching their scout planes. Before they could return from their assigned patrol sectors, a faint gray mass on the northern horizon reduced visibility to 25,000 yards and signaled the presence of a fog bank. I remembered this perpetual fog, formed where warm ocean air from the west encountered the cold California Current, for it had ambushed the *California* every time we made the passage from San Pedro to Bremerton.

It ambushed us again. By 0900 visibility was 10,000 yards; half an hour later it was 400 yards. The planes were called back and recovered in a moist, swirling twilight which alternately lifted and then closed down again.

---

*We lost the *Yorktown*, the destroyer *Hammann*, and many brave pilots. The Japanese lost all four carriers of the First Mobile Force, the *Akagi*, *Kaga*, *Hiryu*, and *Soryu*, and the cruiser *Mikuma*. The cruiser *Mogami* was heavily damaged.

Shortly after dinner Lieutenant Sugg found me idling in the radio shack.

"Ah, Ted," he said genially. "I'm glad to find you here. The *Mississippi* has a plane lost and probably down. We can't pick it up on the CXAM radar, so I've set up a watch on our direction finder. Could you take over at 1600?"

My experience with this seldom-used equipment was limited, so I took a brief refresher from one of the Pennsy radiomen before I reported to the radio direction finder (RDF) shack, a tiny doghouse perched at the after end of the emergency-cabin level.

Bill Fisher was seated at the receiver-amplifier. He manually twirled the compass coil through a full 360 degrees with his left hand while pressing one of the earphones against his head with the right.

"That goddam plane should be transmitting," he growled, "but I can't hear a frigging thing."

"You southpaws," I said in mock disgust. "Hell, you're turning the antenna in the wrong direction."

As usual, Fisher was not amused by my levity. "You should get a job on the radio, Mason," he snorted. "With Fred Allen." Handing me the headset, he scooped up his cigarettes and safety matches and fled.

I began a tense vigil. An OS2U Kingfisher observation plane probably was afloat not far away, its pilot sightless in the fog and its observer-radio operator keying his transmitter and praying that someone would hear his weak CW signal.

In about an hour I did hear it, so faint it was almost indistinguishable from the background noise of the receiver and blanked out often by bursts of static. I made delicate adjustments of the hand wheel to get a maximum signal. Flipping a switch to cut out the vertical antenna, I readjusted the compass coil for the "null," or minimum signal, which produced a more accurate bearing than the maximum. The position pointer indicated the bearing relative to the ship's head.

"RDF to flag bridge," I shouted through the voice tube.

"Flag bridge, aye," came the muffled response.

"Contact with *Mississippi* plane, bearing five oh degrees relative."

The report brought Sugg on the double. "My God, you've found them!" he said. "We're changing course to go down the line of bearing."

"Sir, I just hope this thing has been calibrated recently. I think it was installed about 1920—and now I've lost the signal."

In a few minutes the ship fired a 5-inch, 25-caliber illuminating projectile. Visibility was down to 50 yards or so, and the starshell pulsated feebly against the opaque mass of the fog bank. Providentially, the fog lifted temporarily and a lookout spotted the plane 500 yards off the starboard bow. Within ten minutes it had been hoisted aboard with its happy pilot and radioman.

I was glad to have something to cheer about. In the past three months we had cruised thousands of miles, burned hundreds of thousands of gallons of fuel oil, expended thousands of rounds of ammunition, and consumed many boxcars of provisions. Aside from the personnel-training mission, the accomplishments of Task Force One had been marginal. For all our bristling guns we had not fired one projectile at one enemy ship or plane. No wonder the battleship sailors were now known throughout the fleet as "Market Street Commandos."

On 30 June the *Pennsylvania* broke the baker flag at the foretruck and began taking on more ammo. The next day we fueled to capacity: the ship again was drawing 35 feet of water. On 2 July the planes of V Division flew back from temporary duty at the new Alameda Naval Air Station and were hoisted aboard. Task Force One would be under way soon, probably for gunnery practice and the expenditure of more fuel, projectiles, provisions, and the occasional man.

But without me. On 3 July I received my orders. I was being transferred to the Receiving Station, San Francisco, for assignment to new construction by Service Force Pacific. Two days later, I packed my seabag, lashed it to my hammock with seven marlin hitches, and said goodbye to my good friends Madden, Baker, Moore, Fisher, and all the others. I knew I would miss them very much. But I would not miss the *Pennsylvania.* I had not changed my opinion that this creaky, overloaded 1912-model battleship was a seagoing disaster waiting to happen. Only very good luck would see her through the war.

Surprisingly, the *Pennsylvania's* luck lasted until 12 August 1945, just three days before Emperor Hirohito broadcast news of the Japanese surrender to his people. Torpedoed at her anchorage in Buckner Bay, Okinawa, she began flooding on the aft starboard side and settling heavily by the stern. Only heroic damage-control efforts and the assistance of two fleet tugs saved her from sinking. My evaluation of her structural soundness had been emotional, perhaps, but it was not incorrect.

1942

5

Strange and Glorious Interlude

It is with our passions as it is with fire and water, they are good servants, but bad masters.

—Sir Roger L'Estrange

"No wonder they call it Goat Island," a petty officer said caustically as our bus turned off the Bay Bridge and began the steep, winding descent to the Yerba Buena Receiving Station. "Only a goat would want to live here."

"I'll bet this is where they train the mascots for Navy's football team," another said. With a shrug of resignation, he added, "Hell, if it's good enough for a Navy goat, it's good enough for the enlisted men."

Personally, I thought the receiving station looked rather picturesque from above. The large, U-shaped building had a formal entrance portico supported by six Roman pillars, with flanking porticoes at either end. Above the entrance, a large circular cupola served as a skylight. The architecture was more than a little reminiscent of Thomas Jefferson's Monticello home, judging by the photos I had seen.

The receiving station faced a large parade ground of irregular shape that lay in the shadow of the Bay Bridge. In Yerba Buena's days as a naval training station, this had undoubtedly been the Grinder.

On the other side of the bridge, the old protected cruiser *Boston*, commissioned in 1885, was moored to a pier. In 1940 she had been renamed the *Despatch* and converted to a training ship for radio operators.

A new heavy cruiser *Boston* was building at Quincy, Massachusetts. But to most sailors this sole survivor of the White Squadron was still the *Boston*, for she had been with Admiral Dewey at Manila Bay in 1898.

The station occupied a neck of relatively flat land near the island's east, or Oakland, end. On the steep incline to the west were the white Victorian houses of officer's row, and above them the commandant's mansion. A signal tower occupied a clearing in the Monterey pines and eucalyptuses at the 350-foot-high peak of the island.

A sailor standing next to me at muster on the parade ground looked up at the frieze over the main entrance. "MDCCCXCIX," he spelled out. "What the hell does that mean, Sparks?"

"Roman numerals," I explained. "They add up to 1899."

He reacted with the typical American abhorrence of age. "You mean this goddam pile of wood is that old?"

"That's only forty-three years. They tell me it was built as a training station during the Spanish-American War."

That war was ancient history to the young seaman. "My God," he said. "I gotta get outta here before it falls down in a high wind."

Once inside, I abandoned all thought of Monticello and began to agree with the seaman. The barracks was as big as three barns and just as open. On the main deck hundreds of sailors stood in long lines before a bank of personnel and disbursing offices at the east end, or milled around waiting for something to happen. In the wings on the north side were the mess hall, sick bay, executive offices, and the cubicles of the barber shop, cleaners, and other ship's service stores.

The second deck was nothing more than a wide balcony that ran around all four sides of the main building. There were no bunks, cots, or lockers: apparently one was expected to live out of his seabag and sling a hammock from hooks on the rows of square wooden stanchions. Noting the gurgling steam radiators that lined the wall, I decided to spread my bag and hammock on the worn wooden deck. I had forgotten that heat rises but hadn't forgotten how I had fallen from a hammock onto the steel deck of the *Louisville* during the crossing from Pearl Harbor a few months before.

YBI Receiving Station was a relic of the American Steel Navy of William McKinley and Teddy Roosevelt. Sailors had lived here under these conditions since before the turn of the century. After a trip to the head one deck down, I was not certain that even the plumbing had been upgraded. The building, quite literally, was moldering. It was none too clean and smelled more than a little like its unofficial name. I decided I must find ways to spend as little time here as possible.

But first I had to endure days of processing and nights of discomfort under my two thin blankets on the loft deck. The radiators hissed and spat, but the heat dissipated somewhere in the cavernous spaces of the barracks. By breakfast time I needed both hands to raise a coffee mug to my lips. After muster on the parade ground, where I strained to hear my name above the roar of cars, trucks, and Key System trains on the bridge above, I joined the interminable lines on the main deck "bull pen." It was the only way to eventually get liberty and pay. I constantly perused the transfer lists that were being posted on the bulletin boards. Here at YBI, I found, self-reliance was not merely a virtue; it was a necessity.

At last I found my name on one of the typed lists. The Service Force had detailed me to a ship named the *Pawnee*, under construction in nearby Alameda. All I knew about the Pawnees was that they were a nation of Plains warriors, now confined to a reservation in Oklahoma. I looked for a senior petty officer and soon found a first-class quartermaster with several red hashmarks on the left sleeve of his undress blues. "Wheels, I've just been assigned to the *Pawnee*. Hull AT-74. Could you tell me what type of ship she is?"

"Indian-class ship," he said. "Let's see. Yeah, she's one of the new ocean-going tugs."

I looked at him in dismay. The word "tug" evoked images of the small, squatty harbor workboats, their bulwarks lined with auto tires, which assisted battleships in and out of their berths.

"My God," I said. "An ocean-going tug! Do they really go to sea?"

The quartermaster grinned. "Damn right. They're over 200 feet and around 1,400 tons. Crew of ninety or so in wartime. We use 'em for salvage, firefighting, and deep-sea towing."

"What kind of duty are they?"

"Damn good if you draw an old Mustang skipper—and you probably will, 'cause he's gotta be a salvage expert." He grinned again. "Yeah, they're good duty if you don't mind towing some cripple along at five knots for weeks on end, where you're a sittin' duck for any Nip sub that happens along. Good luck, Sparks!"*

*This conversation with the quartermaster first appeared in *"We Will Stand by You": Serving in the* Pawnee, *1942–1945* (Annapolis, Md.: Naval Institute Press, 1996), pp. 5–6.

From a mighty battlewagon, a force flagship, to a lowly fleet tug! Why not shore duty at Dutch Harbor, Unalaska, or maybe a nice new ammo ship? Then the delicious dark humor of my predicament made me laugh. Why not view this assignment as a promotion? The dreadnought's fifty years of glory had ended in a chaos of fiery destruction at Pearl Harbor seven months before. Better the insignificant *Pawnee* than duty in the new queen of battles, the ungainly and decidedly unmajestic flattop.

While I waited for my new ship, I learned that Goat Island was a very unhealthy place to be stationed. There didn't seem to be any summer there. The sunshine was weak and pale. A chill wind whistled past Alcatraz and invaded every leaky joint of the cattle barn that was the naval receiving station. The dank, cold weather had driven the training station to the friendlier shores of San Diego Bay twenty years before. Half of every recruit company, I heard, had ended up in sick bay. Sick bay remained a busy place, with a long line of sniffling sailors at each morning's sick call. Despite my usual susceptibility to colds, I was not one of them. I ate three hearty meals a day, supplemented by orange juice purchased from the ship's service cafeteria. Or perhaps it was the many cups of coffee I drank every day that kept me going.

Periodically the fog overran its banks outside the Golden Gate and rolled in under the bridge, swallowing up the Presidio, Fort Mason, and Fishermen's Wharf, swiftly engulfing Treasure Island and Yerba Buena, and moving on silently to enshroud the East Bay in its ghostly white mantle. The foghorns and sirens began sounding their mournful mixed chorus in baritone, bass, and soprano. Freighters and oilers and patrol craft inched their way west against the cottony tide, for not even a San Francisco summer sea fog could halt the commerce of war. Lost in the middle of the bay, Yerba Buena seemed isolated from the enemy and curiously safe.

The fog was still there one morning after muster, resisting the efforts of a small, wan sun to burn it away. I was standing on the neo-Roman portico when I saw a crowd gather and heard someone shout for a corpsman. An old-time first-class petty officer had fallen, never to rise. I had seen him before, a stocky man with a bloated red face and an obvious case of the shakes, or worse. He was from the Asiatic Fleet, I was told. His transfer to Yerba Buena made it necessary for him to sober up after many years of dissipation and that, apparently, had killed him. He was, in a way, a casualty of the Japanese attack on the Philippines.

I thought about a 35-year-old seaman first class in the *California*, an alcoholic who was continuously drunk. I had often seen his tall, emaciated form in the third-deck passageways, but he had not seen me; his eyes were crazily focused on infinity. He stood no watches and had no duties, being protected by the chief master-at-arms and other senior boatswain's mates. They were career men who took care of their own, for in two or three years he would have retired with a pension. Now I wondered if he had survived the sinking of our ship. Since he seldom ventured topside, I doubted it. Did it really make any difference whether he died on the third deck of his home, or later in some stinking warren on skid row? Perhaps the former was the more merciful.

By standing in line and asking questions, I learned the *Pawnee* had been launched on 31 March and was still fitting out at the United Engineering yard. Probably, she would not be commissioned before late October or early November. Intentionally or not, the Navy had given me an extended vacation, and I determined to enjoy it to the fullest.

My duty assignments were not onerous. Occasionally I donned canvas leggings, duty belt, and World War I "tin hat" and patrolled the YBI sea wall with a Springfield service rifle. Or I was taken to the Federal Building in the Civic Center. There, with a .45 automatic, I guarded an unmarked door that led to some kind of Navy intelligence facility that operated around the clock.

As befitted a radioman, I always seemed to draw the midwatch, midnight to 0400. The long, tiled corridors were empty; the other offices were still and lightless behind their frosted glass doors. The air was close and musty. When I couldn't sit any longer at my schoolboy-type desk, I fought off the urge to sleep by pacing the hallway. I was saved on more than one occasion by a motherly woman wearing a pince-nez who would pop out of the secret office with a large mug of coffee.

"You poor boy," she would say. "I wish I could do more. It must be terribly boring out here."

"It's all right, ma'am," I would say, grateful for her thoughtfulness. "I've stood many a worse watch at sea."

Soon I was given a more adventurous assignment: patrolling the busy streets of San Francisco. At the police station in the somber old Hall of Justice at Kearny and Washington Streets, I received a nightstick, belt, and Shore Patrol brassard and set out with a pardner on the evening's assigned beat. Sometime after 0100, when the bars closed, I checked in my gear and was free for the rest of the night, with the additional privilege of liberty that afternoon.

The new men of the Shore Patrol detachment drew Market Street as a sort of aptitude (and attitude) test. From the Ferry Building tower to the Civic Center more than a dozen long blocks away, San Francisco's broad, dirty and noisy main stem was always awash with the flotsam of a large city—the lame, the misshapen, the poor, the blind, the self-appointed soul-savers. Now they had to compete for sidewalk space with a flood tide of uniforms in Navy blue, Army khaki, and Marine green. Most of the uniforms were worn by seamen or privates fresh from boot camp or recruit training who had little money and even less sophistication about the ways of sinful San Francisco. Generally, they were too young even to buy a drink.

Restlessly they roamed the great, world-weary street, past the bars, pawn shops, and movie-theater marquees, the hotels, office buildings, and restaurants, each hoping he would beat the odds and meet a girl like (or perhaps very unlike) the one he had left behind. Unless he was a "jive hound" who lucked out at the El Patio Ball Room, the only girl he was likely to meet was a streetwalker, or a "conductorette" who collected 10-cent fares on one of the four streetcar lines that kept Market Street perpetually aroar.

The harshly lighted coffee shops offered a last chance at romance. The waitresses, however, were as blasé as the street itself. They had heard the pitches and propositions of these young men from the hills and farms and towns many times before. Rejected again, the boots and recruits were reduced to congregating at the Fun Center, a penny arcade where they could vent their frustration by shooting Japanese Zeros and warships, drawing a bead on Adolph Hitler, or posing with buddies in front of a cardboard battleship. San Francisco, I learned, could be a cold city indeed. It had a well-deserved reputation as a place where almost anything might happen. But not to naive seamen and privates.

Between Chinatown and North Beach, one long block of Pacific Street was set off by a pair of concrete arches which announced that this was the "International Settlement." It had once been the Barbary Coast, a district more notorious in its late-nineteenth-century heyday than the waterfront of Marseilles, London's Limehouse, or the native quarter of Port Said. Reopened in 1939, its feeble but garish incarnation of bars, cafes, and nightclubs was dedicated to remaining more or less within the law while fleecing the servicemen and tourists. The chiefs and petty officers who hung out in the Settlement had little more chance of "scoring" with a cocktail waitress, hat-check girl, or dancer than the seamen in the coffee shops of Market, and they paid a good deal more for the privilege of trying. They did have a choice of atmospheres and decors, from a Gold Rush saloon with sawdust on the floor to a cabaret of the "lost generation" in Paris, from the grass mats and fish nets of the South Seas to the red plush and gold gilt of the Gay Nineties. Outside most of these clubs, slick-haired barkers in tuxedos tried to lure servicemen to promised, if illusory, delights inside.

My regular pardner, a second-class signalman named Jones, shared my dislike for this beat. We considered the operators of the fancy clip joints as so many human sharks preying on the lonesome. We could not do anything about the watered drinks or the B-girls who got a percentage on the hugely overpriced champagne they cajoled sailors into buying, but we could make the profiteers aware of our presence.

"Nix, you guys," said one pitchman. "The boss doesn't like SPs hanging around his club. It's bad for business, you know?"

"Isn't that too goddam bad," I said. "Move aside." As he well knew, the men of the Shore Patrol could go anyplace they wanted to go. After that, we devoted extra attention to this nightspot, to the great discomfort of the owner.

On Broadway not far away were Mona's and Finocchio's, two famous cafes that catered to homosexuals and curious tourists. Mona's featured male impersonators for its lesbian clientele, and servicemen were permitted. But Finocchio's swarmed with males "in drag," on stage and in the audience, and was strictly off-limits.

When we went into Mona's we were met with flat, blank hostility, very unlike our usual reception from women. But when we had to check out Finocchio's, the reaction was even more disconcerting: whistles, applause, and a variety of lewd suggestions.

The fair-skinned, sandy-haired Jones turned pomegranate red. "Goddam queers," he muttered. "We oughta round 'em all up and put 'em in camps, like we did the Japs."

Just off Columbus was a large basement bar patronized by Filipinos and other Asians, many of whom were Navy officer's cooks and stewards. The presence of a few blonde females increased the tension and lowered the boiling point. Our orders here were explicit: go no farther than the top of the stairs. If there was trouble, as was often the case, call the riot squad. Only those members of the SP detachment who were assigned to the black Fillmore district carried firearms. The rest of us were expected to maintain order with a thin nightstick and the prestige of the yellow and black SP brassard on the arm opposite the rating badge. Usually that was enough; but not in this Oriental enclave, whose customers had no reason to love whites and often were armed with guns and knives.

Chinatown's Grant Avenue bore some superficial resemblance to Honolulu's Hotel Street. It was just as narrow, permitting only one lane of traffic and one of parking on either side. Most of the buildings looked just as old; they seemed to lean against each other for support. But where Hotel was amorphous, neither east nor west, Grant Avenue was a Chinese portrait in an Occidental frame. "It reminds me a lot of Shanghai or maybe Canton," a sailor from the old Asiatic Fleet told me.

Here were pagoda roofs in red, orange, and green, cornices that turned up like celery twists, ornately decorated balconies that overhung the sidewalks. Even the street lamps were housed within miniature temples supported by entwined dragons. Intermingled with the hundreds of specialty shops and open-air stalls lining the avenue were restaurants and cocktail lounges. The names they bore ranged from the prosaic (the Far East and Club Shanghai) to the historical and literary (Kubla Khan, for the founder of the Mongol Dynasty, and Li Po's, honoring the great and bibulous lyric poet) to the evocative (the Lion's Den). The Hang Far Low at 723 Grant was known throughout the fleet, although not necessarily for its cuisine.

Since the sidewalks of this picturesque ghetto were so narrow, the press of pedestrians made Chinatown seem even more crowded than Market Street. Joining the American forces making their aimless rounds were merchant seamen and servicemen from Great Britain, Australia, New Zealand, and a dozen other countries. Some of the 20,000 residents lent the spice of the Orient to the uniformed raree. The younger ones wore Western clothes and looked as Americanized as Chinese ever become. But the elders clung to the attire of their spiritual homeland, whence many would return in old age or death so that their bones could mingle with the dust of their ancestors.

The women, in the traditional embroidered shirtwaists and black silk pantaloons, seemed always petite and attractive regardless of their years. The hair pulled tightly back from their foreheads was dark and shiny: I wondered how they kept it that way. The men were more solemn in loose black coats and baggy pants, some wearing skull-caps and others wide-brimmed hats that gave them a slightly sinister aspect.

It was useless to make an overture of friendship to these patriarchs. They looked through me, uttered a few high-pitched monosyllables in Chinese, and turned away. Even though I was there as a peacekeeper, I walked as an alien in their midst. That, I supposed, was how the Chinese had dealt with the Mongols and other invaders over their long history.

Our beat began at Grant and California Street, an intersection made notable by the triple-tiered pagoda tower of the Cathay House restaurant on one side and the Gothic mass of Old St. Mary's Church on the other. Here, at least, East did meet West, and the effect was oddly harmonious. "Son, Observe the Time and Fly from Evil," read the gold inscription below the clock on one of the church towers. Considering that Old St. Mary's was opened in 1854 and had looked down upon Chinatown's early days of slave girls, opium dens, and tong wars (to say nothing of the white bordellos south of California), the inscription seemed an inspired one.

From California we patrolled the east side of Grant Avenue until it met the oblique angle of Columbus Avenue on the fringes of North Beach and returned on the west side. Often we paused to admire the windows filled with delicately carved statuettes and other art objects in teakwood, ivory, and jade, the bronze and enamel ware and cloisonné. In the tiny markets we shook our heads over Chinese delicacies: sea snails, shark's fins, bamboo sprouts, Cantonese roast duck pressed as flat as a board, eggs that had been aging in mud for a decade or more. In souvenir stalls we examined figures of Confucius, laughed over devil-paper strips that were supposed to aid in escaping the evil one, and purchased incense burners in the shape of joss houses, or temples, for our families.

The shop of the herbalist was a final wonder. There among the rows of bins and bottles were sea-horse skeletons, powdered tiger claws, dried toads, and the finely ground horns of virgin deer.

"Say, what is all this stuff used for?" Jones asked.

The middle-aged apothecary smiled urbanely. "They are ancient treatments for various ailments," he explained. "The jars you are looking at now contain what you would call, ah, aphrodisiacs."

"Huh? What the hell is an aphrodisiac?"

"It is a stimulant, said to increase, ah, sexual power," he said delicately.

"Ha! That's the last thing we need. Let's go, Mason."

In the bars and cafes of Grant Avenue, our reception was much more cordial than it had been in the International Settlement. Most of the owners had been there a long time and intended to pass the businesses along to their sons. They were just as interested in maintaining law and order as the Navy was. Jones and I would be greeted with a smile and a slight bow and escorted to a rear table, where we had our choice of food and beverages. Mindful of the prohibition against drinking on duty, we usually had coffee. Occasionally I ordered an exotic blend of tea, which was brought in a large porcelain pot with a padded silk cover.

Until about 2300 hours there was surprisingly little trouble. We told sailors to straighten their white hats and button their cuffs, broke up arguments that could develop into fisticuffs, helped settle disputes over bar bills (in favor of the servicemen, if possible), and protected the random "cruising" homosexual from violent reprisals. We endured the ancient hostility between the Marines and the Navy, the advances of young ladies who were trying to make their escorts jealous, the peremptory demands for action by officers who had not been saluted or addressed with proper courtesy, and the gibes of merchant sailors in dungarees.

The derisive attitude of the merchant sailors was made all the more irritating by the knowledge that they were paid much more than seagoing Navy men for duty that was usually less hazardous. My pardner finally heard the refrain, "You can't arrest me, you goddam SP, I'm in the Merchant Marine," once too often. "Let's see your I.D., Mac," he said to the taunting mariner.

"What the hell for? I already told you—"

"Yeah, we know," I said. "But it looks like you're wearing U.S. Navy dungarees. I think you're out of uniform. Your I.D., please."

"Who's gonna make me?"

"Why, we are," Jones said, putting a hand on his nightstick. "And if we can't, the riot squad can. And if they can't, the San Francisco P.D. sure as hell can. Hand it over."

The man looked around for support from his companions, but they were maintaining a discreet distance. Reluctantly he dug out his identification card.

We examined it carefully under a dim dragon street lamp. He was an able-bodied seaman. We conferred at some length in low voices about where we were going when we got off duty. Finally, we handed the card back to the now jittery A.B.

"I guess we were wrong," I said with a grin. "I sure hope we don't make the same mistake next time we see you."

"Yeah, you'd better start wearing your monkey suit," Jones growled. "Now shove off."

In the last two hours of our patrol, trouble fueled by too much alcohol and too few women was likely to erupt. We removed drunken sailors from bars and, with the cooperation of the Military Police, intervened in street disputes between rival services or nations. Our aim was to restore order without arresting anyone, but that was not always possible. Then we called for reinforcements and the paddy wagon.

One blond Viking of a seaman was a special problem. It required five of us to wrestle him from a bar to the open rear door of the SP van. There he braced arms as thick as tree trunks against the frame and refused to budge. We got out our nightsticks and began to beat a tattoo on his head, shoulders, and hands. The hardwood billies bounced off as if they were ping-pong paddles. When he finally fell through the door he carried three SPs with him. The struggle was still going on as the patrol wagon roared off toward the police station.

"That big ox just wanted to keep on drinking," I told Jones. "Suppose he'd been mad at us?"

A few nights later, when we came out of a cocktail lounge at Grant near Washington, we saw a pretty Chinese girl across the street. She was running back and forth frantically. "Ess Pee! Ess Pee!" she screamed when she saw us. At her feet two shadowy figures were rolling on the sidewalk. One was wearing a Navy uniform. We sprinted across the street, pulled the sailor off a young Chinese in a dark business suit and spread-eagled him on the pavement.

"Now, what happened?" I asked.

The girl was in tears, near hysteria. The civilian got up and brushed at his clothes, struggling to regain his composure.

"This sailor assaulted my fiancée," he said in unaccented English. I guessed he was in a business or profession.

"Is that true?"

The sailor was slender and darkly handsome in a rather weak, petulent way. He was wearing the red shoulder stripe of a fireman.

"Naw," he said sullenly. "This Jap attacked me."

I knew he was lying. I had to repress a savage urge to take my fists or nightstick to him. Any man who would assault a woman of any race, under any circumstances, did not deserve to wear the uniform of the United States Navy.

In the distance, whistles were blowing. Already a crowd was beginning to gather.

"Would you like to prefer charges?" I asked the Chinese man.

"I certainly would."

"Good. Please file a complaint with the Shore Patrol at the police station. This man will be there soon."

More whistles blew. The crowd was growing and the situation was becoming ominous.

"Get the riot squad over here, Jonesy," I said. "On the double."

Now I was alone in the middle of a circle of angry Chinese. I got a firm grip on the fireman's arm and moved him against a storefront. I got out my nightstick. It wasn't much, but it was better than nothing.

The men began closing in around us. I spotted the ringleader, a tall, gaunt-faced man with a furious, almost fanatical expression, and concentrated on him.

"Stand back!" I commanded, raising my stick. "This man is going to the brig just as soon as the patrol wagon arrives. Everything is under control."

The leader hesitated. The group of thirty or more Chinese hesitated, too. I kept my club raised and repeated my order.

The stalemate continued for what seemed a very long time. At one point the mob started to surge forward again but stopped at my fierce, "Stand back! This man is going to the brig."

At last the paddy wagon rolled up with siren wailing. The crowd dispersed silently, by twos and threes. One of the last to leave was the ringleader. We looked at each other across the abyss of cultures, and I nodded. I hoped he understood that I wanted my fellow-sailor court-martialed just as much as he had wanted more direct punishment. The man had dishonored his uniform. My uniform.

"I hope your skipper throws the book at you, you SOB," I told the fireman as I shoved him toward the other patrolmen.

"You sure saved his ass," Jones told me later while we filled out the arrest reports. "How does a creep like that get in the Navy?"

"Saved my own, too," I reminded him. "Any other district of this city and the creep and I would have been beaten to a pulp. The Chinese are very law-abiding people, thank God."

Still, I was rather pleased with myself. Too pleased, perhaps. The incident had brought a heightened awareness, a tingling excitement, and a vague feeling of power.

"I hope I don't stay on Shore Patrol much longer," I said. "I'm beginning to think like a cop, and that's not what I intend to be."

As if to compensate for its hazards, Shore Patrol carried some special, though unofficial, rewards. Despite the fact that San Francisco was rapidly being taken over by the military, women were easy for an SP to meet. They smiled coyly from bar stools, rushed up seeking protection from too-aggressive sailors, stopped us on the street on the pretext of needing directions. Even the ones with dates sometimes scribbled a phone number on a cocktail napkin and passed it surreptitiously.

"I can't figure it, Ted," Jones said. "We come down here on liberty and the broads ignore us. Then we tie on that goddam SP brassard and we have to fight 'em off with a club. Tell me about women, buddy."

"The guy who could have told you was killed at Pearl," I replied, thinking of my great friend Melvin Grant Johnson. "What little I know I learned from him—and from reading some Shakespeare. Basically, they both said women are devious, illogical, sentimental, untrustworthy, and dangerous as hell. So let's go find a couple."

"Yeah," he agreed. "Tonight we got the brassard. Hell, they'll find us!"

I spent most afternoons drinking coffee with Jonesy and other new friends at the ship's service cafeteria, which occupied the ground floor of the nondescript building adjoining the barracks. We had plenty to talk about beyond the ships we had been detailed to and our liberty adventures in the city.

On 7 August the Marines had landed at a place called Guadalcanal in the Solomon Islands, 10 degrees of latitude below the equator. According to the crude newspaper maps, it was very near Tulagi, which planes from the *Yorktown* had raided just before the Coral Sea battle. The Japanese had begun construction of an airfield on Guadalcanal, posing a direct threat to our bases in the South Pacific and our shipping lifeline to Australia and New Zealand.

Reacting quickly to our capture of the partly completed airstrip, the Japanese sent seven cruisers and a long destroyer racing south from their bases at Rabaul, New Britain. Just after midnight of 9 August they took our divided force of cruisers and destroyers totally by surprise off Savo Island. Sunk were the U.S. heavy cruisers *Quincy, Vincennes,* and *Astoria* and the Australian heavy cruiser *Canberra.* The heavy cruiser *Chicago* was damaged.

Savo Island was the worst defeat at sea ever inflicted upon the U.S. Navy. Once again it brought into question the competence of our commanders. The derogatory phrase "trade-school graduates," which I had first heard in the radio shack of the *Pennsylvania,* was now common among petty officers.

"The trade-school graduates brought us Pearl Harbor and the Java Sea," Jones said. "Now they've brought us Savo Island. What next, for crissakes?"

We wondered how many of our fellow sailors had been lost in the unexcusable debacle off Guadalcanal.

"We'll never know," a petty officer said. "Not till after the war, when it's too late for the civilians to do anything about it."

"You can be sure of one thing," another said. "We're all gonna end up down there—unless the Japs run us clear back to Australia first."

Some were in no hurry to go. They told me that it was sometimes possible to delay one's transfer from Yerba Buena by illicit means. A radioman explained how:

"Every Monday morning I get into line and tell the transfer-desk yeoman, 'I'll bet you two bucks I won't be here next week.' The guy pulls his huge stack of transfer papers, finds mine, puts it on the bottom of the pile, and holds out his hand for the deuce. The next week I do the same. It's been working for two months now!"

While appreciating the ingenuity of this scheme, I knew my conscience was too tender to condone petty bribery. Even if it could, I probably would encounter a yeoman of strict rectitude and get put on report. I had no desire to join the numerous brig prisoners, a large black "P" stenciled on the back of their fatigues, who were always being moved across the parade ground at double-time. The marines who guarded them seemed to take as much pleasure in their work as the ones who had regularly brutalized and beaten up the brig prisoners in the *California.*

The temptation for easy money must have been irresistible to some YBI yeomen. They worked in dirty, cluttered and noisy offices doing endless paperwork in quadruplicate for unending lines of enlisted men.

Everyone in every line wanted something: pay, liberty, emergency leave, transportation, a change of assignment, a transfer—or was trying to forestall a transfer as long as possible. These hectic conditions would continue as long as the war did and probably worsen. To be sure, the yeomen were safe in San Francisco Bay. But I wondered at the price. Were they allowing themselves to be transformed into mindless robots, like the wage slaves in Chaplin's 1936 film, *Modern Times*? I remembered the words of Benjamin Franklin, memorized in high school: "They that can give up essential liberty to obtain a little temporary safety deserve neither liberty nor safety."

During the afternoon bull sessions I learned something of real, immediate value. While waiting for a ship, it was not only possible but also rather easy for a petty officer to get leave by going through channels.

"Just don't ask for too many days at a time," I was told. "Better to take a week and come back later for another week. Hell, they're glad to get rid of you."

I went through channels and got a seven-day leave. I had stumbled across the formula for a glorious life in limbo at the naval receiving station: one week of leave, two weeks of Shore Patrol with liberty every other night, one week of leave.

Only one problem remained: financing all this unexpected freedom. Again, my cohorts at the cafeteria told me how. With so many men being drafted into the military and San Francisco Harbor operating at capacity, a shortage of stevedores had developed. The International Longshoremen's and Warehousemen's Union, directed by the infamous, Australian-born Harry Bridges, was allowing sailors to work on the waterfront by special permit. I signed up at the ILWU headquarters and was soon in the hold of a freighter, unloading canned pineapple and raw sugar from Hawaii or coffee beans from Central America.

The work was hard, but I welcomed it after months of relative inactivity in the *Pennsylvania* and at YBI. Growing up in the foothills of Northern California during the Great Depression, I was no stranger to hard work. At the end of each ten-hour shift I received a piece of round brass that could be exchanged at the company pay window (or almost anywhere else at 5 cents on the dollar) for $17.50. That was two and a half times the average hourly wage in 1942, a great deal more money than I had ever earned. Each ten-hour night in the hold would finance a week or more of liberty or leave.

The name Bridges was anathema to my father and almost everyone else. In 1939 and again in 1940 the government had vainly attempted to deport him as a Communist alien; his case was pending in the courts. But to the longshoremen, the tough one-time seaman from Melbourne was a hero. Over beers in Embarcadero dives they told me about the maritime workers' strikes he had led in 1934 and 1936. The strikes had finally broken, at the cost of several lives and great financial hardship, the tyrannical labor practices of the shipping moguls.

I mentioned two Steinbeck novels about the working class that had greatly moved me: *The Grapes of Wrath* and *In Dubious Battle*. I wondered why no novelist had written about the San Francisco waterfront.

One stevedore, a burly Norwegian of forty, looked interested. He got out a pipe and started filling it with Prince Albert.

"Son, there are good reasons. He would have to have grown up in the Bay Area and lived through the general strikes. Steinbeck is a Monterey novelist who writes about itinerant farm laborers.

"The other California authors are second-raters, at best. Kathleen Norris writes about motherhood and the middle class. Charles Dobie romanticizes San Francisco's criminal past, and Steward Edward White does the same for the forty-niners, the most pernicious band of scoundrels who ever exploited a state. You've heard the anonymous verse?

> "The miners came in forty-nine,
> The whores in fifty-one;
> And when they got together,
> They produced the Native Son."

While the laughter was abating, he lighted his pipe. "That leaves William Saroyan. Once he had possibilities, but he has proved too Armenian and too filled with brotherly love. No, there is only one writer who could have told our story, and he came along thirty years too soon."

The man in the watch cap and worn plaid shirt had surprised me with his language and obvious erudition. "Jack London?"

"Aye, Jack London. If you haven't already, read his *Essays of Revolt* and *The Iron Heel*. London was a drunk, a fornicator, and a sailor"—smiling at me as he said it—"but he wrote like an avenging angel. He was one of us!"

Now I had the means to enjoy my leaves. I clipped my campaign ribbons—American Defense with fleet clasp, American Campaign, and

Asiatic-Pacific with one bronze star for Pearl Harbor—to my dress blue jumper and hitchhiked wherever I went. It was faster and cheaper than riding the overcrowded buses and trains and enabled me to meet a cross-section of civilians: salesmen, waiters, wives and parents of servicemen, farmers, truck drivers, even a professional gambler driving his Cadillac (and his blonde showgirl friend) to Reno.

Once I thumbed the 450 miles of two-lane Highway 99 to Los Angeles. A close friend and shipmate from the *California* and *Pennsylvania* was being held in the county jail there on felony drunk-driving charges and faced a bad-conduct discharge. There was nothing I could do but give him cigarette money and commiseration and promise to write. A couple of times I took the aptly named Skyline Highway to Santa Cruz to see my mother, who had remarried and whom I called Lilah. Usually I went to my hometown and stayed with my foster-parents.

Back in San Francisco I began spending more time with Helen Hazelton. On occasion we took the elevator to the Top of the Mark. The view of the city, the bay, and the bridge through Yerba Buena to Oakland was breathtaking, but the place was essentially a Navy officer's hangout. More often we went dancing at the Music Box, or talked long over drinks at Bimbo's 365 Club on Market, where the mirror image of the nude "girl in the fishbowl," greatly reduced in size, attracted sailors who were not intimidated by the minimum charge and elegant decor.

In late evenings we took the Key System electric train across the Bay Bridge to Oscar's, a sprawling nightclub on the shores of Lake Merritt. One drink before the crackling fireplace in a secluded lounge and we boarded a streetcar. Our last stop was "Irish Johnny" Taylor's bar on MacArthur Boulevard, within walking distance of Helen's home.

Taylor was an irrepressible pugilist who was still handsome after some 125 pro fights. His roadwork seemed to consist of racing the length of the bar while mixing drinks or jitterbugging on the dance floor. He liked Helen because she was a lady and me because I could speak with some knowledge about boxers and boxing. I had been an avid reader of the "green sheet," the sports section of the San Francisco *Chronicle*, all through my school years and had discovered *Ring* magazine when I was serving in the *California*, where intership boxing was the major sport.

"Sure an' boxin' is a lousy racket," Taylor told me, "but it ain't all bad. How else could a dumb Mick like me have made enough moola to buy his own candy store? Oh, I coulda made more—been champ, maybe—but then I wouldn'ta had no fun!"

He fought "Hammerin' Hank" Armstrong, then the world welter-weight champion, a couple of times. Once he was stopped on a TKO in four or five rounds.

"What happened, Johnny?" I asked him a few days later. He didn't have a mark.

"Ah, it was nothin,'" he said with disgust. "The bastard landed a lucky punch, is all. I'll get 'im next time!"

When Helen and I came in, Taylor would set up two drinks on the house. Vaulting nimbly over the bar, he would put some coins in the jukebox and ask her to dance. Watching him on the ring-sized floor, I could see how he had survived so many fights with so little apparent damage. He was as graceful as an ocelot. I didn't worry about him steal-ing my girlfriend away. He took women no more seriously than any-thing else in his life. He had, I thought, an ideal temperament for a fighting man, and I wished I shared it.

Toward the end of October, I was informed at morning muster that I was being transferred to Treasure Island to join the *Pawnee* comple-ment. My strange and glorious interlude of liberty, leave, and love was ending.

Among the ruins of Stalingrad the Russians were still holding off the German Wehrmacht in hand-to-hand fighting. British General Bernard Montgomery had just opened the Battle of El Alamein against Field Marshall Erwin Rommel's Afrika Korps. In the South Pacific the Japa-nese had reinforced their troops on Guadalcanal and were trying to break through the Marine perimeter and recapture Henderson Field (named for Maj. Lofton R. Henderson, USMC, lost in a dive-bombing attack on the carrier *Kaga* during the Battle of Midway). Off the island, the carrier *Wasp* had been torpedoed and lost on 15 September. But the Navy claimed an enemy carrier and four destroyers sunk in the Battle of Cape Esperance on 11–12 October. Obviously, the issue at Guadal-canal was still in doubt. The *Pawnee's* services were needed there, and that is where we would doubtless go.

I tossed my bag and hammock into a stake-body truck and took a last look around the Goat Island Receiving Station. The American eagle atop Jefferson's pillared portico stared to the southwest, its wings half-lifted

in preparation for flight. On the other side of the Bay Bridge the protected cruiser the Navy called the *Despatch* and I called the *Boston*
pointed her decorated ram prow in the same direction, as if hoping for
one final call to battle stations.

Primitive it had been, that great barn of a receiving barracks, erected
during the *Boston*'s war, but it had given me nearly four months of
casual duty in one of the world's most exciting cities, and more liberty
than I had ever imagined I would enjoy in wartime. I hardly could have
asked for more. Now the Navy would expect me to repay its generosity.
I was well pleased.

The Puget Sound Navy Yard in June 1939. In the foreground is the battleship *Maryland*, and behind it is a heavy cruiser. In the background is Sinclair Inlet; downtown Bremerton, Washington, is out of the photo to the right. (courtesy of Puget Sound Navy Yard)

The YMCA building in Bremerton, where young seamen and firemen could find a respite from shipboard discipline and crowded living conditions as they moved from the civilian world to the military. (courtesy of Bremerton Armed Forces YMCA)

Seamen from the USS *Mississippi* mill around the entrance of the Bremerton YMCA in a 1937 photo. Business at the "Y" ebbed and flowed with the arrival and departure of capital ships and fleet units. (courtesy of Bremerton Armed Forces YMCA)

Members of V-3 Communication Reserve in Placerville, California, area were given service rifles but no radio gear. In a snapshot taken by the author in late 1939, members and their advisers prepare to dig the pit for a rifle range. Standing at the far left is F. C. "Bill" Fisher, who served with the author in *California* and *Pennsylvania,* 1940–42.

All through the peacetime decades, the *California* rehearsed for a battle-line engagement that did not come until the Battle of Surigao Strait in the Philippines, 25 October 1944. Above, steaming off the Southern California coast, the state's namesake fires her main battery to starboard. Range clock atop foremast and bearing scale on No. 2 turret indicate that photo was taken in the early 1920s. (courtesy of Los Angeles Maritime Museum and Port of Los Angeles)

California (foreground) and other Navy ships ride at anchor in San Pedro Bay, with the city of Long Beach in background, in the late 1930s. The decision to move the fleet's home port from San Pedro to Pearl Harbor was provocative and disastrous. (National Archives)

On forty-ninth anniversary of Pearl Harbor attack, author gives keynote address at *Arizona* Memorial Visitor Center. Present were some 2,500 visitors, along with representatives of the national and local television, radio, and print media. Mason is wearing Hawaiian shirt, the garrison cap of the Pearl Harbor Survivors, and the traditional lei of red carnations. (courtesy of *Honolulu Star-Bulletin*)

Author on balcony of his Waikiki Beach hotel after his keynote address and book-signing at *Arizona* Memorial Visitor Center on 7 December 1990.

Author's chief radioman in *California*, Thomas J. Reeves, rests at the National Memorial Cemetery of the Pacific (the "Punchbowl") under the gold marker of Medal of Honor winner. During World War II a new destroyer escort, the *Reeves*, was named in his honor. Nearby is the marker for author's best friend, Radioman Melvin G. Johnson. (courtesy of Don Till)

Nevada under repair at Puget Sound Navy Yard in photo taken 26 June 1942. Entire bomb-damaged and burned-out superstructure has been stripped away, leaving only the tripod-mast supports, and the mainmast is being lowered. The gallant old battleship later distinguished herself at the invasions of Normandy, Southern France, Iwo Jima, and Okinawa. All battleship sailors have a special place in their hearts where the *Nevada* and her crew of 7 December 1941 are enshrined. (courtesy of Puget Sound Navy Yard)

Battleship *Pennsylvania* in San Francisco Bay in early 1943. After author left ship in July 1942, inadequate 5-inch/51-caliber secondary and 5-inch/25-caliber A.A. batteries were replaced with the new 5-inch/38-caliber dual-purpose guns. But ship still carries the fleet's first operational radar, the CXAM. Note "bedspring" antenna at truncated mainmast. (National Archives)

The oiler *Neosho* in 1939. The author was transported to Hawaii and his first duty aboard the *California* in this ship. The *Neosho* was moored just astern of the *California* during the Pearl Harbor attack; she was lost during the Battle of the Coral Sea. (National Archives)

Four shipmates who survived the sinking of *California* and were now assigned to the *Pennsylvania* enjoy liberty at the Streets of Paris nightclub in San Francisco in June 1942. From left, the author, Army PFC William P. Hooper Jr. (who joined our party, probably because he wanted to be a sailor), J. K. "Jawbones" Madden, Jim Baker, and Tom Moore.

Sailors on liberty are noted for their pursuit of "bad" girls, but for men far from their own homes a quiet day at the home of a good girl and her family was equally treasured. This picture was taken in May 1942. From left, the author, Helen Hazelton, J. K. Madden, a friend of Miss Hazelton's, and a *Pennsylvania* shipmate.

The Yerba Buena (Goat) Island facility was hastily built as a naval training station during the Spanish-American War. This 1918 photo shows part of main barracks, gym, parade ground (Grinder), and Army Point (right background). By author's time at YBI, former gym, right of barracks, had been converted to a ship's service cafeteria. (Naval Historical Center)

When the naval training station was moved to the friendlier climate of San Diego in the early 1920s, the Goat Island facility became a receiving station. In this 1935 photo, it seems to huddle in the shadow of the San Francisco-Oakland Bay Bridge, then under construction. On hill above receiving station, at right, are white Victorian houses of officers' row, with commandant's mansion above them. At very top of island, center, is the signal tower. (courtesy of Treasure Island Museum)

The author in dungarees on Main Street of his hometown, Placerville, California, during a week's leave in summer of 1942.

The author dances with Helen Hazelton at the Music Box, a nightclub on O'Farrell Street, during his Goat Island interlude.

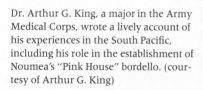

The *Pawnee* was launched on a rainy 31 March 1942 at the United Engineering shipyard in Alameda, California. The sponsor's party included (from left) Mrs. W. W. Anderson; Lt. Comdr. Oscar Steigler of the Twelfth Naval District; his wife, who holds the champagne with which she christened the ship; and R. E. Christy, president of United Engineering. (U.S. Navy photo)

Dr. Arthur G. King, a major in the Army Medical Corps, wrote a lively account of his experiences in the South Pacific, including his role in the establishment of Noumea's "Pink House" bordello. (courtesy of Arthur G. King)

A handful of servicemen gather outside the entrance to the Pink House. Since military authorities were uneasy about the publicity the brothel might generate, this picture was taken surreptitiously with an old Eastman folding camera concealed in a shoe box. Members of the Shore Patrol in the Jeep at left, on hand to keep order, did not notice. (courtesy of Ted Blahnik, editor of Guadalcanal Campaign Veterans' *Echoes*)

Downtown Noumea in 1943 or 1944, photographed by a soldier in the Americal Division. The author thought the town resembled "a run-down, third-rate New Orleans." Noumea's only imposing structure, St. Joseph's Catholic Cathedral, is in the background. (courtesy of N. Harry Martin)

Flavius J. George, admired skipper of the *Pawnee*, shortly after his promotion to commander in 1944. (courtesy of Mary George)

After the *Majaba* was torpedoed at Guadalcanal, Lieutenant George was given command of the boat pool and responsibility for unloading the supplies needed by the beleaguered Marines. For the next three months, he lived on the beach under conditions like these, depicted in a nearby Marine camp. (Defense Department photo)

Following her commissioning on 7 November 1942, *Pawnee* boxes the compass on shakedown cruise in San Francisco Bay. (National Archives)

Lieutenant Commander George climbed to the searchlight platform in the foremast of the *Pawnee* to pose for this photo, taken in the Solomons in 1943. (Naval Historical Center)

Mistakenly attacked by U.S. PT boats in Blanche Channel on the night of 30 June 1943, the *Pawnee* has torpedoes pass ahead, behind, and under her. At right, the abandoned transport *McCawley* explodes after torpedoes set off a magazine; in distance, the destroyer *McCalla* can be seen steaming to intercept the attacker, presumed at the time to be a Japanese submarine. (painting by Richard DeRosset)

The author and his closest friends in the *Pawnee* dubbed themselves "the four musketeers." From left are musketeers Donald J. "Flash" Aposhian (with unidentified friend),
Dale H. Gerber, and Harley A. Schleppi.

Munsee, a sister ship of the *Pawnee*, takes over towing of the crippled heavy cruiser USS
Canberra. (U.S. Navy photo)

Pawnee tows new light cruiser *Houston* in one of the most storied ship rescues in naval history. (U.S. Navy photo)

At top, the *Pawnee* can be seen towing the *Houston* as she takes a new torpedo hit in the stern. At bottom, the torpedo's effect: pillar of smoke, fire, and debris erupts from the cruiser, obscuring the *Pawnee*. (U.S. Navy photos)

(CL 81)
U. S. S. HOUSTON

Heading:

THIS IS MY PLAN CHARLIE X SIX DESTROYERS REMOVE PERSONNEL FROM HOUSTON

CANBERRA PAWNEE AND ZUNI X THEN SINK THESE SHIPS WITH TORPEDOES X

CRUISERS FORM ON SANTA FE SCREENED BY DESTROYERS OF TU 30,3.1 X CARRIERS

WITH THEIR DESTROYERS FORM SECOND GROUP X GROUPS RETIRE IN COMPANY AT

BEST SPEED EASTWARD X PLAN EFFECTIVE WHEN DIRECTED X

ACTION

File No.	Reference No.	Precedence	Date	Method	Operator	Supervisor
	152355		OCT 16	FL		

From:	CTG 30.3				Orig. By:	Released By:

Action:	TG 30.3			TOR	TOD

Info:				Freq.

Capt	Exec	Nav	Gun	Eng	1st Lt.	Comm	Supply	Aviation	AA Officer	Disburs	Medical	Marine	Radio	Signal	Radar	Capt Off	Exec Off	OOD	CWO	

During the *Houston* tow-away, Rear Adm. Laurance T. DuBose formulated three battle plans in case Japanese surface forces caught the retreating task group. Here is the message form on which a *Houston* radioman transcribed Plan C, which called for the scuttling of the *Pawnee*, her sister ship *Munsee* (incorrectly identified as *Zuni*), and the damaged cruisers. (courtesy Cleo B. Isom, USS *Houston* Association)

Heading:

FOR SKILL AND GUTS THE SAFE RETIREMENT OF THE DAMAGED
CANBERRA AND HOUSTON FROM THE SHADOW OF FORMOSA COAST
UNDER HEAVY ATTACK WILL BECOME A NAVY TRADITION . TO
ALL HANDS WHO CONTRIBUTED TO THE JOB , "WELL DONE".

----HALSEY----

ACTION

File No.	Reference No.	Precedence	Date	Method	Operator	Supervisor
			OCT,28/44		Orig. By:	Released By:
From:	COMMANDER THIRD FLEET					
Action:	THIRD FLEET				TOR 1435	TOD
Info:						Freq.

Capt	Exec	Nav	Gun	Eng	1st Lt.	Comm	Supply	Aviation	AA Officer	Disburs	Medical	Marine	Radio	Signal	Radar	Capt Off	Exec Off	OOD	CWO	

The message from "Bull" Halsey congratulating the men and units involved in getting the *Houston* and *Canberra* to safety. (courtesy Kermit A. Lamm, USS *Houston* Association)

Out of harm's way: the author in Sacramento before reporting to pre-radio materiel school in early 1945.

Navy Pier in Chicago after its conversion from a training facility for machinist's mates to an advanced radio materiel school that turned out a class of urgently needed radio technicians every week. (courtesy of William F. Nameny)

A typical classroom at the Navy Pier radio materiel school in Chicago. Facilities and instruction were much the same at the RMS the author attended in Dearborn. (courtesy of William F. Nameny)

Chester W. Nimitz, left, then a rear admiral and chief of the Bureau of Navigation, and Henry Ford Sr. at the dedication of Ford-built school for training machinist's mates at the River Rouge automobile plant in Dearborn, Michigan, in January 1941. School was later converted to primary radio materiel school. Within a year, Nimitz would reach the pinnacle of his naval career as Commander-in Chief, Pacific Fleet. (Naval Historical Center)

Author, left, and "Flash" Aposhian reunite at Chi Chi Club in Salt Lake City in the summer of 1946. The author had completed his first year at the University of Southern California; Aposhian, an electrician's mate in the Navy, had started an electrical subcontracting business.

6

The South Pacific
of James A. Michener

You throw the sand against the wind,
And the wind blows it back again.

—William Blake

The *Pawnee* (ATF-74) was commissioned on 7 November 1942 at the Alameda yard of United Engineering on the Oakland Estuary. She was the eleventh in a class of powerful new fleet tugs named for Indian tribes, and the fourth to be sent to the South Pacific Theater. One, the *Seminole*, already had been lost. A second, the *Navajo*, would be within a year; and the third, the *Menominee*, spent most of her time salvaging a sunken Japanese destroyer, the *Kikutsuki*, from Halavo Bay, Florida Island, under the direct orders of William F. Halsey, Commander South Pacific. All during the critical months of 1943, *Pawnee* was the sole ATF operating in support of the cruisers and destroyers of the Third Fleet in the Solomon Islands. That she survived without losing a man was something of a miracle.

Summarizing those months of almost nightly runs up the Slot and Blanche Channel in "*We Will Stand by You*," I wrote:

The slow and lightly armed *Pawnee* had led a charmed life. She had a superb commanding officer. He had been given the time and the hazardous assignments that together had coalesced some ninety-five men, gathered at random from all backgrounds and all parts of the nation, into a spirited ship's company. Luck and skillful handling (and, perhaps, the notoriously defective American torpedoes) had spared us off Rendova

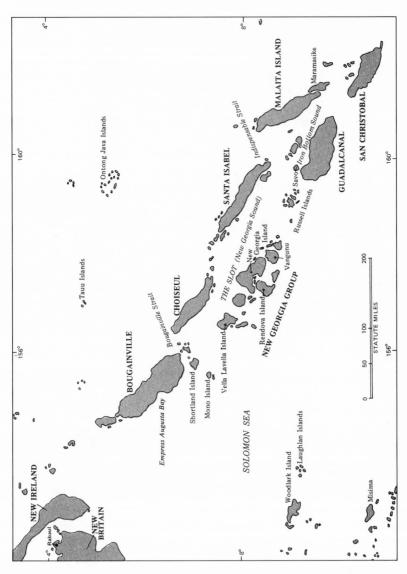

The Solomons, scene of eight months of exhausting and dangerous operations for the *Pawnee*. "Whatever they were—a gateway to hell, a last paradise, a fall from grace—nothing was ever like the Solomons." (map from Paul S. Dull, *A Battle History of the Imperial Japanese Navy, 1941–1945*)

[during the invasion of the New Georgia group in the Central Solomons]. At other times, the enemy had saved his ammunition for bigger game, or had missed us . . . or had been foiled in the last seconds [by the providential arrival of friendly aircraft]. . . .

From San Cristobal to Bougainville, death had crouched in waiting, as it did in all the war theaters. But here it assumed an aspect so brutal and alien that King Solomon's Islands might have belonged to another age, or another planet altogether. Here among the jagged coral heads, the dripping rain forests that marched up mountain slopes toward towering thunderheads, the smoke-breathing volcanoes, here under the implacable sun, there was nothing to relate to, nothing to remind one of home. Only the 100,000 ebony-skinned aborigines seemed to have some tenuous identification with the place, and that only as squatters tolerated indifferently by Nature.

Here the vastness of scale reduced man and his engines of destruction to insignificance. Steaming up the Slot against the huge cyclorama of ocean and islands and sky, our warships were plastic toys, our weapons popguns, ourselves Lilliputians led by posturing popinjays. The phosphorescent blue water swallowed our toys, the crawling green jungle quickly covered the scars gouged by our petty disputes, the voracious fauna of both stripped the flesh from the bones of our dead in a wink of time.

Here among these savage beauties, this bursting chaos of Nature, we and our enemies were the aberration, as out of place as the first man in the first garden. I thanked "whatever gods may be" that I had not died here, where death was so commonplace—and so unmourned. Here the individual counted for no more than a falling leaf; here only life en masse had value. Perhaps the islands were as much a state of mind as an actual location in the South Pacific.

Whatever they were—a gateway to hell, a last paradise, a fall from grace—nothing was ever like the Solomons.*

When I returned to civilian life, I did my best to forget the ordeal I had survived in the South Pacific, chiefly the Solomons, except for periodic reunions with *Pawnee* shipmates who had become close friends. One day the title of a paperback caught my eye, and I paid $1.75 for a copy of *Tales of the South Pacific,* by James A. Michener (Fawcett Publications, Inc., Greenwich, 1973). I had seen the film musical *South Pacific* and labeled it a fantasy, but I hoped Michener had come closer to the facts of the real South Pacific in his book. Reading it, I realized that I should

*"*We Will Stand by You,*" pp. 146–47.

have paid more attention to the flexible definition of tale ("a narrative that relates the details of some real or imaginary event, incident, or case; story") and was glad I had not paid the price of a hard-cover copy.

Michener's tales are a blend of a little fact with much fiction. The author uses a mix of actual and imaginary settings: the real Noumea in New Caledonia, Segond Channel in the New Hebrides, Tulagi in the Solomons; a fictional coral atoll he called only "the rock," an island he named Kuralei, Red and Green houses of prostitution (one for enlisted men and one for officers).

A few of his characters, unavoidably, are real: Admirals Halsey, J. S. McCain, Aubrey W. Fitch; Generals Alexander A. Vandegrift and Alexander M. Patch. Invented are Admiral Millard Kester and nearly all Navy and Marine Corps personnel, along with Nurse Nellie Forbush, French planter Emile De Becque, and Bloody Mary, who gave her name to the popular hangover drink of vodka and tomato juice. (One assumes that Michener, a graduate of Swarthmore, was aware of the original "Bloody Mary." She was daughter of Henry VIII, queen of England [1553–58], and wife of Prince Philip of Spain; her persecution of Protestants brought her the "bloody" sobriquet.)

The narrator of *Tales* is a Reserve officer of commander rank in the South Pacific "through the bitter days of '41 through '43," a paperwork sailor who never served in a warship. "I was a new type of naval officer," he writes in unnautical language that makes his point abundantly clear. "I was a man who messed around with aircraft, PT boats, landing barges, and the vast shore establishment." His status as a "qualified messenger" apparently gives him carte blanche to travel throughout the theater, occasionally carrying briefcases stuffed with secret documents. Mostly he does little but observe. The majority of his associates do little, either, at least until the climactic, bloody landing on Kuralei; they fight boredom, jungle rot, and malaria in the rear areas and wait for orders. Occasionally one finds a woman; he is an officer, of course.

In his depiction of life in the South Pacific Theater, Michener's elitism is but a reflection of the Navy's class system. In *Battleship Sailor* (pp. 68–69), I likened it to a medieval town "with a rigid hierarchical structure of peasants, artisans, clergy, and nobility, all answerable to the *seignior*, or lord of the manor." In the feudally based naval society, the knights, or officers, live in a different world than that of the serfs (seamen) and artisans (petty officers). The author's narrator, as one of the especially privileged knights, reflects this perspective.

Michener writes engagingly of such exotic places as the old convict island of Norfolk, where the inbred survivors of the *Bounty* mutiny and Pitcairn Island now live; and of fictional Bali-ha'i, where the French sequester the young women of the New Hebrides—native, Chinese, Tonkinese, and French—to protect them against rape by American servicemen. This is the island of song, where 1st Lt. Joe Cable of the Marines seduces Tonkinese virgin Liat, daughter of Bloody Mary. Only officers such as Cable and Ens. Bill Harbison of land-based Aircraft Repair Unit Eight on an island of the New Hebrides, whose target is Navy nurses, are permitted the privilege of seduction.

The enlisted men, deprived of contact with women not only by infrequent liberty but also by a caste system that forbids fraternization with nurses, who were categorized as officers, have the dubious choices of celibacy or, if Noumea were a port of call, a brief encounter with a prostitute at the famous Pink House (about which I will write presently). To be sure, Michener allows two sergeants to marry daughters of De Becque, but they are half-castes, French and Javanese, whom officers and gentlemen would not be permitted to marry. One officer, a Reserve "expediter" with a huge capacity for alcohol, marries the third daughter, but in a secret Buddhist ceremony at midnight. He is killed in the landing on Kuralei.

The writer of the cover blurb for the paperback edition rhapsodizes that *Tales* "is the story of soldiers, sailors, and nurses playing at war and waiting for love in a tropic paradise." Michener's officer-narrator seldom goes to sea. Customarily, he flies from island to island, offering what seems a romanticized description of the experiences of a relatively few members of the ever-swelling shore establishment. Since I was serving in the *Pawnee*, and seldom got ashore, I cannot comment on the accuracy of Michener's observations and characterizations. But I am certain of one thing. His *Tales* largely ignore the sacrifices of the seagoing and airborne men who were there for the real purpose of the war, the enforcement of Halsey's fierce injunction: "Kill Japs, kill more Japs." That reality was to be found in the grim, gray ships of the Third Fleet which Michener's messenger never visits, anchored between engagements in the Great Roads of Noumea, Segond Channel at Espiritu Santo, Purvis Bay of Florida Island in the Solomons. They were in the South Pacific to drive the Imperial Japanese Navy and Army from the Solomon Islands and Bismarck Archipelago; the sole purpose of the massive shore establishment described in the *Tales* was to lend all necessary logistic support to the Marine and Army divisions that were making the landings and to the Navy's combat and service forces afloat.

While Michener's messenger-narrator was "playing at war," writing of such trivia as the "Bouncing Belch," an old TBF torpedo plane used to ferry beer and liquor to officer's "wine messes" around the Solomons, the real Navy fought a series of major engagements that were more savage and bloody than any in American history.

Battle of the Coral Sea, 7–8 May 1942:

Our losses were the carrier *Lexington,* oiler *Neosho,* destroyer *Sims.* Carrier *Yorktown* was damaged. The Japanese lost the light carrier *Shohu;* the carrier *Shokaku* was badly damaged. We saved Australia and New Zealand from a possible Japanese invasion.

Battle of Savo Island, 9 August 1942:

The Navy had been at war for eight months but suffered a devastating defeat reminiscent of Pearl Harbor. The Japanese, although little superior in strength, nearly annihilated our force of cruisers and destroyers. The causes of our gross failures in leadership are still debated. We lost the heavy cruisers *Quincy, Vincennes,** *Astoria,* and the Australian cruiser *Canberra.* Damaged were heavy cruiser *Chicago* and destroyers *Patterson* and *Ralph Talbot.* The price of this defeat was 1,023 killed or mortally wounded in the seven ships (370 in *Quincy* and 332 in *Vincennes*) and 719 wounded (167 in *Quincy* and 258 in *Vincennes*).

Battle of the Eastern Solomons, 24 August 1942:

Third of the great carrier engagements, following Coral Sea and Midway (4–7 June 1942). This indecisive action, marked by timidity on both sides, saw the first offensive use of a battleship, the new *North Carolina.* Carrier *Enterprise* was heavily damaged, with seventy-four killed and ninety-five wounded. The Japanese lost the light carrier *Ryujo;* the carrier *Shokaku* and seaplane tender *Chitose* were damaged.

In the battle's aftermath, dive bombers from Guadalcanal's Henderson Field damaged the light cruiser *Jintsu* and the transport *Kinryu Maru* on 25 August. Flying Fortresses from Espiritu Santo appeared that same morning and sank destroyer *Mutsuki,* the first destroyer sunk by high-level bombers. On 28 August fast minelayer *Gamble,* a converted four-piper, sank submarine *I-123* east of Guadalcanal. (One of her crew was

---

*Unlucky *Vincennes* was to make the news again on 3 July 1988 when her namesake shot down an unarmed Iranian Airbus in that nation's territorial waters, killing all 290 civilians aboard. Her captain, Will Rogers III, was placed under a death threat by a Muslim extremist group.

Seaman Richard "Dick" Hansen, now historian of the Naval Minewarfare Association.)

Battle of Cape Esperance, 11–12 October 1942:

Rear Adm. Norman Scott achieved, with a large measure of the luck which is always a factor in naval engagements, the classic crossing of the "T." His Task Force 64 sank heavy cruisers *Furutaka* (killing Rear Adm. Aritomo Goto) and *Fubuki*, and damaged heavy cruisers *Aoba* and *Kinugasa*. Destroyers *Natsugumo* and *Murakumo* were sunk by air attack on 12 October. We lost the destroyer *Duncan*. Heavy cruiser *Salt Lake City*, light cruiser *Boise*, and destroyer *Farenholt* were damaged.

Battle of the Santa Cruz Islands, 26–27 October 1942:

In what was essentially a carrier-plane battle, we lost the carrier *Hornet* (111 killed, 108 wounded), destroyer *Porter* (15 killed), and, in a separate action in Ironbottom Sound, fleet tug *Seminole*, sister of the *Pawnee*, and YP-284. Damaged again were the valiant *Enterprise* (44 dead, 75 wounded) and destroyer *Smith* (28 dead, 23 wounded). New battleship *South Dakota* (which shot down 26 planes) and antiaircraft cruiser *San Juan* suffered minor damage.

Naval Battle of Guadalcanal, 12–15 November 1942:

Phase I, night action of "Bloody Friday the Thirteenth," as it will always be known. In a desperate melee, five of the thirteen American ships were lost: antiaircraft cruiser *Atlanta*, destroyers *Barton*, *Cushing*, *Laffey*, and *Monssen*. The badly damaged antiaircraft cruiser *Juneau* was sunk the next day on the withdrawal of Task Force Sixty-seven to Espiritu Santo by submarine *I-26*, with the loss of nearly 700 men, including the five Sullivan brothers. Badly damaged were the flagship *San Francisco* (with the loss of Rear Adm. Daniel J. Callaghan, Capt. Cassin Young, and nearly every other man on the bridge) and heavy cruiser *Portland*. Light cruiser *Helena* and destroyers *Aaron Ward* and *Sterett* suffered lesser damage.

The Japanese losses were battleships *Hiei* and *Kirishima*, damaged during the surface action and later sunk (see below), and destroyers *Akatsuki* and *Yudachi*. Damaged were destroyers *Amatsukaze*, *Ikazuchi*, and *Murasame*.

Phase II, air attacks: As the *Hiei* withdrew from the Savo Island area on the afternoon of 13 November, she was sunk by air attack.

On the morning of the fourteenth, heavy cruiser *Kinugasa* and light cruiser *Isuzu* were damaged by planes from Henderson Field. Later that same morning, planes from the *Enterprise* sank *Kinugasa* and damaged heavy cruisers *Chokai* and *Maya*, light cruiser *Isuzu* (again), and destroyer *Michishio*.

On the afternoon of 14 November a group of enemy transports sent to reinforce Guadalcanal were heavily attacked by fliers from Henderson Field; seven were sunk.

Phase III, battleship surface action: New battleships *Washington* and *South Dakota*, with a screen of four destroyers, engaged a Japanese heavy bombardment group that included the battleship *Kirishima*, two heavy cruisers, two light cruisers, and a squadron of destroyers. In one of the very few line-of-battle actions of World War II, the *Kirishima* was heavily damaged and scuttled. The destroyer *Ayanami* was sunk; cruisers *Atago* and *Takao* were damaged.

Three American destroyers were sunk: *Benham*, *Preston* and *Walker*. The *South Dakota* was heavily damaged, as was destroyer *Gwin*.

Battle of Tassafaronga, 30 November 1942:

In a debacle reminiscent of Savo Island, Rear Adm. Carleton H. Wright led a scratch team of four heavy cruisers, one light cruiser, and six destroyers into torpedo waters of Ironbottom Sound against a squadron of destroyers on a reinforcement mission. The heavy *Northampton* was sunk (along with Wright's reputation); the badly damaged heavies *Minneapolis*, *New Orleans*, and *Pensacola* were lucky to reach the safety of Tulagi. Only the light cruiser *Honolulu* and the six destroyers were undamaged. The Japanese, brilliantly commanded by Rear Adm. Raizo Tanaka, lost only destroyer *Takanami*.

Battle of Rennell Island, 29–30 January 1943:

On a mission to relieve the last Marine element remaining on Guadalcanal, Task Force Eighteen, under another commander new to the South Pacific, Rear Adm. R. C. "Ike" Giffen, came under determined torpedo attack from Betty bombers. Heavy cruiser *Chicago* was lost; destroyer *La Vallette* was badly damaged.

Battle of Kula Gulf, 6 July 1943:

Following an invasion of the New Georgia group of islands in the Central Solomons (see next chapter, "The South Pacific of Capt. Flavius J. George"), three light cruisers and four destroyers of Task Group 36.1, under Rear Adm. Walden L. Ainsworth, intercepted the "Tokyo Express," as the reinforcement groups to Guadalcanal were called, in Kula Gulf. "Happy *Helena*," one of our proudest and most battle-tested light cruisers, a veteran of Pearl Harbor and "Bloody Friday," was torpedoed;

she jacknifed and sank, with heavy casualties. Of the ten Japanese destroyers, we sank *Niizuki* and *Nagatsuki*. *Suzukaze* and *Amigiri* were damaged.

Battle of Kolombangara, 12–13 July 1943:

An American task force of cruisers and destroyers, again under Admiral Ainsworth, met light cruiser *Jintsu,* five destroyers, and four destroyer transports of the Tokyo Express off the island of Kolombangara. We sank the *Jintsu,* killing Rear Adm. Shunji Izaki, but all the enemy destroyers escaped. We lost the destroyer *Gwin,* which exploded and sank with very heavy casualties. The New Zealand cruiser *Leander* was torpedoed, as were our light cruisers *Honolulu* and *St. Louis.*

Battle of Vella Gulf, 6–7 August 1943:

In a brilliantly planned and executed action, the six destroyers of Comdr. Frederick Moosbrugger sank three of four enemy destroyers— *Arashi, Hagikaze, Kawakaze.*

Battle of Vella Lavella, 6–7 October 1943:

In another destroyer action against a Vella Lavella evacuation force that was not nearly so well fought, we lost the *Chevalier. O'Bannon* was damaged in a collision with sinking *Chevalier; Selfridge* was torpedoed but saved. The Japanese lost only the *Yugumo.*

Battle of Empress Augusta Bay, 2 November 1943:

In a cruiser and destroyer engagement following our landing on Bougainville, our destroyer *Foote* was torpedoed but towed to safety by fleet tug *Sioux.* Heavy cruisers *Denver* and *Montpelier* and destroyer *Spence* were hit by gunfire, causing minor damage. We sank cruiser *Sendai* with gunfire and torpedoes; sank destroyer *Hatsukaze* with gunfire; lightly damaged heavy cruisers *Haguro* and *Myoko.*

Battle of Cape St. George, 25 November 1943:

In the final engagement of 1943, the five destroyers of Destroyer Squadron twenty-three, under Capt. Arleigh A. Burke, sank Japanese destroyers *Onami, Makinami,* and *Yugiri* while sustaining no damage. It was a nearly flawless action by "31-Knot" Burke, similar to Moosbrugger's victory at Vella Gulf.

Of the above battles, Michener's officer-messenger mentions only the Coral Sea, which is acknowledged in passing for saving New Zealand. He does devote a good deal of space to enlisted men, but from a lofty, elitist perspective, depicting them as naive, ignorant, semiliterate, and as trying to waylay nurses with intent to rape.

When he asks for volunteers for a dangerous reconnaissance mission on an enemy-held island, eight of the ten brave men are described as "average unimpressive American young men." The other two are Seabee Luther Billis, "big, fat, and brown," a fast-talking operator-type with tattoos, a gold ring in his left ear, and several bracelets; and his acolyte, Hyman Weinstein, "a thin Jewish boy, scared to death."

Embarked at last on a war vessel, an LCS (large infantry landing craft) for the climactic landing on Kuralei, the narrator listens to some enlisted men. He has them talk as no enlisted men in the history of the Navy ever talked. The only comparison is to Hollywood war movies, where the screenwriters labored under the same double handicap as Michener did: a "tin ear" for the argot of the lower classes, and a proscription against the four-letter profanities with which they sprinkle (sometimes saturate) their conversations.

During a shore bombardment, a fireman says: "I tell you, sir! I haven't seen anything prettier than that since Market Street on a Saturday night!" (Quite aside from the impropriety of the comparison, Market Street has been called many things, but pretty is not one of them.)

A cook describes how he picked up a girl there. "Well, this babe— and I ain't kiddin', fellows. She was just about through her dessert, and there I was on me soup. It looked to me like she was givin' me the eye, but you know how it is. A smart girl. Maybe she is. Maybe she ain't. She sort of puts it up to you. . . . So quick as a wink, I ditches my soup and steps beside her. . . ." (In the war films, variations on this improbable dialog were usually uttered by actors such as John Garfield and Richard Conte.)

A married machinist's mate describes how the visit of his wife to Frisco resulted in a pregnancy. "At the first sign of encouragement he whipped out a picture of as undistinguished a baby as I have ever seen. . . ." (Even the offspring of enlisted men are not allowed to be attractive.)

Earlier in *Tales*, a Marine corporal facing an invasion proposes by letter to a "snub-nosed little girl in Columbia, South Carolina" he has met but once. The letter uses the lower-case *i* for first-person singular, *was* for *were* (as in "you was very sweet to me"), and spells *brought* as *brot*. The corporal is killed in the first wave of the landing on Kuralei, but the narrator is philosophical: "To Florence, though, who would never be married in a hundred years anyway, that letter, plus the one the chaplain sent with it . . . well, it was almost as good as being married."

This offensive condescension extends to the narrator's repeated references to enlisted men as would-be rapists. In the real South Pacific, hundreds of thousands of virile young men were confined to ships and bases and deprived of all feminine companionship. The few women who were present in the theater, Navy and Army nurses, were prohibited from associating with enlisted men; their social life, was restricted to officers. On occasion (although I can find no record of it) a nurse may have been attacked by a man unable to contain his pent-up libido, and perhaps enraged by the grossly unfair caste system. One of the few truthful notes in the musical "South Pacific" was a chorus of frustrated enlisted men bawling the plaintive "There Is Nothing Like a Dame."

Michener's nurses, while "waiting for love," had a choice among officers, and the occasional French planter. For the hapless enlisted men, there were no "dames," and the wait for one was likely to last for many months, even a year or two, dependent upon a transfer to the States or an R & R cruise of their ships to Australia or New Zealand. As for the "tropic paradise," the humid beauties of jungle and coral atoll concealed the fact that they were the breeding ground for malaria, dysentery, dengue fever, poliomyelitis, tuberculosis, yaws, elephantiasis, even leprosy. Sailors fortunate enough to escape these diseases could almost certainly count on athlete's foot, mild-to-severe ear infections, and prickly heat (commonly known as "the crud").

In the hard male world of wartime, the services provided little relief from the loneliness, deprivations, and resulting low morale. For a pragmatic solution, although admittedly a partial one, the Navy had only to draw upon its experience in Honolulu, where the military cooperated with the civic authorities and private enterprises in a number of bordellos for enlisted men only. The girls, brought from stateside by the Matson Lines, were inspected weekly for venereal disease by Army and Navy doctors. (I described a visit to a typical Honolulu brothel in *Battleship Sailor*, pp. 17–19.)

Michener makes passing references to the famous Pink House in Noumea, as well as a Red House and a more stylish Green House for officers on "Luana Pori." The Pink House was real. Former officers willing to discuss such things disclaim any knowledge of bagnios for officers (which does not mean that none existed).

In his absorbing *Vignettes of the South Pacific*, Dr. Arthur G. King, then a major in the Army Medical Corps, describes the origins of the Pink House:

Venereal disease has been from time immemorial a medical problem for armed forces of every country, and New Caledonia in 1942 was no exception. . . . It was when the American troops flooded in and the U.S. Navy anchored off-shore that the New Caledonians began to worry.

It is not known whether it was for medical or sociological or perhaps financial reasons, or whether the initiative came originally from the American commanding general or from local entrepreneurs, but a project was soon started to establish in Noumea a "military bordello" for American troops only. The first I heard of it was when General Patch [Maj. Gen. Alexander M. Patch, commanding Americal (America-Caledonia) infantry division, U.S. Army] called the Island Provost-Marshal and me, the Island Medical Inspector, to a closed door meeting of just the three of us. He outlined the project briefly to us, assured us that it was a totally French idea and directed us to obtain the details from the French chief of police and to work with him. His parting words to us were: "Remember, gentlemen, that no matter what happens I am never to know that the house exists or that its activities are connected in any way with the United States forces."

The chief of police, with whom each of us had had dealings before, was very affable as he explained the background and the plan of operation. A consortium of several French citizens, including the Intendant-General and himself, had purchased a house called "Chateau Moreau" on the rue Paul Bert. They had repainted it pink and installed a great many toilets; they had arranged private rooms for ten "girls" under the direction of an older "experienced" woman. A former policeman would also live there to do the work about the place and maintain order if any civilians gave any trouble. The madame would select the girls and have them examined every week by the French Health Service which would stamp their health cards each time.

The Provost-Marshal and I made a reconnaissance and talked to the madame and the bouncer. Upstairs the spacious chateau did indeed have ten rooms, each with a bathroom attached, and the downstairs included several large rooms which were nicely, if sparsely, furnished. The traditional piano was not in evidence. A prophylactic station was, of course, essential, but the kitchen proved to be unsuitable for that purpose. The house and small back yard were surrounded by a ten-foot-high stone wall pierced in front and the side by two tall gates, each of which might be locked. We decided to use the front gate, guarded by an M.P., for the single entrance, and the side gate, with an M.P. stationed there, for the only exit. In the side yard we decided to erect a small tent, with water supplied by hoses from the kitchen, and a "client" would have to pass through the tent and receive the standard venereal prophylaxis treatment by a medical corpsman. The M.P. there would enforce the rule.

The madame explained that the charge for each soldier or sailor would be $4.50; ... However, she was vague when asked about the distribution. She pointed out that the total had to "take care of" not only the girls but herself and her "husband" and the chief of police and the Intendant-General and the original investors. She then tried to impress us with how kind she was to the girls, such as that they need not work while they were menstruating!! On the other hand she later wheedled an order for a case of lubricant which I authorized on the grounds of humanitarian aid for use when business was "brisk," and it often was. Except for checking frequently on the "cahiers," the Health cards each of the girls had to have stamped regularly after examinations by the French Health Service, and supervision from time to time of the functioning of the "pro station." I had very little to do with the Pink House except to worry about the possible publicity.

In the four months of operation [June to November 1942] there were only occasional brawls in the house, most of which the M.P.'s handled informally but successfully. The "bouncer" cooperated with them and only very rarely telephoned the French police, whose chief interest was to avoid publicity. The French population maintained the pretense of ignorance and in general approved of the Chateau Moreau "for the sake of their wives and daughters." From the records of the prophylactic station and spot checks by the Provost-Marshal it was determined that there had been over 24,000 man-visits in those four months, and not a single case of venereal disease was ever traced to the "Pink House."

It was a thriving operation, treated discreetly by the Army authorities who maintained that it was exclusively a French institution. There were many jokes in our Army and Navy about the Pink House in Noumea, but rarely was a question asked about why a "house of ill-fame" was tolerated by the American brass hats. The most common inquiries were about how the fees were distributed and why the charge was $4.50 instead of an even $5.00. It was generally believed that $2.00 went to the girl, $1.00 to the madame and $1.00 for police protection. When pressed to explain the extra 50 cents, some wag explained that it was for the towel supplied to each customer.

The quip about the towel proved the undoing of the whole project. After the Americal Division moved to Guadalcanal a new Inspector-General was assigned. In a routine audit of the Medical Supply Depot, he found a number of inventory discrepancies, including a large number of towels. When one of the sergeants there was interrogated at length, he joked about taking a small bundle of them from time to time to pay for services at the "Pink House." However, the Inspector-General was "not amused." He went to the Chateau Moreau in an effort to search the place (possibly also to satisfy his curiosity) and to obtain evidence of stealing. At the front gate the American M.P. would not let him in to what was obviously French property. He was similarly rebuffed at the side gate even though he could see an American tent set up and an American corpsman working.

He then came to my office, as I was then the Service Command Surgeon, responsible among other things for all medical property. I felt that I was still under the orders of General Patch that he "must never know that the house exists," which posed a difficult administrative situation. Hoping to be evasive without accepting responsibility I tried to explain the value of the "Pink House" for the morale and health of the troops, and insisted that it was entirely a French installation. . . .

It was touch and go, but I finally calmed him down and pointed out the inevitable damage to the prestige of the Army if the newspapers got wind of the affair. Publicity would be an intolerable price to pay in order to punish the theft of a few dozen towels, an infinitesimal fraction of all the government property lost or discarded in the war zone. He insisted that he was not concerned with sexual morality but that he had a duty to perform. Gradually he agreed that this was an unusual situation best settled by the new Commanding General.

That evening we made an informal report to the new general in his quarters. He pretended to be astounded to learn that a house of ill-repute was being operated in the vicinity and was grateful that we had given him an opportunity to take care of the problem without the risk of involvement. This mollified the Inspector-General, who conceded that publicity would be unacceptable, and so agreed not to mention the house in his report. The general ruled that the theft of the towels would be adequately punished if the sergeant were transferred to a unit up-country. The prophylactic station and the M.P.'s were to be withdrawn immediately, and the "Pink House" placed off-limits.*

We must not leave the original Pink House without an eyewitness report from one of the very few former enlisted men who admits visiting the place. A crewman in one of the ships of the Service Force who later saw much action in the Solomon Islands writes:

I believe it [the Pink House] sat on a hill above the town and was to the left of downtown from the boat-landing quay. It was quite a distance

---

*Arthur G. King, M.D. (Col. AUS-Ret.), *Vignettes of the South Pacific* (Bloomington, Ind.: ALMAGRE Books, 1991), pp. 57–61. Reprinted with permission.

from the harbor, as I recall; maybe as much as half a mile. When we first went there [in late September or early October 1942] there was no line outside. One could walk into the place, buy a drink, talk to the girls and take one's time about going into the rooms. I believe a Frenchwoman was the madam, but I can't recall what she looked like. I know that most of the prostitutes were white girls; but there was at least one black Melanesian. . . .

The reception area where the guests were greeted was a large room, and there were small rooms upstairs, where the men went with the girls. . . . The building was surrounded by a concrete (or stone) wall with broken bottles buried in the concrete at the top. It was about seven or eight feet high, as I recall.

It was probably on our next trip to Noumea that I went there again, because I remember a long line of men in front of the Pink House. I took one look and decided I did not wish to wait in line. So I went around behind the building and climbed over the wall. I had some trouble with the broken glass buried on the top of the wall, but managed to make my way over it. I dropped down the other side and entered the building. I might have availed myself of the services of the girls, but I don't recall that I did. I just had a drink, talked to some of the sailors, and left. I did not get caught climbing the wall. At that time I believe there was a wrought-iron gate at the entrance, and Shore Patrol or MPs guarding it and along the line. I seem to recall that the line was several blocks long. That was the last time I was ever in the Pink House.*

Nor is that the end of the tale. By the time *Pawnee* arrived in Noumea in early March 1943, the Pink House had been reincarnated. It was now located a few blocks north of the fleet landing, on the Rue Jules Ferry.

"The whaleboat deposited us at the fleet landing on a rubble-filled embankment called, rather grandly, the Grand Quai," I wrote. "A left turn and a short walk, we had been told, would bring us to the most famous establishment in Noumea, the Pink House. The only enlisted men's brothel in the South Pacific, it was a joint venture among the Army, the Navy and the civilian authorities and a model of efficiency. The line extended along the waterfront for a block or more. Upon entering the drab premises, you surrendered your I.D. card, paid your five dollars and took potluck. That might be a Javanese, a Chinese, a half-caste Polynesian or, if the luck was running good, the single

*Letters to author, 12 and 26 September 1994; 28 February and 17 March 1995. Name withheld by request.

Frenchwoman. Before your I.D. was returned, you were required to take a full-service prophylaxis."*

The Pink House was still there when *Pawnee* returned from a week of R & R in Sydney in early February 1944. It may have been shut down at its original location on the Rue Paul Bert, but commanding generals, and admirals, come and go. The demand was great, and the leading citizens of wartime Noumea were eager to supply it.

It is not known who gave authorization for the Pink House to resume its humanitarian services to the enlisted men. Although Dr. Arthur King is fluent in French and still has friends in Noumea, even he has been unable to penetrate the Gallic curtain of bureaucracy.

One friend, Emery La Vallée, who arrived in Noumea in November 1943, suggests that "in 1942–43 probably the Army called it off limits but the Navy left it open for their personnel." In 1943, he adds, "there were several similar institutions, one very near Admiral Halsey's residence, another in the Vallée Des Colons, and a very secluded one at Pont de Français, several kilometers from Noumea."†

Should M. La Vallée be correct, as is very likely, Michener may have come closer to truth than to fiction in his statements about Green and Red Houses for officers and enlisted men. One certainty remains. There was a Pink House on the Rue Paul Bert. It was closed by Army fiat, and reopened along the waterfront, on the Rue Jules Ferry.

Let us leave the last words to the cosmopolitan Arthur King, a prominent Cincinnati obstetrician-gynecologist before retiring from medical practice:

What remains of historical importance is the *name* which almost everyone in the South Pacific during World War II will recognize: "*The Pink House in Noumea.*" Although it existed under strict Army supervision for only four months, without a single case of venereal disease traceable to it, its name became a euphemism for military bordellos in the area. Perhaps the structure *does* deserve some sort of plaque or memorialization.‡

In another letter, he offered a learned comment that has special relevance today:

"We Will Stand by You," pp. 36–37.
†Letter to Dr. Arthur King of 21 October 1994. Quoted in Doctor King letter of 11 November 1994 to author, Ted Blahnik, Richard Hansen, and Emery La Vallée.
‡Previously cited letter of 11 November 1994.

I never liked General Patch, even though I was on his staff and served faithfully, but I felt that his initiating the Pink House was a courageous act. Of course my view was that of a physician with responsibility for the health of the troops. Apparently the idea of a military bordello "took." Just the other day I noted a report that the worst danger our soldiers, sailors and Marines face today in Haiti is getting AIDS. An adequate number of properly supervised "Pink Houses" will save many lives, but most officers are too frightened at what is considered "politically correct" to do anything significant about it . . . other than to preach abstinence.*

*Letter to Richard Hansen, copies to author and Ted Blahnik, 28 October 1994.

7

The South Pacific of Capt. Flavius J. George

For honour travels in a strait so narrow
Where one but goes abreast.

—William Shakespeare, *Troilus and Cressida*

Under different circumstances we might have become friends. But true friendship is only possible between peers, and Lt. Comdr. Flavius J. George was commanding officer of my ship, while I was his first-class radioman. That gulf was unbridgeable.

If he gave me any special consideration, it was the flattery of keeping me aboard and in hazard. When *Pawnee* was allowed one man for Officer Candidate School, he passed me over and sent a third-class soundman, even though I was a survivor of the Pearl Harbor attack who was known to be studying for college on his own time. If I had been C.O., I had to admit ruefully, I would have made the same decision. We were making hazardous, unescorted runs up the Slot and Blanche Channel almost nightly in support of the cruisers and destroyers of the Third Fleet. An inexperienced soundman could be replaced easily, but a radioman who had been trained in two battleships could not.

The captain's only acknowledgment that he regarded me differently from other crewmen was that he called me by first name rather than by surname, the customary impersonal address to enlisted men. He seemed to know that I would not take advantage of the familiarity.

Our special relationship was affirmed by two events in the Solomons, which I related in *"We Will Stand by You."* "Once, during our first days in the Russells [late July or early August 1943], I copied an air-raid warning before the 0600 reveille. I went to the captain's cabin less than fifteen feet away and knocked on the door.

"'Good morning, captain,' I said after I had received permission to enter. 'Condition Red. Enemy planes approaching.'

"George sat up in his berth and looked at his watch, an elaborate wrist chronometer of the type favored by navigators and pilots. I noticed he slept in his T-shirt, like the enlisted men. He seemed wide awake.

"'Well, Ted, they're a little early this morning, aren't they?' he said casually. 'I think you'd better have the bridge sound general quarters.'

"'Most C.O.s would have leaped from their bunks and raced up the ladder shouting orders. . . . But George was calm, cool and collected. There was no sweat. Now that's the kind of a C.O. I want up here!'

"A couple of weeks later I witnessed an even more striking example of George's panache. One murky night in Blanche Channel, I happened to be standing beside him on the port wing of the bridge. As usual, *Pawnee* was operating alone. The ship was in condition of readiness two and materiel condition Baker, with lookouts posted and the 20-mm. and .50-cal. guns manned and ready.

"Without warning, a Pete night fighter came diving at us out of the broken cloud cover. I heard the whine of its powerful radial engine before I spotted it, a dark shape hurtling down from an altitude of less than 2,000 feet. . . .

"'Open fire,' the captain ordered. Nothing happened. Our gunners, taken by surprise, were trying desperately to get the target in their sights.

"The seconds passed, each one stretched as long and taut as a bowstring just before the release. At such moments, time is relative.

"'Do you think he's going to get us, Ted?' George asked in a nonchalant tone.

"'Yes, sir, I think he will,' I replied in the same tone. From the angle of his dive, I judged the Pete's wing bombs would hit in the pilothouse area. My stomach tied itself into the old familiar knots. I could visualize my broken body, torn apart by shrapnel.

"At the penultimate moment, we were saved like the heroine of the old *Perils of Pauline* serials. One of our new P-38 Lightning fighters came rocketing down on the tail of the Pete, its machine guns spewing red-hot tracers. The enemy plane pulled out of its dive and fled north with the twin-fuselage P-38 in close pursuit.

"The captain and I looked at each other. I shook my head and gave a low whistle of relief. He smiled briefly and shrugged his shoulders. Then he went into the pilothouse.

"We had been very close in those elastic seconds, not a ship's captain and one of his petty officers but two men looking together into the face of death. It was probably only my imagination that I saw his legs trembling a little. I hoped he hadn't noticed mine." *

All through our nightly roundelay in the Solomons, the captain demonstrated this kind of grace under pressure, an insouciance which gave the crew confidence in his abilities and valor. Like a number of the other petty officers, I admired these qualities and did my best to emulate them. My regard for Flave George was only increased when, many years later, I was given a copy of the journals he kept beginning in May 1942 and continuing through his wartime career as commanding officer of five ships. In these diaries he confided his true feelings, which were never divulged to officers and enlisted men of his crews in the *Catalpa, Majaba, Pawnee, Chain,* and *Vesuvius.* He learned early that being a ship's captain was a lonely occupation. Distance must be maintained, lest familiarity interfere with unhesitating execution of orders during some emergency. At the same time, he was sure enough of his presence and authority to participate with his men in softball games against other ships. (I relate one example on pages 94–95 of *"We Will Stand by You.")* Many other officers I have known did not care to risk such close association with their crews.

George reported to *Pawnee* on 13 April 1943 under a burden of resentment from the enlisted men. Our commissioning skipper, Lt. Frank C. Dilworth, had been summarily relieved of his command by Admiral Halsey's Comsopac headquarters for our failure to expeditiously get the refrigerator ship *Delphinus* off Nomobitigue Reef near Noumea. Dilworth, who had come up "through the hawsepipe" of enlisted rates and chief warrant boatswain, had run the ship with a controlled permissiveness, giving his chiefs and senior petty officers wide latitude, and was greatly admired by his entire crew. His was the first "happy ship" I had ever served in.

---

* *"We Will Stand by You,"* pp. 124–25.

"If George was aware of our resentment, he certainly didn't show it," I reported in "*We Will Stand by You*" (p. 50). "He moved and spoke with a kind of debonair assurance which hinted at a privileged background. What that background had been no one knew, but he looked more like an English gentleman than a salvage expert. A high-bridged nose dominated a thin, intelligent face. His smile was rather perfunctory and his eyes seemed to survey the world with a cool skepticism. He was a man, I thought, who would trust his own judgment and confide in no one. I hoped he would prove half as competent as he gave the impression of being."

From Noumea the *Pawnee* went to Tulagi Harbor and Guadalcanal. At Lunga Roads on that now-famous island, we joined an armada of attack transports, destroyer-transports, the new LSTs (tank landing ships; already the sailors joked that the acronym stood for "large slow targets"), and our destroyer screen for the landings on the islands of New Georgia, Rendova, and Vangunu in the Central Solomons.

In four terrifying minutes off Rendova on the night of 30 June, when the damaged attack transport *McCawley* and *Pawnee* came under torpedo attack that sank the "Wacky Mac" and very nearly destroyed *Pawnee*, George earned the lasting respect and fealty of his crew. (Ironically, our attackers were U.S. PT boats that failed to heed warnings that we were operating in the area.) And the *Pawnee* acquired a reputation among the destroyers and other ships of the Third Fleet as a lucky ship with a charmed life.

That self-assurance of Flavius Joseph George which hinted at a privileged background was in part a performance that fitted his concept of command presence. He was born in Seattle on 10 January 1909, the first of two sons after a pair of daughters. His father, also Flavius, as were several generations of Georges before him (the name was apparently taken from Titus Flavius Vespasianus, emperor of Rome, A.D. 69–79), was an engineer who spent a number of years working on the Canadian Pacific railroad.

The young Flavius was attending the University of Washington when the Great Depression made it impossible for the family to help with expenses. Demonstrating his drive and resourcefulness, he resolved to work his way through college. It took seven years, with frequent time away from classes for a variety of jobs in Alaska.

In his final year at university he was cadet captain of the Naval ROTC unit. "That's when I met him," Mary George writes, "and you never saw a handsomer man in a uniform! At graduation in 1932 he was commissioned an ensign in the Naval Reserve.

"Even with his shiny new Business Administration diploma, the best job he could get was pumping gas and selling tires for Firestone—I think for $80 a month. He headed south and sold gent's wear at the Emporium [in San Francisco], then drove a big rig for Union Oil. But Flave wanted more than eating money, so he ended up in Ecuador. There he worked for the Guayaquil and Quito railroad as a paymaster, and hunted for gold with the Cotopaxi Exploration Company: not a lot of money, but three years full of adventures.

"He was called back to Seattle in 1940, when his parents died within a few months of each other. The next call, that same year, was to active duty in the Navy." *

As a lieutenant (junior grade), George was commissioning officer of the net tender *Catalpa* (AN-10) at Alameda on 22 May 1942. His private journal entries began that day and continued as his duties permitted through his commands of the auxiliary ship *Majaba* (AG-43), a boat pool on Guadalcanal, *Pawnee* (ATF-74), the salvage vessel *Chain* (ARS-20), and the ammunition ship *Vesuvius* (AE-15). Since they were written in a clear, colorful, and candid style, I will quote liberally from them through his service in the *Pawnee*, with annotations. They provide an unforgettable look at duty in small ships of the Service Force in the South Pacific Theater, as seen through the eyes of a man who was a leader in all he did, cheerfully accepting whatever hazardous assignments he was given. Fortunately for history, he also confided to his diary—and only to his diary—those moments of doubt, trepidation and anxiety which come to every man, and with special force to an officer bearing the lonely burden of command:†

Sunday 24 May 1942
Heaved up the anchor and got underway for Suva, Fiji Islands, at 8:20 this evening. Following us out of S.F. Bay were the S. S. *Henry Knox* and *YN-10*.

---

*Letter to author, 6 September 1994. She and then-Commander George were married in 1945 when he returned from the war. In that year he became head of industrial relations for Mobil Oil Company in Venezuela, where the Georges lived until his retirement in 1961. Moving to Hawaii, they lived there until his death on 9 November 1990. Captain George was buried at the Punchbowl in Honolulu with full military honors.

†War Diary, 24 May 1942 to 7 January 1944: Papers of Capt. Flavius J. George, USNR; Operational Archives, Naval Historical Center, Washington, D.C.

The weather was wet, windy and black and the sea was rough and our little convoy had trouble keeping together from the start as we were completely blacked out. By the time we reached the spot past the Farallons where we changed course to the south the other two had been lost in the blackness.

The rough sea threw the poor little Catalpa around like a water-logged cork and a lot of our boys were sick before we got out of the main ship channel. Most of the rest were sick before morning.

Monday 1 June
Noon dist. from S.F.   1836 mi.
Made good since last entry   1116 mi.

We have settled down to a more or less unvarying routine of General Quarters at dawn, breakfast at 7:30, energise Degaussing coils until 8:00, turn to on ship's work until noon chow, secure from ship's work at 1600, supper at 1730, General Quarters again from dusk to dark, and complete black-out thruout the night, which means everyone not standing a watch is in his bunk by 2030. . . .

We are lucky in having a following sea which boosts us along a good mile per hour faster than we would ordinarily go. The resulting motion of the ship was rather disconcerting for the first few days until we all gained our sea legs. A fast moving swell will approach from astern and as it catches our little ship under the counter her stern will lift skyward while her nose dips deep and she will skitter through the water like a surfboard rider. Then as the swell passes amidships the downward swooping motion ceases and she settles back on her haunches ready to leap aboard the next swell. Working hand in hand with the forward swooping motion is an interesting sidewise waddle resembling that of a drunken duck that always seems to leave the deck a couple of inches higher or lower than where you are placing your foot.

[The wooden-hulled net-laying vessels of the *Aloe* class displaced but 560 tons. Dimensions were 146 (163 oa) by 30½ by 11½. The one-shaft diesel-electric drive was capable of 13 knots. Armament was a single 3-inch gun and miscellaneous small-caliber machine guns. The crew complement was forty-eight.]

Sunday 14 June
A British patrol boat met us several miles off the entrance to Suva harbor and guided us thru the entrance in the coral reef. Inside the harbor were anchored several U.S. destroyers, a British cruiser, and along-

side the one adequate dock was a huge troop transport that had brought in several thousand American troops a few days before.

The shore control station blinkered us instructions to come alongside the dock forward of the transport and as we threaded our way thru the anchored ships one of our main engines had to choose that moment of all times to poop out, after bringing us across five thousand miles of tossing ocean without a murmur. And of course it had to be that engine that was giving us power for our steering engine, so we found ourselves without rudder control.

On top of that, the electrician at the main control panel, a new man, got rattled and threw the switches on both main engines so we couldn't even back down and as a result almost rammed the British cruiser. Ah me, sometimes being a skipper isn't all it's cracked up to be. We finally got everything under control again and docked without further incident. . . .

After checking in with the authorities and getting all urgent business squared away for the time being, I toured the island with a couple of other officers. It is very quiet and colorful with a very small business district and many attractive little homes[,] all with beautiful yards and a profusion of cultivated and wild flowers.

We wound up at the Defense Club, a nice little place for officers and the only place in Suva where a drink is obtainable on Sunday. Met a number of pleasant British and New Zealand army and navy officers. All in all Suva is a very cozy little South Sea Island settlement and we will all be probably bored to death with it inside of a week.

Thursday 25 June
Notification of my promotion to full Lieutenant came thru yesterday and this morning I took my physical and was sworn in by Commander Holmes.

Monday 29 June
Yesterday the S.S. President Coolidge docked and [I] went aboard with Cmdr. Hillsinger to visit with the Captain, who was an old friend of his. Capt. [Henry] Nelson invited us to his quarters and we sat around all afternoon drinking Scotch and chewing the rag. When we left, just barely able to navigate, the skipper presented us both with a quart of his special stock. Got as far as the First Mate's cabin and he dragged us in and we had to have several more with him. Staggered out of there and were stopped by the Chief Engineer. Fortunately he took pity on us and brewed us some black coffee which sobered us up enuf so that about nine we were able to make it back to the Catalpa. . . .

[On 25 October 1942 the *President Coolidge* entered a protective mine-field at Segond Channel, Espiritu Santo, and sank. Two lives and all supplies were lost; reinforcement of the Guadalcanal garrison was delayed for weeks. More details below.]

Thurs. 2 July

Started to work in earnest on the nets yesterday. Started at 6 A.M. loading chain, buoys and 3-ton clumps [clump blocks], laid four moorings[,] hooked up a 10 panel A/T net, and unbrailed it, finishing at 4 A.M. this morning. We laid the net parallel to, and 400 ft. outboard of, the Suva dock, to give the ships alongside some protection against aerial torpedoes. . . .

Found myself in the storekeeping business yesterday. Since the ship has been in service I have allowed one of the Electrician's Mates to run a private canteen on board as an accommodation to the men who don't get ashore often enuf to keep in smokes and candy and toilet articles. His stock has always been small and the few dollars profit only a just return for his time and initiative. However, since arriving here he got a little too ambitious, bought $450.00 worth of goods from one dealer, jacked his prices, and with his greatly increased profits started an undercover loan shark business on board. Most of the youngsters on board were easy meat, they are always broke between pay-days and willing to pay thru the nose for some pocket money when ashore. I finally heard about it, made a little investigation, and stepped on him hard. Had two of the officers take an inventory of his stock and bought him out completely for $650.00. With luck I may get it back in ten or twelve months. In the meantime we now have an official Ship's Service Store managed by one of the other officers and assisted by two of the enlisted men. Profits will be used for setting up a non-interest loan fund for the men and the purchase of recreational gear. Should have court-martialed the fellow but knowing him as I do figure that the loss of his lucrative business will be a much more dreadful blow.

[The captain dealt firmly but fairly—rather too leniently, some may think—with a universal problem afloat or ashore: greed. It may also be noted that George has not yet converted entirely to twenty-four-hour nautical time.]

Mon. 20 July

I flew over to the other side of the island in a PBY [a pontoon patrol plane] to check with the Ebony [AN-15] on her work so we could take up where she left off and flew back to Suva that same evening. The trip only takes an hour by plane and is an extremely scenic one. The big flying boat taxied to the far end of Suva Harbor, turned into the wind, the beat of the motors swelled to a mighty roar and the ship leaped forward with the surface of the Bay flashing by the machine gun blister where I was perched. The slapping of the surface waves against the hull gradually decreased as the ship raised higher on her step and then ceased entirely as the Bay fell swiftly away below us. The roar that filled our ears diminished as the motors were throttled back and we circled the city to gain altitude, then headed out to sea and turned north. Fifteen hundred feet below us the ocean was a deep blue up to the scalloped line of white lace that marked the surf beating on the outer coral reef. Inside the reef the water was a light green so clear that the coral formations could be plainly seen. Then came the golden colored beach rimming the island, backed up against groves of coconut palms under which tiny grass huts could be seen, and the cultivated squares of sugar cane, taro, and other island products. In the center of the island jagged volcanic peaks reared skyward, their tips wreathed in mist, and their sides covered with tangled tropical growth.

In an hour we were circling over our destination, the seaplane base, where we settled gently onto the water and a few minutes later were rowed ashore in rubber boats.

[This passage demonstrates George's powers of close observation coupled with a gift for vivid description.]

Sunday 9 August

We returned to Vatia [from Nandi] Friday nite and Saturday morning met the new Governor-General of the Fiji Islands who came aboard for a short visit. He is a South African Major General who has been fighting in Libya for the past two years and seems to be quite a pleasant old boy.

We knocked off work Sat. noon and after chow had a ball game between our boys and the men at the Base, which we won 9 to 8. That evening we threw a party on the dock for the men at the Base. Mixed up 60 gals. of punch made out of fruit juice into which we poured 5 gals. of 190 proof grain alcohol from the ship's stores. Made a very innocent tasting drink but what a hidden wallop it contained. We were joined by some of the native troops who brought their guitars and ukes and had a swell party under the stars singing and listening to the music, must have been about a hundred and twenty men present. Everyone got a little tight and a good percentage passed out cold. Sent three men up to the base camp with a pitcher of punch for the men on watch there. They evidently decided to drink it up themselves and save time—we found them a couple of hours later stretched out in the middle of the road.

Anyway, everyone had a good time and worked off a little steam and only three men fell off the dock. The Navy would undoubtedly frown on such goings on, but the boys there are so isolated from all pleasures and amusements that I believe it did them a lot of good.

[A classic Navy party organized by George in contravention of regulations (and in the absence of high-ranking officers). When he was C.O. of the *Pawnee,* the grave situation in the Solomons did not permit such levity. (The crew would have loved it!)]

Wed. 12 Aug.

Never a dull moment in the Navy. Arrived back in Suva Monday morning and immediately went to work as operations on this side were completely snafu. First job was to untangle the Indicator Net gate which was fouled up and couldn't be completely opened. It was a hurry-up job as the Pres. Coolidge was ready to sail and her Skipper was howling bloody murder over the narrow spaces he had to steer his ship thru. . . .

Returned to the dock and was told Cmdr. Mare[,] the Port Director[,] wanted to see me. Went up to his office and was informed that I was to take command of the USS Majaba and proceed to Auckland the next morning. Just like that. Seems that her Skipper, a Lieut. Cmdr.[,] had just gone to the hospital with a nervous breakdown or something, and none of the other officers on board knew anything about ship handling. I wasn't very keen on the idea but on being assured that it was only temporary duty and that I would be returned from Auckland by first available transportation to resume command of the Catalpa, I assented.

So, at noon today, I shoved off in my new command, accompanied by two small mine sweepers which will stay with us for 400 miles and then turn off for New Caledonia while we continue the next 800 miles alone.

The Majaba is a rather decrepit old girl, slow and evidently not too seaworthy. She is loaded with a couple thousand tons of sugar for New Zealand. She's about 300 ft. long which makes her considerably larger than the 160 ft. Catalpa. Had no chance to find out how she handled before going up on the bridge and backing her away from the dock and between another ship and the A/T net paralleling the dock. As I stood up there with two of the other officers miles away up in the bow and the third miles away at the stern, gawd how lonely I felt.

However, it will be a swell experience and I'll learn a lot about handling larger ships, and it will look pretty good on my record, so I'm glad of the chance. However, one of these days I'm liable to bite off more than I can chew.

[The "decrepit old girl" George was pressed into taking to Auckland was acquired by the Navy as the steam schooner *El Capitan* from the E. K. Wood Lumber Co. of San Francisco in April 1942. Built in 1919 by the Albina Engine & Machine Works in Portland, Oregon, she operated for more than two decades in the coastal and intercoastal lumber trade. The Navy renamed her *Majaba* (an island in the Philippines) and converted her for service as a miscellaneous auxiliary (AG-43).]

We docked in Auckland at 4:30 this afternoon [18 August] after an uneventful six days trip from Fiji. The city looked very attractive as we steamed in the harbor but I'm too damn tired to step off the ship so will turn in early and wait until tomorrow before going ashore. . . .

We had hardly made fast at the dock when we were boarded by the local U.S. Navy Doctor, Supply Officer, Operations Officer, and Repair Officer, who without loss of time made all arrangements for necessary supplies, repairs, and so forth. First time I've ever known that to happen and gave me a very high opinion of our Naval Administration here.

Anyway, to heck with it. I'm going to bed.

Friday 21 August
Went ashore yesterday morning and didn't return to the ship until this afternoon, and had me a good time ashore.

Together with Lt. Roberts, my Exec, had a spot at the Auckland Club, then we went to the lounge at the Station Hotel and had several more before eating a very enjoyable dinner there. The liquor shortage here is getting serious and you usually have to take what is offered, with little choice in the matter. We had to alternate between Scotch, beer, and brandy as we could never get two consecutive drinks the same.

Left Roberts about 7:30 P.M. and looked up a blind date fixed up for me by one of the local officers. Name of Clare Darbey and not bad. We took a cab out to the apt. of Cmdr. Rylander and Lt. Cox and sat around until 11:00 drinking gin. Nice setup those two have, the shortage of men in New Zealand being as acute as it is.

Left there and went dancing at a local night-spot then took Clare home to her sister's where we had tea and toast, then back to town where I had to call almost a dozen hotels before I could get a room for the night.

[My *Pawnee* skipper could handle his liquor as well as he did his ships. All that and tea and toast, too. . . .]

Friday 4 Sept.

The poor old Majaba is certainly a mess these days what with all the repairs taking place. . . . I had hoped to get away long enuf to do a little sightseeing over the countryside but have been tied down every minute. As in the other British ports, the Americans are the only ones here that work a seven day week and from morning to night. The local forces muddle along at the old peacetime pace and aren't quite sure whether they approve of our methods or not.

The officers stationed here with the ComSerOnSoPac [Commander Service Squadron South Pacific] are a grand bunch of fellows and have certainly cooperated in fixing up the ship. I take quite a razzing in the Officers Mess about the Mighty Majaba and have to submit to such rumors as the one that I have to steer around floating seaweed so the bow won't get stove in, and that the men chipping rust in the holds have to wear life-preservers in case one of them chips clear through the side. Very funny.

Sunday 6 Sept.

Went to a formal dance at the Officers Club last night and had a grand time. The club is the nicest spot in Auckland, having been organized by the Naval officers stationed here who all chipped in enuf to equip it in a big way. Each officer has his own liquor locker behind the bar, from which the bartender fills his orders. Music is furnished by the ship's orchestra of the USS Rigel, and each member of the club has his own key to the door. Had a blind date that was very nice, all the girls there being about the most attractive ones in Auckland as an invitation to the club is much sought after.

Friday 11 Sept.

At sea once more and glad of it after the rush and confusion of three weeks overhauling, and taking on our cargo. . . . Every available inch of the Mighty Majaba is crowded with cargo, army rations, airplane parts, cement, and ammunition. We'd be a nice haul for the Japs.

Saturday 12 Sept.

Got thru the Hole-in-the-Wall ["a secret passage thru the reef that winds among the islands and is bounded by hidden mine fields"] just at sunset. . . . I have the nice feeling one has when just starting on a vacation. Now that we are safely out in the open ocean I can relax with a pleasant six days at sea ahead before arriving at Tongatabu. There will be plenty to do in the way of ship's work, and lifeboat and gunnery drills,

and navigation, but it's at sea that the pleasure of being in command out-
weighs the worry and stress of operations in restricted waters.

Sat. 26 Sept. [Suva Harbor]
Have received my orders to proceed to New Caledonia and am anxious
to get underway. May see some action.
The horrors of war were visibly demonstrated to us yesterday. One of
the big flying boats tried to take off for Australia to have a damaged
motor repaired, but due to the load she was carrying, the remaining three
motors couldn't lift her off the water. So she unloaded several hundred
sacks of mail and tried again. Still too much weight, so she sent ashore
parachutes, life jackets, a spare machine gun and most of her ammunition. But to no avail. So they had no alternative, they were forced to leave
behind the eight cases of whiskey they were carrying, and finally succeeded in taking off.

[George's ironic tone only underscores the brazen discrimination
which was practiced throughout the South Pacific Theater at the
expense of the enlisted men. In this instance, their mail was offloaded
in favor of whiskey for officers' clubs.]

Monday 12 Oct.
Our loading [at Segond Channel, Espritu Santo] is almost completed
and we should be ready to sail early Wed. morning. Our destination is
Guadalcanal where our Marines are holding a small area recently won
from the Japs. So the latter part of this week will see us chugging happily
along at our usual nine knots thru submarine infested waters, with the
good old Majaba crammed to the gills with aviation gas, high explosive
bombs, and aerial torpedoes. Ordinarily I prefer to travel independently
but this time I'd just as soon they sent a destroyer escort along with
us. . . .
The crew have been working like dogs getting the cargo aboard and I
often wonder that they don't rebel at the sight of the Merchant seamen in
the ships alongside drawing several times the salary for an easy eight
hours with time and a half for overtime, and a fat bonus for venturing in
the war zone. Sent half the men ashore yesterday for a swimming party,
the first time they've been ashore in the eight days we've been here, and
the other half went ashore this afternoon. They really have a lot to put up
with on this old ship, cramped and makeshift quarters, water for washing their hands and faces only three times a day just before meals and no
water at all for a shower while we are in an area like this where there is

no way of replenishing the limited amount of fresh water we carry in our tanks.

Wed. 28 Oct.

Due to a ball-up in communications, tonight finds us anchored in Segond Channel once more, instead of steaming towards the Solomon Islands. . . .

Since here we've got a lot of news[,] most of it very bad. Last Monday the Japs sank the new carrier Wasp off the Solomons and we haven't even the consolation of knowing we got some of them at the same time. In addition the Enterprise was hit and damaged, and the cruiser Chester which had filled us with water just a few days ago limped back here yesterday with a huge torpedo hole in her side. But most tragic of all, because of someone's criminal stupidity, the beautiful big President Coolidge came in here two days ago by the wrong channel, struck one or more of our own mines and went to the bottom only a few hundred yards from where we are now anchored. She blundered into the minefield at 10 A.M., in broad daylight, and altho she had some 5000 commando troops aboard, only a half dozen or so were lost. But all the terrific amount of new and modern equipment they had with them was lost. God what a crime, as [if] the Japs aren't sinking enough of our ships.

[That "criminal stupidity" caused the loss of the Army transport *President Coolidge* can hardly be denied. Who bears the responsibility has been debated ever since.

[Although all but one of the 5,050 troops of the 172nd Infantry, 43rd Division, and all but one of the 290 merchant sailors aboard were saved, all of the soldiers' military equipment went to the bottom of Segond Channel. The reinforcement of the hard-pressed Guadalcanal garrison was delayed for weeks. Not the least of the losses was 519 pounds of quinine sulfate, the entire reserve supply for the South Pacific Theater.

[The Navy, at least initially, had no problem fixing the blame. At Noumea in November 1942, a Court of Inquiry on board the destroyer tender *Whitney* found that the loss was caused by "the gross negligence and culpable inefficiency" of the ship's master, Henry Nelson. The court's recommendation was for further proceedings and prosecution.

[At the military commission that followed, Captain Nelson was tried on a charge of "through negligence suffering a vessel of the United States to be lost." He was acquitted.

[Many years later Dr. Arthur King decided to investigate the sinking and its aftermath for a chapter of his *Vignettes of the South Pacific*. With some difficulty, he received the proceedings of the Court of Inquiry. Upon analyzing the findings, it appeared to him that "the sinking was the end result of a sequence of incidents for which different individuals and the U.S. Navy itself were responsible."*

[The sailing orders from the port director at Noumea were delivered to Captain Nelson by a young Navy ensign an hour and a half before the *President Coolidge* sailed for Espiritu Santo. A "special information" half-sheet contained specific instructions for entering the heavily mined Segond Channel, which had claimed the destroyer *Tucker* on 4 August. It was paper-clipped to the many pages of sailing orders. Nelson, at the Court of Inquiry, claimed he had never seen the half-sheet. It seems likely that the messenger accidentally picked up the original enclosure intended for the ship's master when he assembled all the duplicate sets. "For Want of a Navy Staple," a ship may well have been lost.

[Several facts emerged from the transcript of the Court of Inquiry. The captain, being a civilian, was never notified by the port director of the presence of mines guarding Segond Channel. Dr. King notes, "When questioned, as they all were, every officer, both civilian and military, testified that he had no criticism whatever of the conduct of the master, Henry Nelson. . . . [N]ot a single witness who had been aboard the ship stated when questioned under oath, that he had ever seen the crucial and mysterious 'Enclosure B, Special Information' which was supposed to direct the vessel safely out of the mine-field."

[Dr. King concludes: "Although Henry Nelson was acquitted of negligence and culpability[,] the Opinion of the Navy Court of Inquiry, which had completely exonerated the Navy system and performance, had been widely publicized. It was war time and the good name and reputation of a distinguished mariner were considered just another sacrifice in behalf of maintaining U.S. Navy morale. One wonders how different might have been the outcome if the 'Special Information' sheet and more explicit orders so tardily delivered to the ship's master, had been firmly stapled together."†]

Thurs. 29 Oct.
[W]e are expecting to shove off within an hour, and this time we're going on thru, Jap navy or no. The situation at Guadalcanal is extremely

---

*"For Want of a Navy Staple," *Vignettes*, p. 47.
†Ibid., pp. 54, 56.

critical and unless our cargo of avgas and bombs gets up there without further delay our planes will be unable to continue operating. This trip we will have three destroyers with us and one other supply ship, and we must get there.

Monday 2 Nov.
Dropped anchor a half mile off the beach at Guadalcanal at 0700 this morning after an uneventful trip from Santo. . . .

Anchored close by is another supply ship and a troop transport, while further offshore several destroyers circle back and forth in an arc to screen us from sea attack. A short distance up the beach a destroyer is noisily throwing 5″ shells up in the hills where the Japs have guns that might range us. At eleven A.M. five Jap planes attempt to reach us but are driven off by our fighter planes that take off from the close-by flying field. As our planes glide back in to refuel and rearm, they go into a Victory roll overhead, the signal that Mr. Moto isn't having any more for the time being.

I requested a working party of 40 Marines to help handle cargo, 92 turned up for the reason that after the nerve racking battling of the last few weeks, to be able to get away from the island on board a ship for a few hours is a welcome divertisement. And for another reason—they only get two meals a day on shore and most of them are ravenous. We served them cafeteria style and one boy went thru the line four times.

The water between here and the beach swarms with Higgins boats, tank barges, and lighters, shuttling back and forth with cargo to the beach. On this end it goes rapidly, we can lower a lot of cargo over the side working our four booms. On the beach end it's slower, the boats ram their noses as far as they can and long files of men splash out and lug it ashore by hand. The heavy stuff is lifted by two light cranes. The black natives are coming into camp in ever-increasing numbers to work for us, it took weeks to overcome the fear instilled in them by the Japs.

Tuesday 3 Nov.
Last night was one of the worst I've ever put in in all my life.
At 4 P.M. word was received that a strong Jap fleet was approaching from the eastward. Immediately every ship heaved up its anchor and got underway. We were to follow the destroyer Southard [DMS 10, high-speed minesweeper converted from a four-stack destroyer] eastward thru Skylark Channel [actually, Sealark Channel] then turn north and lose ourselves in the broad expanse of waters between San Cristobal and Malaita Islands. By the time we passed thru the narrow and treacherous channel it was pitch dark, blowing a gale and rain was coming down in

sheets. Running without lights it was extremely difficult to keep the Southard in view, tho it was just idling along to keep its speed down to ours. It was important to keep her in view as our magnetic compass was away off due to the metal cargo we were shifting around, and we were dependent on the Southard's Gyro to guide us safely thru the blackness.

Or so we thought. Shortly after eight a signal gun flickered faintly from ahead. It was the Southard informing us new orders had just been received directing that we turn back alone and anchor at Tulagi, eighteen miles from Guadalcanal, for the night. We were dumbfounded, not only would it be difficult at best to return thru Skylark in the pitch blackness with an unadjusted compass, but Tulagi harbor always required a pilot even in the daytime and we would not have one. As we swung around on a reverse course the Southard blinkered a final, and not very optimistic, "Good Luck."

We guessed at a compass error of 15, and set our course accordingly. . . . From Guadalcanal came an emergency plain language radio message that an enemy destroyer was close off-shore and almost simultaneously the Jap cut in his searchlite as he headed into the west end of Skylark. We had to get clear of the beam, and fast, so to hell with coral reefs and shoals, full right rudder and full speed toward Florida [Tulagi Harbor]. A reef would sink us but a shell would blow our explosive packed ship, and us, sky high. It felt like dashing blindfolded thru a strange and furniture cluttered house. We couldn't see a damn thing. The minutes dragged by and no rending crash threw us off our feet as we strained our eyes futilely ahead. The minutes became a half hour and ages later three quarters, so we must be close to shore. By this time the driving rain had drowned the gleam of the searchlite so we came left again and once more let caution gain the upper hand. . . .

Why, O why did I ever join the Navy. We turned to the left once more, and by this time I was so groggy from lack of sleep and strain that all I wanted was an anchorage, any old anchorage, and blessed oblivion. Land must be somewhere close ahead, so we walked down the anchor to 40 fathoms and edged slowly in. Finally it hooked on something, how securely there was no telling, but we weren't a bit choosy by this time, we had something to hold on to and nothing short of the Judgment Day would pry me loose until the blackness ended. So we veered out an additional 40 fathoms of chain, and I turned in for an hour's sleep before General Quarters at 5 A.M.

By 5:30 it was light enough to make out our position, we were a couple hundred yards off a rocky shore and about a mile north of Tulagi Harbor entrance. By 6:30 we were safely inside and standing by for instructions from the shore station.

Wed. 4 Nov.

About 7:30 the Southard came steaming in and as soon as it spotted us calmly at anchor burst into a frenzy of enthusiastic blinker signals— "Congratulations"—"Well done"—"Excellent" etc. I immediately became a little suspicious, and my suspicions were soon confirmed when the Southard rather shame-facedly confessed she had decoded the message concerning us all wrong the night before, and sending us off alone was a mistake. So all night long her skipper had been in a stew over the questions that would be directed his way when we were discovered sunk by the Japs or a reef.

[Probably the radio message was garbled, either in transmission or reception, and the *Southard,* under radio silence, could not ask for a repeat. Still, the C.O. of the DMS showed poor judgment in abandoning a slow, lightly armed ship whose cargo was desperately needed for the Guadalcanal garrison. As captain of the *Pawnee,* George was the victim of another communication foul-up that did not end so happily; see chapter 8.]

Friday 6 Nov.

Left the ship [at Guadalcanal] in the morning and went ashore with one of the other officers on a little sight-seeing expedition. Thumbed a ride on a gas truck to the fighter field just back of the center of our line [Henderson Field] and talked to the Marine pilots there. Youngest bunch of Majors and Lt. Colonels I've ever seen, and all with many Jap planes to their credit.

From there we decided to visit the front at our right wing where there had been heavy fighting for the last few days. Rode on an ammunition truck for about nine miles to the end of the road then hit into the jungle. . . . From the end of the road it was only a half mile by trail to the advance Command Post. There we met the Colonel in command and he seemed quite pleased to see us. Said he's been wondering where in hell the Navy was, they certainly weren't around to stop Jap destroyers from landing troops in his rear every so often. It was rather quiet at the C.P. so we left there and start[ed] wandering around in the bush with a couple of Marines as guides. It was very hot and humid and the air reeked with the stench of decomposing bodies. Especially in one area where 350 Japs had been slaughtered in one group and there hadn't been time as yet to bury them. They had been pretty well picked over for souvenirs so when our guides mentioned that one of our patrols had knocked off half a dozen Japs just a few hours before and that their bodies were a few hundred yards ahead we decided to take a look-see on the chance of obtaining a Jap sword and a rifle or two.

Back of us our field pieces and mortars were booming away and ahead of us the Japs were replying in kind, while an occasional burst of machine gun fire or the crack of a sniper's rifle kept reminding us that the surrounding jungle wasn't as deserted and lifeless as it appeared to the eye.

Finally a couple of shells burst uncomfortably close and we could hear the shrapnel ripping through the foliage overhead. I called a halt and told the two Marines that a few souvenirs weren't worth getting bumped off by a Jap shell. One of them replied, "Hell, them ain't Jap shells, them's ours, we're in Jap territory." And both of them were genuinely disappointed when [Ensign] Turner and I simultaneously did an about face and headed back with no further desire to hunt souvenirs in that particular area. And when we reached our first machine gun outpost concealed beside the trail, how positively beautiful those dirty, ragged and bearded boys looked to us.

It was rather touching the way all the groups we met were so glad to see us, and how the word would spread that a couple of naval officers were present, and we would be plied with questions as to when the Navy would be able to put a stop to the nightly shelling by enemy vessels, and when would reinforcements arrive so they could be relieved. This particular outfit, the Sixth Marines, had been in the jungle without relief since last August.

Wed. 18 Nov.

So much has happened during the last two weeks I'll only be able to touch lightly on the highspots.

First and foremost, the poor old Majaba finally reached the end of the trail. On the morning of Nov. 7 we shoved off from Tulagi at dawn, dropped our hook in 15 fathoms about a thousand yards off the beach at Guadalcanal and started lightering ashore the balance of our bombs and landing-field mat. We had worked straight thru the previous night and had put ashore at Tulagi the balance of our avgas—thank God.

I had been on my feet for the past 30 hours, so as everything was progressing smoothly, no enemy planes were in the vicinity, and two of our destroyers were at hand screening our unloading, I hit my bunk at 8:30 to grab a couple of hours sleep. About an hour later I was awakened by a confused shouting on deck, the General Alarm buzzer started sounding off, and I stumbled groggily and only half awake towards a port to see what the trouble was. Then—CRASH—the most terrible explosion—

concussion—burst of flame—seemed to envelop everything. The deck buckled under my feet and threw me against the bulkhead. The doors on either side of my cabin smashed outwards and roaring steam from below blotted everything from sight. It was like a terrifying nightmare, I was much too dazed to know what was going on.

Then the steam thinned slightly by my portside door but still blocked my way aft to the ladder from the boat deck to the main deck. A guy-line from the fore-mast slanted down forward so down I went hand over hand. For the first time I was able to size up the situation. A Jap sub had fired a torpedo at us from the center of the channel, it was set too deep and passed completely under us but its wake warned the lookouts and the alarm was sounded. Almost immediately came the second torpedo and this time it got us, almost exactly amidships, demolishing the engine room and fireroom, blowing a huge hole in our starboard side and ripping and twisting steel plates and frames from the keel up to the main deck.

By now the ship had a decided list, and many of the crew were in the water, some having been blown overboard by the explosion and others having jumped. Both our lifeboats were smashed but several liferafts were floating close by. In a few minutes shore boats started coming alongside and we started lowering the injured over the side, most of them suffering from burns or scalds, others with cuts or wrenched ankles.

When all the casualties had been transported ashore I had the anchor chain cut with a torch and all shore boats started pushing and pulling us shorewards and we were able to beach the ship just before she went under.

That night I stayed aboard with half a dozen men to keep any possible raiding party from boarding us before we could collect all the confidential gear that had been scattered around by the force of the explosion. Next afternoon I went ashore for the first time and reported to the C.O. of the shore base. He was very sympathetic and promised to evacuate us by the first available transportation, which should be in a couple of days. In the meantime we were to make out the best we could in tents on the beach.

[The *Majaba* was torpedoed by enemy submarine *I-20*. The *Bobolink* (a World War I-era minesweeper reclassified as ATO-131 in June 1942) towed George's ship eastward along the coast of Guadalcanal from Lunga Roads and beached her that afternoon off the mouth of the Tenaru River. Two months later *Bobolink* and new fleet tug *Navajo* (ATF-64) towed *Majaba* to Tulagi Harbor. Reclassified as IX-102, she served as a floating quarters and materiel storage ship at Florida Island for the rest of the war. Her captain and crew received one battle star, and almost no other recognition, for their harrowing experience.]

Our first and most vital job was for all hands to dig themselves foxholes, as the Japs were just starting a big offensive to regain Guadalcanal. "Condition Red," the signal of approaching enemy planes or naval units, was sounded frequently day and night, and each time you grabbed your steel helmet and dove for a foxhole. It's funny how each bomb, as it whistles earthward, sounds like it's making a bee-line right for your hole. Nearby soldiers & marines were killed or wounded each raid but somehow our crew escaped unscratched. Our fighter planes were Grummans, which while sturdy and deadly, just weren't fast enough to take off and gain sufficient altitude to turn back the bombers before they got overhead. Then one day a number of trim and speedy P-38s arrived to bolster our forces and as they flew in men all up and down the line jumped to their feet and waved and cheered. Reminded me of the cheering section at a football game when the first team goes in.

One night an enemy heavy cruiser and destroyer steamed in under cover of darkness and for two hours shelled the hell out of us. They concentrated most of their fire on the airfield to prevent the planes from taking off.

In the meantime almost the whole crew came down with malaria or dysentery or both due to the lack of fresh water for washing & poor sanitary conditions. Had to send my three remaining officers in an ambulance to the field hospital. Ens. Turner had previously been flown out due to a head wound at the time of the torpedoing, and Pierce had been transferred to the hospital ship Solace at Espiritu Santo due to illness.

By this time our transportation out had arrived in the shape of two supply ships and a troop transport which unloaded hurriedly and cleared out again. I went to see the local naval commander concerning his promise to evacuate us but was told that he had decided to keep us all here permanently as he wanted more men ashore to handle cargo. And so ended all my hopes of ever getting another ship and of any further promotion. And how I hated to break the news to my crew who had taken the torpedoing and sickness and discomfort all in stride on the assumption that we would all be at sea together again soon.

While the three auxillary [sic] naval vessels were here I witnessed one of the most spectacular sights I ever expect to see. About ten one morning word was radioed in from a scouting plane that eighteen twin-engined enemy torpedo planes protected by fighters were heading in from the eastward and should arrive in half an hour. Immediately the three ships got underway and headed for the open water where they could maneuver while their escort of the cruiser Atlanta and four destroyers placed themselves between them and the enemy. In a few minutes we spotted them, black, deadly looking planes flying in low over the water in perfect formation. As they bored in the fighting ships opened up with their A.A. and in front and around the planes black puffs started blossoming out. Soon they seemed to be flying into a regular wall of fire but on they came, seemingly impervious to damage. The whole scene had a slow-motion quality, the big black planes seemed to float along only a few feet above the surface through the countless black balls of smoke that appeared in front of them and then dissolved lazily behind them. Only the flames spitting from the defending vessels' guns reminded you of the sweating men unceasingly ramming home the shells. Then as the range decreased the illusion of invulnerability ceased. One plane, then another and another exploded in a burst of flame or nosed over into the sea with a tremendous splash. In a matter of seconds only four were left and these launched their torpedoes wildly, and frantically banked away from the deadly fire. Overhead the naval fighting planes had been zooming in a mass dogfight but down from the melee streaked several of our Grummans and Aircobras to pounce on the hapless four and neatly bag them. Score: all enemy torpedo planes downed and three Zeros, against two of our planes lost and no damage to the ships.

[Few of the war correspondents covering the South Pacific Theater could have done as well in describing this air attack. With his gift of language, perhaps a Welsh heritage, it is regrettable that George chose not to write his memoirs.]

Shortly thereafter news was flashed in that a strong enemy task force was headed our way to arrive late that night [12–13 November], so all further unloading was cancelled and the three ships fled southward leaving behind the five war vessels. About eleven that night our tiny naval force was bolstered by the last minute arrival of five more cruisers and six destroyers that blinked their recognition lights as they filed by us in the blackness. Even so we knew we were going to be terribly outnumbered as the enemy force was known to include two battleships whose mighty guns and heavy armor alone should have been more than a match for our thin-skinned force. At shortly past midnight the two forces suddenly made contact just this side of Savo Is., a few miles to the west.

The stabbing beam of a Jap searchlight skewered the Atlanta and from both sides at point-blank range enemy shells poured into her, reducing her in a few shocking seconds to a twisted and scorched hulk. By this time the whole sea and sky was aflame with gun flashes, with arcing bridges of red tracer shells connecting the combatants, while the earth under us trembled from the concussion as we watched with fascinated anxiety. Occasionally a blinding flare and rumbling blast would indicate that some ship had blown up and we would catch momentary glimpses of black and smoke shrouded shapes belching flame. We hardly dared hope when we first noticed the battle seemed to be shifting northward and away but by two in the morning it was evident that our little force had somehow outshot and outfought the heavier enemy force. We were all so damned proud of them we could have bawled. Gradually the firing dwindled away in the distance but the sky remained alight with the flames from burning warships until dawn, when numerous columns of black, greasy smoke marked the locations of those still afloat.

I was dispatched with all available Tare boats and lighters to start bringing back survivors and raced thru a sea thick with oil and debris of every description to the side of the smoldering Atlanta. That once beautiful ship presented a picture of desolation and ruin that is indescribable. Her entire superstructure had been shot away and her three forward turrets were like shattered egg crates out of which stuck distorted and twisted guns. Her main deck was almost awash and on it huddled the grimy and dazed remnant of her crew. I climbed aboard and searched out her senior medical officer, who I found in the shambles of the wardroom working feverishly with his assistants over the burned and blasted bodies that covered every inch of deck space, and arranged for the transfer to the shore hospital of all cases that could be moved. Then back to my Tare boat and over to the cruiser Portland with the balance of my small boats, some of which dropped out on the way to pick up the men clinging to the wreckage in the water.

The entire stern of the Portland had been blown off by a torpedo and her hull [was] punctured and pockmarked with shell holes. Arrangements were made to have her towed to Tulagi Harbor, and in the meantime another rescue party headed for one of our beached and burning destroyers. In the distance one of the Jap battleships listed helplessly and nearby a destroyer gushed black smoke, but modern war isn't merciful and we knew that at any moment our bombers were due to appear to administer the coup-de-grace.

Then the Atlanta flashed word that she couldn't remain afloat much longer, so every available boat and tank lighter was ordered to come alongside her and remove all remaining personnel. All day long we worked with feverish haste to get the survivors ashore and the Portland towed to safety before the Jap bombers could succeed in breaking through the protective screen of our fighter planes and add to the destruction. It was really touching the way the faces of the tattered survivors of the Atlanta lit up with relief and hope when it came their turn to climb into a boat headed for shore and safety. Late in the afternoon the last man went over the side and shortly thereafter demolition charges hastened her final and tired-looking lurch to the bottom.

The tug with the Portland in tow [the *Bobolink*] made slow progress toward Tulagi, finally reaching there in safety at eleven-thirty, just as the beam of a Jap heavy cruiser cut the darkness in search of her. Robbed of her hoped-for victim, the Jap sprayed a few shells shoreward and disappeared in the night.

Back on shore we received the summary of the night's action: Jap losses were one battleship, a cruiser and six destroyers; our losses were one cruiser sunk, one damaged, and four destroyers lost. What a showing against a much stronger force!

[A moving and emotional description of the First Naval Battle of Guadalcanal, known to sailors as "Bloody Friday the Thirteenth of November." Our outnumbered Task Force Sixty-seven —whose actual composition was five cruisers and eight destroyers—turned back a Japanese bombardment force whose mission was to deliver a knock-out blow to Henderson Field. (For the actual losses, see page 115.)]

Dec. 6, 1942

This is certainly no place for reading, writing or keeping up a diary. Our day's work starts before dawn with 4:30 A.M. reveille, hit the beach and man all boats so the unloading can start at daylite (I forgot to add that our usual "Reveille" is around 3 A.M. when the Jap bombers visit us and by the time the "All Clear" is sounded and we get up and out of our fox-holes it's too close to 4:30 to make going back to your cot worth while), work at top speed all day transporting cargo ashore from the ships that arrive daily at dawn, secure when they leave at dusk, eat the evening chow (of corned beef) in the gathering darkness, sit around in the complete darkness of the nightly blackout planning the following day's operations or just bulling for an hour or so, then hit the bunk around 8:30 P.M. That is when we don't have to work all nite picking up survivors or unloading a ship that has run aground or some such thing. We lead a busy life.

To go back a few days to the Atlanta incident [the night action of 13 November], we learned a couple of days later why our Navy sent such a comparatively weak force against the Jap task unit. Our scouting planes brought word of another and even bigger Jap force including eight crowded troop transports and four big supply ships that were due to hit us about midnight. But this time our main battleforce was lying in wait for them, having been held back for just such a purpose. The result was disastrous for Tojo's boys, in their frantic efforts to escape the 16″ salvos of the Washington & South Dakota the Jap war vessels completely deserted the twelve auxillaries [sic], eight of which were sunk immediately and the other four run aground by their Jap skippers. There our dive bombers took over and blasted them to bits. It was officially estimated that over thirty thousand Japs were wiped out in the engagement.

[George is describing the results of the air attacks of 14 November and the battleship surface engagement of 14–15 November. Battleships *Washington* and *South Dakota* were not held back by plan; they were too far south to reach Guadalcanal until 14 November. The Japanese lost seven of eleven transports and a heavy cruiser. For the ship losses on both sides in the air attacks and night surface engagement, see chapter 6, pages 115–16.]

To return to more peaceful topics, after I had been attached to N.O.B. [Naval Operating Base] for a couple of weeks, our Commanding Officer, Lt. Cmdr. Fewel, was detached from here and given command of all naval activities at Tulagi, and I found myself in his shoes here, with twelve officers and three hundred men under me. The Naval establishment here at Guadalcanal is made up of three separate groups, each with their own camp and jurisdiction. The "Sea-Bees" (6th Construction Battalion) number some eight hundred men and do all engineering and construction work here, building roads, airfields, and so forth. The Cub-Ones number about three-fifty and handle all supplies and equipment ashore. Our job is to handle all waterfront activities, bring all cargo ashore from supply ships, handle passenger and mail trips, and furnish water transportation for all special expeditions. Our facilities consist of an armada of self-propelling pontoon barges, towing barges, big tank lighters, ramp boats, and personnel boats. Our biggest problem is trying to keep the boats running, they take an awful beating with never any time out for overhauling or repairs until they break down. Then we have to struggle and sweat to fix them up, with few tools, no facilities such as chain hoists or a marine runway, and a completely inadequate stock of spare parts. Sometimes a dozen or more boats will break down in a couple of hours. Fortunately we have a fine bunch of men in our Repair gang, Chief Machinist Mates and Motor Machinist Mates and Electricians, all experts in their line with years of experience behind them.

We have about fifty boats for all purposes and frequently receive additional boats from the transports that unload here, which take away with them an equal number of damaged boats that our repair facilities can't handle. That should be a good system, but unfortunately the skippers of the transports don't want to lose their best boats so leave us all their cripples which soon break down and leave us worse off than ever.

[It is a tribute to George's ability and leadership that he, a lieutenant of the Naval Reserve, was entrusted with such responsibilities. His opposite numbers in charge of the Seabees and the Cub-Ones were "brass-hat" commanders.]

On the night of Nov. 30–Dec. 1 there was another big sea battle just off Savo Island, a few miles west of here, and our side didn't come out so well, as the cruiser Northhampden [heavy cruiser *Northampton*] was sunk, the Minneapolis had her bow blown off up to number two turret, the New Orleans had her bow blown off up to number one turret, and the Pensacola took a couple of fish aft. However the three damaged cruisers were successfully towed to Tulagi and eventually will reach a major repair base, but it will be many months before they are in service again. The Japs were said to have lost nine war vessels of various sizes in the encounter but we didn't see anything at all of them the following morning, and anyway nine for four is lower than our usual average.

[George is describing the disastrous Battle of Tassafaronga, where Rear Adm. Carleton H. Wright took five cruisers and six destroyers against eight Japanese destroyers, blundered into torpedo waters, and came away with one undamaged light cruiser and his destroyers. George didn't find the wreckage of nine enemy vessels, for the enemy lost only one destroyer. Nor was that the last blemish to Wright's reputation. As commandant of the Twelfth Naval District, he played a leading role in the Port Chicago Mutiny. On 17 July 1944 an ammunition explosion at Port Chicago, California, destroyed part of a loading dock and two cargo ships, killing 320, of whom 202 were black sailors loading ammunition, and injuring 390, including 233 black enlisted men. The mutiny resulted when the survivors were ordered to resume loading ammunition at Mare Island without receiving any leave or formal counseling. At the ensuing general courts-martial, fifty of the black mutineers were found guilty and sentenced to dishonorable discharges after prison terms as long as fifteen years. The other 208 defendants were found guilty of refusing to obey a lawful order and received lesser punishments. This disgraceful chapter in naval history was accorded book-length treatment by a black sociologist, Robert L. Allen, in *The Port Chicago Mutiny* (New York: Warner Books, 1989).]

Dec. 15, 1942

Life at Guadalcanal is about as busy, rushing, confusing, disorganized, and completely snafu as it could possibly be. . . . Right now we have three troop transports and five cargo vessels waiting to be unloaded, all in imminent danger of being torpedoed, as were the Majaba and Alchiba, and all screaming madly for more boats so they can finish up and get the hell out of here. When they first come in I put on my other shirt and board each one in my capacity as Port Director. Each Captain greets me warmly, compliments us on our accomplishments here, and an atmosphere of cordiality and good fellowship envelops one and all. By noon each one starts sending signals to the beach requesting more boats be assigned to his particular ship, and by nightfall when all steam out in search of better protected waters until the following dawn, my ears have become considerably singed from the unkind remarks directed my way.

On the second day I visit the Captains again and try and explain the situation, also assuring them that all the boats they see idly at anchor are broken down, and that I'm not . . . holding them back just to be mean. By the third day none of us are on speaking terms, and by the time we finally get them unloaded and they shove off for good everyone is wondering was it worth while taking this place back from the Japs after all. The only nice side of the picture is my nightly interview with Captain Compton, Comdr. Nav Base Cactus, the responsibilities of his job have made him almost a physical wreck, but he usually greets me with "Hello George, have you read this latest dispatch from Admiral Turner [Richmond Kelly "Terrible" Turner, Commander Amphibious Force, South Pacific Force] giving us hell about the unloading?" and then he grins and we have a drink.

Dec. 16

One of those things you dream about but seldom if ever experience happened to me the other nite. Got back to my tent after dark and almost fell over two huge mail sacks sitting in the middle of the deck. . . . Thought it was the mail for the entire camp but was told it was all for me. So I laughed heartily at the joke and took a closer look with my flashlite—and I'll be damned if it *wasn't* all for me. Four month's accumulation of letters, magazines and packages. I really felt guilty and selfish when the men gathered around and watched me empty the sacks, with understandable envy on their faces. There were packages of cookies & cakes, and Xmas presents, and bundles of funny papers and magazines, and cartons of cigarettes and soap and razor blades, and stationery & stamps and stacks of letters from as far back as July.

Kay, bless her heart, had sent a brand-new portable victrola with dozens of the latest records, and no sooner had I torn off the wrapping than the men set it up out in the open and soon the first music we had heard for many long weeks came drifting out of the darkness, while the tiny red tips of cigarettes formed a broad circle around it, marking where the men sat listening. Kay had intended the victrola and her packages for the crew of the Catalpa. They would have been very welcome aboard ship, but to the men stationed here, where there are no amusements of any kind, the pleasure they brought was beyond measure.

Jan. 9, 1943

The Army has now taken over all operations and most of the Marines have been evacuated. . . . Most of the Cub Ones have been evacuated so they number only a hundred or so, mostly staff. On the other hand, my outfit has grown until I now have sixteen officers and about five hundred men.

For awhile N.O.B. was at a pretty low ebb, with overwork and malaria and dysentery raising hell with both health and morale. At one time I was down to seven officers and with the boats manned by men still weak from their second or third bout with malaria, it really hurt to see some of the men, who had been healthy, husky youngsters on board the Majaba, reduced to walking skeletons, and of course the same situation existed to an even greater extent with the boat crews which arrived before we did. The situation is still serious but with new men arriving in ever increasing numbers I have been able to evacuate most of the more serious cases. . . . I can see no chance of getting away from here for at least a couple of more months, unless I'm evacuated because of health, and so far the only thing I've suffered from is lack of sleep, which doesn't arouse the least spark of sympathy from the local medical unit.

[George's resistance to disease, particularly the endemic malaria, was remarkable and doubtless a factor in his ability to lead. In addition, as he describes below, he had access to one powerful anodyne which was denied the enlisted men.]

Jan. 28, 1943

We have been busier than ever the past week or so which together with the loss of sleep due to nightly air-raids have made us all a little punchy.

Had a bigger than usual raid the other night and once again my armada took a beating, about a dozen boats being pretty well riddled by shrapnel. Had four night duty crews sleeping out in the boats and by some miracle only one boy was wounded. My private gig, a snappy little job with a big wicker chair and a canopy, was set on fire which gives me an added grudge against Tojo. The unfortunate part of it is that we have no night fighters and consequently the Jap bombers cruise overhead at will, with nothing but A.A. fire to worry them, and they can keep up high enuf to be out of range.

Feb. 13, 1943

What a whale of a difference just a few days can make. Three days ago the Japs evacuated all their remaining troops from Guadalcanal, thus ending the six-month struggle for this area. First decisive victory over the Jap army since the war began. . . .

A new unit known as the Amphibious Force Boat Pool has arrived, headed by Lt. Cmdr. Holtzman of the Coast Guard, and complete with all facilities to set up a machine shop and marine railway and everything necessary for a self-sufficient organization.

For the past month or so all the new boats and crews I've received have been designated for the Boat Pool, so to avoid the confusion of dual command I turned the whole works over to Cmdr. Holtzman, camp, galley, boats, and the remanents [sic] of the crews, that arrived here about the time I did. So, in theory at least, I'm now a man of leisure with nothing to do but take it easy until the arrival of my orders to New Zealand for rest and recreation. In reality, however, I'll probably have to keep running the outfit for several weeks more until Holtzman gets on top of all the angles.

In the meantime life shouldn't be too unpleasant here. I have a radio and even an electric fan in my tent, and a good stock of liquor including Scotch, gin, Vermouth, Orange Curacao, Creme de Menthe and Creme de Cacao, beer, and also Coke and soda pop. My supply is the envy of every officer on the island. . . .

Have been recommended for advancement to Lt. Cmdr. due to my work here. By the time the letter reaches the Navy Dept. in Washington and [is] acted upon, I'll probably have made it anyway due to seniority, but feel rather pleased about it anyway.

While George was stockpiling liquor "liberated" from the cargo ships unloading at Lunga Roads, the chances are that the several hundred enlisted men under his command were fortunate to receive an occasional can of beer. When he was C.O. of the *Pawnee*, the crew received no beer at all.

I discussed the R.H.I.P. (rank hath its privileges) policy about liquor in *"We Will Stand by You"* (p. 93): "It was well known that Admiral Halsey was a two-fisted drinking man who . . . mistrusted teetotalers. No sooner had a forward naval base of shacks and Quonset huts been established than an officers' club opened for business. It was stocked with bourbon, Scotch, gin and brandy shipped in as essential war supplies from the States.

"Where the enlisted men had access to bars and liquor stores, they didn't care. 'Let 'em have their goddam officers' clubs' was the prevailing sentiment. 'I wouldn't want to drink with 'em, anyway.' But in the Solomons the booze-for-officers-only policy was blatantly discriminatory, and was deeply resented by many sailors."

It is doubtful that Commander George gave the matter much thought. It had taken him seven years to graduate from college, and eight years at a variety of jobs in and out of the country while taking the required Naval Reserve courses and cruises that eventually earned his jay-gee half-stripe and command of his first ship, the *Catalpa*. The emoluments of command, such as officers' clubs and private stocks of liquor, were accepted by him as no more than his due. He who assumes the responsibility, he undoubtedly believed, deserves the privileges and the plaudits. Where failure results, he alone must shoulder the blame. While many enlisted men envied his captain's cabin, attendants, and other perks, few who were aware of the price he paid would have exchanged places. It is lonely at the top; most men are unsuited for the altitude.

Being an exceptionally ambitious man, with a courage to match, George gladly accepted responsibility and, indeed, sought it out. Outwardly, he was reserved and seemingly modest. When the *Pawnee* officers posed for a group photo, he elected to stand in the back row with the warrant officers, rather than front and center, the position commanding officers always assumed. Since everything he did had its purpose, it was likely he chose the occasion to send a subtle message to his officers. Customarily, he sat at the head of whatever table he graced. He served in five ships and was C.O. of each one. Cast on the beach after *Majaba* was torpedoed, he was soon, as a mere lieutenant, placed in charge of Naval Operating Base, Guadalcanal, when the issue was very much in doubt. The Navy authorities loved men like Flave George, who never turned down a hazardous assignment, bringing to each one grace and style, and a measure of the luck that is always a factor in naval operations. (He also startled on occasion with ironic humor. When he assumed command of the ammunition ship *Vesuvius,* he told his officers: "This ship will never sink. If anything happens, we're going straight to heaven.") The Navy's love for George was reciprocated. Wartime offered opportunities for adventure and advancement, coupled with the routine and discipline which gave his ambitions form, and that respect for authority which plays such a large role in the sea services.

He was an autocrat without appearing to be one. In his journal he seldom mentioned a subordinate officer by name, and never an enlisted man, whom he designated by his rating specialty. The officers who merited names were almost always senior in rank, commanders and captains, ranks which he intended to, and did, achieve.

If all the officers I served with and under had shared the qualities I admired in Flave George, I still would have disliked the class and caste system for its manifest inequalities and injustices. At the same time I would have admitted without rancor that a special man such as George, "Nature's own Nobleman," in Martin Tupper's well-turned phrase, deserves special respect and consideration. Unfortunately, the privileges of commissioned status rest arbitrarily upon bands of gold, irrespective of merit. Where R.H.I.P. operates, as my *Pawnee* shipmate and close friend Donald J. Aposhian observed, "The rankest seem to have the most privileges."

8

The *Pawnee*'s South Pacific

Nothing is ever done in this world until men are prepared to kill one another if it is not done.

—George Bernard Shaw

The destinies of Lt. Comdr. Flavius J. George and the ninety-five officers and men of the USS *Pawnee* would soon interact, but only after a series of improbable events.

On the morning of 7 November 1942, when *Majaba* was torpedoed at Lunga Roads, the *Pawnee* was dockside at the United Engineering yard in Alameda, preparing for the commissioning ceremonies the next morning (which was 7 November on the west side of the international date line).

During the terrifying First Naval Battle of Guadalcanal on 13 November, which George described so vividly from his temporary duty with Naval Operating Base ashore, *Pawnee* was making daylight shakedown cruises around San Francisco Bay. In late afternoon we moored at South Pier in the Port of Tradewinds on Treasure Island, and half the crew was given liberty.

On the morning of 9 December, *Pawnee* departed the continental limits of the United States, setting our course west-southwest for Pearl Harbor to pick up *ARD-5*, a floating dry dock, and tow her to Espiritu Santo in the South Pacific. George had been given charge of N.O.B. and its boat pool and was living in a tent and taking refuge in a foxhole during the frequent Japanese air raids and shore bombardments.

On 29 January 1943 *Pawnee* picked up a pilot to negotiate the dangerous minefields at Segond Channel, which had already claimed the destroyer *Tucker* and transport *President Coolidge,* and released her tow. She spent the next four weeks at Espiritu Santo on a variety of minor towing and salvage duties. During this time George was relieved of his N.O.B. command and pronounced himself "a man of leisure" while he awaited orders to New Zealand for R & R. But he quickly grew impatient for action. His journal entry for 18 March 1943 reads:

Seems I was a little previous in thinking I was due for a little leisure time before heading south. About the middle of last month I heard of plans to take over the Russell Islands, some 60 miles to the westward of Guadalcanal, and as I was getting somewhat bored with things here, volunteered for advance reconnaissance duty. So, at midnight of Feb. 18, with several Army & Marine officers, I was put ashore at Reynard Sound on Banika Is., one of the Russell group. For the next two days we thoroughly explored Banika and Pavuvu, the engineers checking air-field possibilities and water supply and roads, while my job was to check the coastline in a small motor boat we'd brought along and pick out the landing beaches to be used by our troops.

We found many indications of Jap occupancy and learned from the natives that the main force of Japs have been evacuated to New Georgia the day before we landed, leaving behind only a few patrols which we carefully avoided.

At midnight of the third night we were picked up by a PT boat and returned to Guadalcanal where we made our reports to Admiral Turner and the Commanding General [John Hester, an Army major general] and his staff. The occupying force was divided into three groups to be landed simultaneously at Wernham Cove, Paddy Bay [at Pavuvu, the largest island], and Renard Sound, the only places I had found where the beaches were at all feasible for landing craft. At midnight of the 21st we set out with some fifteen destroyers crammed with troops and supplies and at dawn the landing was made without a shot being fired and under such complete air coverage from Henderson Field that not a Jap plane got thru to us.

I remained at Renard Sound in charge of naval operations, with Lt. Smith, Lt. Barnes and about fifty seamen. . . .

After about a month in the Russells received dispatch orders to report to ComSoPac in Noumea so at present [18 March] am packing my gear here at Guadalcanal and expect to catch a ship south tomorrow. About the time ComSoPac orders arrived, another dispatch was received from Admiral Turner, ComAmphFor, directing that three officers be nominated for an advance reconnaissance of the New Georgia Islands, and suggesting I be one of the three. So Admiral Halsey's orders take precedence, I'll probably miss out on the New Georgia deal, and don't know whether to be glad or sorry.

By the end of March George was in Auckland, where he was assigned to the *Talamanca* (AF-15, a refrigerated store ship) as gunnery officer. "Have been here four days now," he reported in his journal for 1 April 1943, "and more or less worn myself to a frazzle trying to make up for all the parties I've missed out on during the last six or seven months. Hope to be able to maintain the present pace for three more days until the Talamanca shoves off on her regular run."

But he never sailed in the *Talamanca*. On 26 February *Pawnee* stood out of Segond Channel for Noumea, towing a rusty coastal transport which had been holed amidships by a torpedo that passed clear through without detonating. We put our tow alongside *ARD-2*, a veteran of the Pearl Harbor attack, and spent most of the next two weeks moored portside to the *Argonne*, another Pearl Harbor survivor known to all as the "Agony Maru." At Noumea she had been the flagship of Vice Adm. Robert L. Ghormley, the first Commander South Pacific, and his bolder successor, Halsey. When the latter moved ashore in November 1942, the *Argonne* became a miscellaneous auxiliary.

On St. Patrick's Day 1943 we were ordered to Nomobitigue Reef on a crucial salvage job. The "beef boat" *Delphinus* had gone aground there with a full cargo of chilled and frozen provisions destined for the forward areas, and Commander South Pacific wanted her off without delay. As I described in detail in *"We Will Stand by You,"* Chapter Three, it took us nineteen days. Our beloved commissioning skipper, "Captain Frank" Dilworth, was relieved of his command. Detached from the *Talamanca* as his replacement was Lt. Comdr. Flavius J. George.

Two ironies must be noted, which some may attribute to mere chance and others to the force of destiny. George was in Auckland for R & R, followed by duty in the lightly armed *Talamanca*, a former United Fruit "banana boat." It was an assignment far below his capabilities. When the hasty decision was made to relieve Lieutenant Dilworth, he was available on short notice.

The other irony is that Admiral Turner, following George's successful survey of the Russell Islands, requested his services for the more dangerous reconnaissance of the enemy-occupied New Georgia Islands, which were scheduled for invasion in June. If Admiral Halsey's contrary orders hadn't taken precedence, George could not have been given command of the *Pawnee*. The unanswerable question: Under another skipper, would we have survived the torpedo attack of PT Squadron Nine that sank the *McCawley* and that *Pawnee* escaped partly by great good fortune and partly by superb ship-handling?

George's journal continues with an entry dated only "April '43":

From Guadalcanal I went to another advance base for a month, then south to Noumea, then by plane to Auckland, and finally back to here [Noumea] to take command of the USS Pawnee, a Fleet salvage tug. My new ship is very nice, brand new and with twice the power of the Catalpa and quite a bit bigger. Wish I had a little more experience with the salvage game, it's going to be rather rough duty until I get onto the ropes.

[Fortunately for George, he was never tested with a salvage assignment that was truly difficult from a technical standpoint, like the *Delphinus* stranding on Nomobitigue Reef. What were tested were his strengths: leadership and ship-handling.]

Sat. 3 July

The long planned assault on the Japanese held New Georgia Islands got underway last Wednesday, a division of our cruisers, screened by destroyers, blasting away at shore installations while our troops poured down the sides of six big transports into surf boats and dashed ashore to secure beach-heads at three strategic points.

The Pawnee had departed from Guadalcanal at 0300, arriving at the Russell Islands at 0700 where we stood by for further orders. At 1000 they came—procede [*sic*] to Blanche Channel, New Georgia Islands, and take the destroyer Zane in tow. We got underway immediately and steamed west unescorted. About halfway to our destination the cruisers and part of their destroyer screen passed us at full speed heading back to the safety of our own waters. They made a beautiful sight as they sliced by us, but would have looked twice as good had they only been heading in the same direction we were.

About 1400 we sighted the New Georgia Islands and shortly thereafter steamed thru the opening thru the reef into Blanche Channel. An hour or so before sundown we sighted the Zane, and congratulated ourselves over the prospect of getting her in tow before dark and then a nice fast trip back to safety, as towing a slim, light destroyer would make very little difference in our speed.

Our optimism was premature. Down the channel foamed four of our transports shepherded by most of the rest of the destroyer force, and from the flagship came a signal to continue on our course towards the Jap air fields at Munda and take in tow the huge transport McCawley which had just been disabled by a Jap Torpedo Plane attack. Another tug was assigned to the Zane job.

So on we went and as darkness fell sighted the McCawley up ahead being towed by the transport Libra and guarded by our last two destroyers [*McCalla* and *Ralph Talbot*]. By the time we reached them it was blacker than pitch due to no moon and low hanging rain clouds.

We edged in alongside the Libra in the inky blackness to transfer the tow line, those of us up on the flying bridge almost getting crushed as we slid under one of the Libra's lifeboats hanging out over her side invisible in the darkness.

The Libra secured a wire messenger to the tow line leading over her stern and passed it to us, then to our dismay blithely lit off an acetylene torch to cut herself loose from the tow wire. We felt sure every Jap plane, gun, and submarine in the South Pacific must be bearing down on us as we lay revealed in the glare. Finally there was a splash and a jerk on our wire messenger as the tow wire parted and slipped off the Libra's stern, the Libra immediately going full ahead to be swallowed by the darkness and taking one of the two remaining destroyers with her.

We started heaving in on the messenger to secure the heavy tow wire, only to find a frayed end—in her hurry to get the hell out of that area the Libra had got under way too soon and her screw had severed the line.

I was really discouraged by that time, how was I going to get another tow wire aboard the helpless and abandoned McCawley looming dimly in the blackness a hundred yards away. The only possibility was to go alongside her, bow to stern [should read "bow to bow"], put a party of our own men aboard, and hope they could heave up and secure our own tow wire to her bow by brute strength. And all the time the precious minutes were flying by, if dawn should catch us still in Blanche Channel the Japs would be on us like hornets.

With our lone destroyer escort [the *McCalla*] circling uneasily around us, we inched in toward the McCawley's port side. A volunteer boarding party [Coxswain Norman Hazzard, Boatswain's Mate Winston "Pappy" Schmidt, and Motor Machinist's Mate Rodney Wolcott] stood ready at our bow to scramble aboard her. The peculiar, oily, dead smell of a torpedoed ship tainted the night air.

Due to the blackness I came alongside her at too great an angle, so ordered the men to wait while I backed off and swung in more parallel. We were less than a hundred feet off when out of the darkness a silent white streak of foam and phosphorescence appeared, pointed straight for our starboard bow.

Our screw churned full astern and the men on the forecastle, too paralyzed to move, watched the torpedo flash by, a scant five feet from our bow. A few seconds thereafter two torpedoes struck the McCawley almost simultaneously, the first on her port quarter, the second just forward of the bridge, the latter hit causing a further explosion probably due to the ignition of a magazine.

A fourth white finger came streaking toward our bow, and behind it a fifth pointed at our stern. I didn't see how they could miss, and slipped the heavy binoculars from around my neck while flexing my knees to keep the explosion from breaking my ankles. A short distance off we could dimly see the bow of the McCawley rise a hundred feet in the air and momentarily hang there almost vertically. We were still going astern and at the last possible second I called for full ahead with full left rudder as the leading torpedo skimmed past our bow. The Pawnee skidded around on her tail and wagged it just out of reach of the last torpedo, while the McCawley disappeared beneath the surface with a dull rumble.

During this time the destroyer had been hidden in the darkness on the far side of the McCawley, and now she churned into view, sweeping across our bow as she headed in the direction from which the torpedoes had come. She signalled us to head for sea at maximum speed as she disappeared in the blackness. We were in hearty agreement with the idea, the further we could get from that particular spot the better we liked it, and the Pawnee practically took off from the surface as the engine room poured on the juice.

Our troubles weren't completely over even yet. A heavy rain squall hit us and the stinging drops blotted out what little visibility we had. During our maneuvering to take over the tow we had lost all track of our exact position[,] and just what course would take us safely thru the reef-fringed entrance of Blanche Channel into the open sea, still several miles away, was pure guesswork. We made the best estimate possible and continued thru the wet blackness without slacking speed, and then, glory be, from astern came the phosphorescent gleam of the destroyer's bow wave [the McCalla]. As she passed us, of the destroyer herself we couldn't see a thing, we signalled her to lead us thru the entrance and gave her our speed, and from then on it was duck soup. She plotted her course by radar bearings of the encircling mountains and we glued ourselves to her wake. [The Pawnee as yet had no radar.] We saw not a sign of the entrance as we slipped thru and our first intimation that we were once more in the open ocean, wonderful place, was when the Pawnee started burying her nose in the heavy ground swells outside.

The destroyer soon left us to our own devices, she had other duties to perform, (incidentally the sub eluded her) and we continued alone thru the night the two hundred or so miles back to Guadalcanal, but none of us cared. We knew nothing could stop us now from returning safely.

[George's account of the loss of the *McCawley* and *Pawnee*'s narrow escape from destruction closely parallels my description of the same action in *"We Will Stand by You,"* pp. 70–77. The *Zane,* which he identified as a destroyer, was a high-speed mine sweeper converted from a flush-deck destroyer. At the times he wrote his action report and journal entry, he still believed that a Japanese submarine had attacked us. In fact, the attack was by PT Squadron Nine, under Lt. Comdr. Robert B. Kelly. Writing many years later, I had the benefit of eyewitness accounts, Commander Kelly's action report, and even a witness to Admiral Turner's reaction to Kelly's initial claim of sinking a Japanese transport.]

July 3
Tonight we are anchored quietly off the entrance to Wernham Cove in the Russell Islands, ready to go steaming off to the rescue of any of our ships that get into trouble in the still developing New Georgia occupation.

We had hardly dropped anchor when Lt. Barnes came bounding aboard to give me all the gossip since I left the shore base here last March. He feels quite lost now as Lt. Smith has also left to return to the States, leaving Barnes the sole survivor of the Unholy Three still on the island.

When we first occupied these islands last February, I was in charge of the Naval establishment at Renard Sound, and never was a man more cursed, or blessed, with two more wacky assistants than Smith and Bonzo [*sic*]. Smith was a hard-bitten former Merchant Marine officer who would rather fight than eat and was never happier than when engaged in a bitter dispute with some high-ranking Army or Navy officer. I remember one evening he returned to our joint quarters looking happier than he had for weeks, and proudly announced that he had just bawled the living be-Jesus out of a couple of snooty, newly arrived colonels. I told him that was liable to get him into pretty hot water, but Smitty only smiled contentedly and said there wasn't a chance, he'd taken the precaution of telling them his name was George!

Tuesday 6 July
Tonight finds the Pawnee anchored inboard of the reef encircling the S.E. shore of Vangunu Island of the New Georgia group. We left Tulagi at 0300 this morning, arriving here about 1300, and our job is to pull one

of our LST's [*sic*] off the beach where a storm tossed it high and dry two nights ago.

This is indeed a lousy place to lie at anchor, with the Japs still in possession of the major portion of this group of islands, with their airfield at Munda only forty some miles to the N.W., and a night prowling force of their cruisers and destroyers as likely as not to come steaming by, in which case Pawnee will be sunk before she knows what hit her.

However, it could be worse, so much so that this place seems like a haven of peace and safety. Our original orders, when we left Tulagi this morning, were to procede [*sic*] at top speed to Kula Gulf, near Kolombangara Island just to the north of here, and tow the cruiser Helena to safety. She was jumped by a Jap Task Force early this morning and badly shot up. It was a hell of an assignment for us, for as we steamed westward thru the night encoded radio dispatches showed the situation there to be growing steadily worse, with more and more Jap cruisers, destroyers, subs, and planes unexpectedly turning up, and our surface units taking what had all the appearances of a first class shellac[k]ing.

I don't mind admitting that the thought of steaming into the center of that mess with the poor little Pawnee didn't appeal to me a bit. Then, just as we were on the fringe of the danger zone came an Urgent Priority message directing us to come here instead. The Helena was beyond saving and was sinking.

Our relief at the change of orders was lessened as we received further reports concerning the survivors, some five hundred men were still struggling in the water and clinging to life-rafts, our fastest destroyers were attempting to pick up as many as possible before Jap planes and ships could return to machine-gun them, at best the loss of life is going to be heavy. It wasn't pleasant to visualize what those men are going thru, blasted and burned from the destruction of their ship, the surrounding islands affording no hope what with the Jap garrisons controlling them, helpless to avoid either the Jap ships or planes that are sure to return.

Naval warfare, as fought in the South Pacific area, is anything but chivalrous. In the good old days two ships or two fleets slugged it out in the open, the loser going down with his flag flying, or at worst hauling it down and putting an end to useless slaughter. Here, war is a matter of stealth and extermination in the darkness. Ships venture into enemy waters only under cover of night and blast away by radar control, while the skulking subs fire acoustically. You rarely see what you are firing at except by the momentary glare of an exploding ship. In several blind melees in this area our ships have poured shells into each other, and the Japs have made the same blunder even oftener. Survivors who are unfortunate enough to be sighted clinging to life-rafts or floating in their life-jackets can expect a hail of machine gun bullets if it's the enemy that spots them first. It's a glorious war all right.

Thurs. July 8

Finally pulled the LST 322 about 1100 this morning after two days of mule hauling, and two nights of expecting to be visited by Jap bombers at any minute.

Just now an emergency appendectomy is being performed in our Sick Bay. The doctor with the shore forces came aboard and requested the use of our facilities as there is yet no adequate spot on shore for surgery. It has only been a few days since we drove the Japs out of this place, killing some four hundred of them with a loss to our side of thirty three men. The hundred or so of our wounded were immediately flown out in PBY's for treatment at Guadalcanal.

[The vessel *Pawnee* pulled off the beach near Oloana Bay, Vangunu Island, was a tank landing craft, *LCT-322*, rather than a much larger LST, a tank landing ship. For a fuller description of this rescue, which employed a bulldozer borrowed from the Seabees to run the two-inch towing hawser ashore, see pages 78–80 of *"We Will Stand by You."*]

Tues. July 13

For the past couple of days the Pawnee has been taking a well deserved rest, peacefully at anchor in Purvis Bay, which cuts thru Florida Island.

This morning several of us took advantage of the lull in activities to explore the upper end of Purvis in the ship's motor launch. The scenery was delightful as the Bay narrowed to a winding channel cutting between high jungle-covered hills that had a glistening greenish tint from the recent rains. Pure white parrots flashed from tree to tree and as we rounded a sharp bend we came close to a huge crocodile peacefully sunning himself on a projecting ledge of rock.

At the upper end of the channel we saw the thatch huts of a native village half hidden behind coconut palms and banana stalks. We beached the launch and soon made friends with a husky young Solomon Islander named Tomi. Tomi knew a few words of English learned from the missionaries of pre-war days and conducted us thru the village, where he introduced us to the chief, an ancient old fellow whose once black and kinky hair was now gray. The chief spoke no English but thru Tomi informed us that he and his people were very grateful to the Americans for driving away the Japanese who had mistreated them, and most serious of all, taken their pigs and chickens away from them.

The Solomon Islanders are much more primitive than the Melanesians of the New Hebrides and Fiji. The men are fairly well built but of a smaller stature, and both men and women wear nothing but a short skirt, with sometimes a bright flower stuck in their bushy hair. Most of them have tattoo marks on their faces, and reddish stained teeth from chewing betel nut.

Cannibalism evidently was never prevalent in these islands, beyond eating a piece of flesh from an enemy's chest in order to absorb part of his courage and strength. However head-hunting used to be considered one of the finer arts before the British Constabulary more or less curbed it.

[I used to long to make this sort of sightseeing tour, especially since it was unlikely I would have another opportunity to visit the South Pacific, but only officers could commandeer the use of our motor launch or whaleboat. The only times I was ashore in the Solomon Islands were twice in the Russells to play in softball games organized by Captain George (no beer for the players) and once on Guadalcanal in search of spare parts for our radio gear.

[The result of this discriminatory policy was to keep enlisted men ignorant of everything outside the immediate area of their rating specialties. What should have been a broadening educational experience, despite the war, was lost. Consequently, most men returned from World War II nearly as unenlightened about the world as they had been before leaving home.]

Sat. July 17
After a couple of peaceful days in Purvis Bay another night action was fought in Kula Gulf and over the air [on the Fox schedule broadcast from Pearl Harbor] came orders for the Pawnee to go up and tow back the destroyer Gwin.

As we steamed westward thru the night we were able to get a fairly good picture of the action from the reports being radioed to the base from the ships involved. We had quite a good force there, our cruisers Honolulu and St. Louis, the British cruiser Leander, and about ten destroyers. While prowling thru Kula Gulf they had made contact by radar with a Jap task force of one cruiser and five destroyers. Both sides opened fire with radar control about two in the morning and the Jap cruiser and at least three destroyers were soon sunk. On our side the Leander took a torpedo amidships which put her out of action but she remained afloat and was able to crawl along toward home at about five knots.

Then our side suddenly ran into some hard luck. Out of nowhere a second force of at least four Jap ships appeared (on the radar screen that is, in the blackness nothing was visible to the naked eye) and before our ships could maneuver out of danger our two remaining cruisers were hit by torpedoes, as well as the Gwin.

Both the Honolulu and the St. Louis were hit near the bow so that their engines were undamaged, and so excellent was their watertight integrity that they were still able to procede [*sic*] at fifteen knots. The Gwin, however, was hit aft and put totally out of commission, so our job was to try and tow her to safety.

Incidentally one of the seamen on the Gwin had one of those freak escapes that seem unbelievable. He was down in the after magazine when the fish hit, and the explosion blasted him up thru two decks where he landed on the fan-tail. He was cut off from the rest of the ship by a fierce fire so dove off the stern and swam for over an hour. Then what does he do but bump into an undamaged motor whale boat drifting unmanned, so he climbed aboard, started up the engine and putt-putted thru the darkness on an easterly course and at dawn overtook the destroyer standing by the crippled Gwin, where he returned aboard. Ripley [cartoonist Robert Ripley of "Believe It or Not" fame] would have a hard time beating that one.

However, with daylight the Jap planes came out in force to try and finish off the cripples. As we passed the three cruisers struggling along toward Guadalcanal and safety the flagship blinkered us to take our orders from the destroyer guarding the Gwin. It soon became evident that to try and save the Gwin would only mean the loss of the Pawnee and any other ships remaining in that area, so the other destroyer [the *Ralph Talbot*] ordered us to reverse our course and hit for home, while he put another torpedo in the Gwin to hasten her finish.

At present we are anchored in Renard Sound in the Russell Islands and standing by for further engagements up the Slot. However, while we took some pretty hard blows, the Jap Navy evidently was temporarily at least cleared out of the New Georgia area, for our nightly sweeps by our ships have resulted in no more contacts with Jap units.

[George is describing the Battle of Kolombangara where, contrary to the optimistic reports of the commanders, the Japanese lost only the cruiser *Jintsu* and her outstanding admiral, Shunji Izaki. On our side, the *Honolulu* and *St. Louis* were out of action for many months, and the *Leander* for the rest of the war, while the *Gwin* was lost.]

Nov. 22, 1943 [This is the first entry after a four-month gap in George's journal.]

For the past few months the Pawnee has been kept so busy that I gave up all attempts to keep any kind of written record. We were kept on the go morning and night for weeks at a stretch without a single night at anchor and a chance to relax from the continual strain and tension. The trouble was that there were only two Indian class tugs in the Solomons area, the Pawnee and the Menominee, and the Menominee was tied up with the job of raising a sunken Jap destroyer in Halavo Harbor near Tulagi. So that left the Pawnee to do all the work "up the Slot" in the combat area. And there was plenty of work to do.

[In *"We Will Stand by You,"* pp. 115–16, I describe how the C.O. of the *Menominee,* Lt. Comdr. Emile C. Genereaux, got the assignment of raising the *Kikutsuki* from Halavo Bay, Florida Island, from Admiral Halsey. Halsey wanted to present the enemy destroyer to Admiral Nimitz, essentially as a war trophy. Consequently, we lost the services of the *Menominee* during the critical months of the New Georgia and Vella Lavella campaigns.]

Following the landing of our forces in the New Georgia area there was a period of a couple of months during which the Japs kept bringing in reinforcements in an effort to save the situation. But when we finally wiped out the last man of the Munda garrison and gained possession of the airfield, there was nothing the Japs could do but attempt to evacuate as many of their men as possible to Bougainville. From New Georgia Island they fled in barges under cover of darkness to Vella Lavella or Kolombangara, and from there to Choiseul, and from there a small shot-up remnant finally made good their escape to Bougainville.

During the reinforcement phase the Pawnee was kept busy towing to safety bombed or shot up units of our Amphibious force that came to grief while bringing up troops and supplies. One of the big LST's was struck amidships by a torpedo one night off Oliana Bay [Oloana Bay, Vangunu Island] and broke in half[,] going down like a rock and taking with it 21 out of 22 Army and Navy officers aboard it. One of those lost was Lt. Cmdr. McClelland Barclay, the illustrator. The forward half remained afloat and we were given the job of towing it down to Tulagi, a rather unpleasant three-day job as we were given no protective escort and expected every moment to catch a torpedo ourselves, being able to make only seven knots and unable to maneuver ["in irons," in the nautical phrase] to dodge a "fish" if we did see one headed for us, due to the hulk we were towing. It's a funny thing how after a few sleepless nights of straining your eyes into the blackness you can see anything you want to, like numerous torpedo tracks streaking toward you or the dim shape of a surfaced sub, if you don't keep a tight grip on yourself.

Another LST was bombed and gutted by fire and still had a number of scorched bodies littering its deck when we went alongside it to secure the tow wire. One victim lay on his back near the rail with a leg hanging over the side and casually swinging back and forth with the roll of the ship. I had to put the Pawnee right alongside in order to put a working party aboard and in so doing scraped the leg with the bow, wiping away the seared flesh and leaving just a pinkish leg-bone with a shoe on the end of it. A couple of the newer crew members got rather sick.

[Although George describes two crippled LSTs, I believe there was only one: *LST-342*. He reconstructed these events from memory four months later. Even if he had consulted the deck logs, they would have been of little value. Handwritten until 1 January 1944 under the strictures of wartime censorship, they described neither ships nor ports by name. I describe the ordeal of *LST-342* in *"We Will Stand by You,"* pp. 87–90.]

We almost invariably traveled alone at night and developed quite a fatalistic attitude concerning our chances of being torpedoed or bombed.

On a number of occasions we would be steaming peacefully thru the darkness, not the least bit mad at anybody and almost forgetting there was a war going on as the soft moonlight and balmy tropical air worked its enchantment on us, when suddenly and without warning WHOOM! WHOOM! and columns of flame and foam would leap skyward ahead or abreast of us. We'd immediately go into a violent zig-zag while vainly searching the black velvet sky for a trace of the goddamned Jap bomber that had sneaked in on our wake to drop his eggs undetected due to the muffled roar of our own exhausts and blowers. [I describe one such incident, when we were saved by a P-38 Lightning fighter plane, on pp. 124–25 of *"We Will Stand by You."*]

One little APc [coastal transport] had the misfortune to go aground on a reef one black and stormy night and in between our nightly trips up the Slot we attempted to refloat it. Her skipper with his two other officers and crew moved aboard the Pawnee as the APc was almost on its beam end. We couldn't get closer than six hundred feet due to the heavy surf and would spend all day ferrying across portable pumps and towing gear, then just as we would be about to take a strain and everyone's hopes would be high, we would receive radioed orders to get underway and procede [*sic*] up the Slot in support of that night's Task Force operations. So all of our preparatory work would go for naught and away we would steam while the poor skipper of the APc would sink into gloom. That sort of thing continued for five days, until I finally radioed headquarters that the hulk had been so battered in the meantime that it was no longer worth saving. I really pitied the skipper, he was just a young fellow with his first command, and to have his hopes raised so high each day only to be dashed down again was really cruel.

So, we were then ordered to bring the officers and crew back to a rear base one day's steaming away, and accordingly started out, but when within only a few hours of our goal in came the usual "Proceed immediately" orders, so back we turned for another night's session up the Slot. And that sort of thing continued for five more days and nights until the APc boys started to get a wild gleam in their eyes and I began to fear they would leap overboard en masse and start swimming home the next time we reversed course on them. We finally made it to our destination, and while they all liked us fine personally, I never saw a group of men so happy to see the last of us.

[This incident demonstrates the stress of our nightly "session up the Slot" or Blanche Channel in response to the almost daily "OP" (operational priority) message copied in the radio shack one deck below the wheelhouse. I describe these grueling months when *Pawnee* was the only operational ATF in the Solomons in considerable detail in Chapter Seven of *"We Will Stand by You,"* beginning on page 109.]

When the Japs finally gave up hope of trying to save the New Georgia group of islands, they at first tried to evacuate their forces on destroyers but our own surface forces made it so costly to them they soon concentrated entirely on dozens and dozens of motorized barges that would attempt to cross the sixty or seventy miles of open water to Choiseul under cover of darkness. And nightly our cruisers and destroyers would range back and forth blasting them to bits. . . . We didn't escape scot-free and the Pawnee had to assist home a number of our destroyers, the Selfridge, the McCalla, the Patterson, the Southard, and so on while a very few never came back at all.

[George is describing the enemy evacuation of some 10,000 men from Kolombangara to Bougainville, using Daihatsu diesel-powered barges. Our destroyer blockade proved far less successful than was reported at the time. It destroyed only one-third of the barge fleet and less than 1,000 men. See Morison, Vol. VI, pp. 242–43.

[*Pawnee* did indeed stand by the *Selfridge* on her ten-knot withdrawal to Purvis Bay after she was torpedoed during the Battle of Vella Lavella, 6–7 October 1943.

[I can find no record of assistance to the *McCalla* or the *Patterson*. Neither destroyer suffered significant damage in the Solomons, although mechanical breakdown or other problems might have required *Pawnee* to stand by.

[While the *Southard*, a high-speed minesweeper, was not damaged in the Solomons, the *Montgomery*, a light minelayer (both ships were converted from flush-deck destroyers) did suffer extensive damage in a turning collision with her sister ship *Preble* off Vella Lavella. *Pawnee* took her in tow alongside, mooring her to the floating drydock in Purvis Bay eighteen hours later. See *"We Will Stand by You,"* pp. 114–15. George should not be blamed for the inadequacies of our deck logs.]

During this time the Pawnee gained quite a reputation due to the fact that while the fighting ships would be relieved and sent south every couple of weeks, every nightly operation for months included the Pawnee in some capacity or other. And when our swift and powerful cruisers and destroyers would depart at top speed from the scene of action to avoid the swarms of Jap planes that would be after them at dawn, they would frequently pass the Pawnee heading all alone and oh so lonesome in the wrong direction to throw a line on a cripple and tow it to safety.

Finally the last Jap was shot, drowned, or safely evacuated, and the Pawnee was summoned to the Admiral's headquarters at Guadalcanal [Rear Adm. Theodore S. Wilkinson, "Terrible" Turner's replacement as Commander III Amphibious Force] where we were complimented on the job we'd done and promised a nice long rest period in the rear area as soon as a couple of more tugs arrived. In the meantime we were to go back up to the Russell Islands and rest up for a few days and catch up on the ship's repair work.

So we dropped anchor that night in a secluded cove and all turned in for the first uninterrupted night's sleep in weeks. Except that at 1:00 A.M. we were ordered to get underway immediately and go to the aid of a ship that had just been hit by night bombers and was blazing and out of control.

So for the next two days we fought fire in a vain attempt to save the big Liberty ship. She was an inferno from her bridge forward, with seven thousand drums of gasoline burning in her forward holds, plus a ton of TNT and a ton of fulminate of mercury in Holds #1 & 2 which we expected to blow up in our faces at any moment. On the second day the wind shifted and we had to move the Pawnee away from alongside. We cut the burning ship's anchor chain and beached her stern first but over night she capsized and lay almost totally submerged. As the intense heat had warped and twisted her forward half out of shape she was written off as a total loss.

[And there she remains, in shallow water off Koli Point. George's account of the loss of the *John H. Couch* differs from mine in some details (see *"We Will Stand by You,"* pp. 127–29). His journal entry has the benefit of immediacy, being written within six weeks of the event. For my report I checked the ship's deck logs and found them useless, since they named neither the *Couch* nor the actions we took to save her. The quartermaster's notebook, which did have an accurate summary, had long since been destroyed. (One shipmate joked that we should have let the *Pawnee*'s deck logs fall into the hands of the Japanese as a counter-intelligence measure.) The entries in Morison and the other sources are too sketchy to be of any value. But I acquired, from the Naval Historical Center, a copy of a memo to the captain from Ens. J. R. Moodie titled "Summary of fire-fighting aboard S. S. *COUCH*, by U.S.S. *PAWNEE* on October 12, 1943." I also had the recollections of Quartermasters John Day and William J. Miller and Yeoman Le Roy E. Zahn, and my own vivid memories of the loss of the Liberty ship.]

Now that everything around New Georgia had quieted down, three new sister ships of the Pawnee and Menominee arrived on the scene and we departed these waters for our long looked forward to period of rest and relaxation. The crew was pretty well worn out and in need of a rest and I had got so run down that the Malaria bug had gained the upper hand and was giving me a bad time.

The Pawnee left a couple of days before the Menominee and we assured them that we'd think of them when we got down to Auckland and that we hoped they would get a trip down there later even tho they never had once in all these months made a trip up the Slot but had remained safely at anchor and enjoyed a good sleep every night.

We were sadly disillusioned when we reached Noumea. It seems that the Menominee Skipper [Commander Genereaux], an old-timer who was a boon companion of the brass-hats of the Service Squadron[,] had come down by plane to arrive ahead of us and had talked his pals into sending the Menominee back to Auckland for a month's rest and yard overhaul and himself back to the States for a month's leave. As for Pawnee, we got two weeks availability in Noumea during which time our own ship's force had to work night and day to try and repair our badly worn engines, and at the end of the two weeks back we went up to the Solomons with our overhaul only half completed. It was a tough break for the crew and when the Menominee passed thru Noumea on her way south they had the decency to feel pretty ashamed about it.

It worked out to our advantage after all, however, as otherwise we would have missed out on the attack on Bougainville and some of the most exciting action we'd so far experienced.

[The influence of Emile Genereaux, already well and unfavorably known to the crew of the *Pawnee* as "Black Jack," extended beyond the Service Squadron of Rear Adm. C. H. Cobb to Commander South Pacific himself. I described (pp. 115–16, *"We Will Stand by You"*) how Halsey gave Genereaux the assignment of raising the enemy destroyer *Kikut-suki* from "somewhere around Guadalcanal." His success at a near-impossible (but militarily insignificant) salvage job resulted in his promotion to full commander in charge of all salvage operations in the South Pacific. It is a good thing for the morale of the *Pawnee* crew that we did not know how Genereaux used his influence to get the R & R we had been promised. In the event, it was late January before we got under way for Sydney, under a new commanding officer.]

We arrived back in Tulagi [from Noumea] the morning of the 13th of Nov., fueled up, and left the next morning for New Georgia to await results of the occupation of Empress Augusta Bay on Bougainville. The night of the 15th we headed west and at dawn made rendezvous with a large convoy of LSTs and destroyers headed for Empress Augusta Bay with troops and supplies. All went well until about 2:00 A.M. of the morning of the 17th when we were standing in toward the Bay which we expected to reach at dawn. It was a beautiful moonlit night and on each of the twenty-some ships of the convoy the gun crews doubled their vigilance as we knew it was now or never if the Japs were going to try and stop us. It was now—and suddenly out of nowhere appeared an uncounted number of Jap planes scattering torpedoes, bombs, and machine gun bullets right and left. Our ships opened up with everything we had and the entire sky became a close-uneven pattern of vivid red as thousands of rounds of arching red tracers streaked in every direction. To the right and left we could see the black outlines of the Jap planes glide by skimming the surface between our columns, hoping we would slacken our fire for fear of hitting our own ships in the adjacent columns. The strategy didn't work. A big bomber glided by to starboard and as he crossed our bow just a short distance ahead flames started licking at his wings. The pilot knew his time was up so banked to the right in a last desperate attempt to suicide crash the LST just ahead of the Pawnee. He didn't quite make it and plowed into the ocean, the plane immediately exploding into a terrific mass of flames that lit up the night for miles. It was rather an awesome sight to see. Astern of us other explosions marked the end of other planes and a thick curtain of black oil smoke signalled the end of the APD McKean as a torpedo hit her amidships. The battle continued with gradually decreasing intensity until dawn lightened the horizon at about 5:00 A.M. when the Japs withdrew to escape our arriving fighter planes.

With the arrival of daylite we steamed into the Bay and the work of ferrying ashore the troops from the APDs swiftly commenced, while the LSTs stuck their shallow draft noses up on the beach and started disgorging their cargo of guns, trucks, and heavy equipment thru the rolled back doors in their bows.

Our surroundings looked forbidding and threatening. A narrow, level area covered with tangled jungle bordered the sea, and then the mountains rose up straight and jagged, topped by eight and ten thousand foot volcanoes that sent columns of grayish smoke and steam up into the quiet morning air.

At about 8:00 A.M. Condition Red was flashed and almost simultaneously geysers of water soared up from alongside a destroyer screening the unloading from the east as Jap bombers streaked in with the sun at their backs. Once more the sky became filled with A.A. fire as the dive bombers zoomed down and the ships maneuvered in violent zig-zags to avoid them. With the shore batteries to back us up the Japs soon withdrew having inflicted little damage and losing several more planes. One downed pilot prolonged his life a few futile minutes by abandoning his sinking plane in a rubber life raft. From the beach streaked a Higgins boat, its machine guns whipped the water to a froth at close range and that was that. The Jap might have furnished valuable information to our Intelligence officers if taken alive, but to the trigger-happy youngsters in the boat he merely represented a supremely valuable target.

Once more unloading operations got underway. From the westward appeared squadron after squadron of our own planes returning from a strike at Rabaul. As one formation passed low overhead we saw an almost unbelievable sight, a fighter with most of its port wing shot off yet holding its course as steadily as the rest of them. You felt a warm surge of admiration and pride for the undaunted pilot who had held his plane up for so many miles by sheer will power. But one wing and the prayer weren't enough, suddenly the plane nosed over and plunged downwards. We watched the pilot tumble from the cockpit and somersault downwards, holding our breath for his parachute to open. But he was too low, and his body smashed into the sea a short distance from his plane.

By six in the afternoon all the unloading was completed and all ships except one ready to get out into the open sea to avoid being caught in such restricted waters by the Jap bombers who were sure to come with darkness. The one exception was an LST which had stuck its nose too far up the beach and with the falling tide was unable to back clear. From the Convoy Commander came a signal for the Pawnee to stay behind and attempt to pull it off, while the rest of the convoy headed out to sea and home some four hundred miles to the eastward. It wasn't a pleasant assignment for us but then our assignments seldom were, so we steamed in as close as we could, dropped our anchor to hold us steady and commenced the difficult job of passing a heavy towing cable in to the stranded vessel. By nine o'clock we had it hooked up and in the inky blackness, the moon wouldn't be rising until after eleven, commenced taking a strain. And of course it had to be then, when we were held immoveable by our anchor leading forward and the tow wire leading aft, that the Jap planes appeared on the scene. They came in low in a search for the lately departed convoy and the 90 millimeter A.A. guns on the beach opened up with an ear splitting din and the giant searchlights swung lower and lower in [an] attempt to locate the planes. Maybe they did, I don't know, we were illuminated from stem to stern and completely blinded by their glare, and bombs could have dropped within spitting distance without us knowing it[,] so shaken and deafened were we by the guns blasting in our faces. It was most unpleasant while it lasted and we were all mildly surprised to find ourselves still in one piece when it was all over.

We tugged and we chugged, breaking one tow wire and having to do the arduous job of passing another wire all over again, but at midnite that damned LST was still firmly aground. We had just decided to secure operations until high tide at 2: A.M. [*sic*] when we received a dispatch to leave the LST there and high-tail it out to sea and make contact the following afternoon with another Bougainville convoy. Ordinarily steaming out to sea alone in an area so thickly infested with enemy subs, ships, and planes wouldn't have appealed to us at all, but after our recent experiences it didn't seem to matter a hell of a lot, so we hauled in our tow wire (to the accompaniment of some terrific squa[w]ks from the LST which didn't mind being left behind but definitely didn't want to be left helpless on the beach)[,] threaded our way out the coral reef studded entrance to the Bay, and headed east thru the darkness. Far ahead of us we could see the red flash of A.A. bursts in the sky where our recent convoy companions were once more being attack[ed], and soon astern of us the A.A. fire opened up from the spot we had just quitted, but we evidently had been leading a pure life and dawn found us well on our way and unmolested. About that time I remembered I hadn't had any sleep for several days so turned in and played dead until noon.

[George is describing, with typical flair and color, the adventures of Task Group 31.6, a reinforcement echelon for the Marines at Cape Toro-kina. His account has some pungent details I was not able to include in my account of this operation (*"We Will Stand by You,"* pp. 139–45.) Since we were standing condition 2 watches or were at general quarters most of the time, I was largely confined to the radio shack, and had to augment my memories with eyewitness accounts by shipmates. But I was able to check Morison and other naval historians for facts George could not have known. The brittle old *McKean,* for example, suffered heavy casualties, sixty-four crewmen and fifty-two marines lost, when she was torpedoed by a Japanese Betty in what the Japanese called the "Fifth Air Battle of Bougainville." The *McKean* had been converted to a "high-speed transport" from one of the oldest of the World War I-era destroyers, DD-90.]

At present ["Nov. '43"] my idea of heaven isn't a place where there are lots of beautiful women, free drinks, and Guy Lombardo's orchestra. Just give me the job of skippering a ship in a non-blacked out area with lots of navigational lights and not a coral reef within a thousand miles. If I ever get to the point of cutting paper dolls it won't be because of Jap subs or bombers, what drives me nuts is the necessity of picking my way through these poorly charted groups of islands in pitch blackness, and most of our operations are at night. When the fathometer shows a hundred fathoms of water under us, then fifty and then twenty and we still can't see a damn thing in front of us (no radar on Pawnee) and don't know whether we're merely passing over a shallow spot in the channel or are heading right for a reef, and don't know whether to continue on and risk the loss of a couple of million bucks worth of ship I'm solely responsible for, and don't even know whether there is room to turn and still clear the islands that you know are close on either side in the darkness, well it's slightly nerve-racking to say the least.

All continues as usual, lots of work, little play and I seem to have recovered completely from the malaria I picked up on Guadalcanal. Only physical oddity due to the rather strenuous life I've been leading is the callouses on the insides of my knees where they frequently knock together. I haven't even a smidgeon of hell left in me, it's all been scared out of me on various occasions.

For all men desirous of a glamorous yet safe career in the Navy I have some definite advice, by all means steer clear of auxillary [*sic*] vessels of the Pawnee type. But for the maximum amount of time far removed from the combat zone, and frequent opportunities to impress the Gentler Sex with your natty dress whites, pick a fighting ship, preferably a battleship. In a year and a half in this benighted area my whites are still virginal, alas.

[A few Navymen may not appreciate his advice, employing the ironic humor he favored, to avoid ships of the *Pawnee* type in favor of combatants, preferably battleships. But nearly all must agree that his delightful candor, coupled with a good reporter's powers of observation and the instincts of a born seaman who almost never made a questionable decision, make his journal a rewarding and pleasurable reading experience.]

Jan. 1944
FROM: COM TWELFTH NAV. DIST.
TO: LT. CDR. F.J.G.
SUBJ.:   CHANGE OF DUTY

LTCOM FJG HEREBY DETACHED PRESENT DUTY PROCEED NAPA CALIF. REPORT TEMPORARY CEO CHAIN ARS 20 AND DUTY ON BOARD WHEN COMMISSIONED AS CO

When George left the ship on the morning of 7 January 1944, some two dozen crewmen assembled in the mess hall and along the starboard weather passageway to see him off. Quartermaster Bill Miller stepped out to lead them in the traditional but now rare three cheers. I was taken by surprise but glad to join the others on the second and third "Hip hip hooray!"

When Lt. Frank Dilworth was relieved of his command, he was presented with an emotional letter of appreciation and a farewell gift to which all hands, including officers, gladly subscribed. We felt that our fine commissioning skipper had been made a scapegoat by a Navy that previously had not even pretended to possess the expertise to accomplish difficult salvage operations. These problems had been turned over to firms such as Merritt, Chapman & Scott Corp. on a "no-cure, no-pay" basis. The Navy did not even have a salvage manual.

George was too remote from his crew to command that kind of hail and farewell. But he had presented us a gift of a far different order. The commands passed down through Chief Quartermaster Earl Clark from the flying bridge during the torpedo attack on the night of 30 June may have saved all of us. Even then we needed more, which some crewmen attributed to luck and a few of the more religious ones to Divine Providence. One of the torpedoes fired at us by the PT boats of Lt. Comdr. Robert B. Kelly was aimed squarely amidships. Instead of blowing us out of the water, it had either "kissed the keel" or otherwise failed to detonate. In the final analysis we had George to thank, with an assist from our Navy's notoriously defective torpedoes.

Lt. Comdr. Flavius J. George was indeed a happy choice by Commander South Pacific for *Pawnee*'s grueling and hazardous runs up the Slot and Blanche Channel. The lesser men who followed him were a constant reminder of the qualities of leadership he possessed and they lacked. One was a martinet of a Mustang who tried, I say with only mild exaggeration, to run the *Pawnee* like a battleship. The other, a Reserve of loud voice and coarse manner, was a blustering bully.

The other eight officers were an eclectic mix of wartime Reserves ("ninety-day wonders," sometimes relabeled "ninety-day blunders" by the crew) and old-line warrant officers. I used to wonder about the subjects of their wardroom conversations. What do men talk about who have nothing in common but a ship and a war?

For the enlisted men of the *Pawnee* the subjects of common interest fell into a few clear categories. Girls. Drinking. Liberties they had made. Their hometowns. Their families, "sweethearts," and wives (for the few who were married). Their (expletive deleted) officers with their chickenshit regulations. The States. Girls.

The sailors were more or less typical of wartime rosters. They were drawn from all parts of the country, with the eleven states of the former Confederacy over-represented, only a few from the Atlantic Seaboard, and the other sections of the country represented in roughly equal proportions to their populations. The exception was California. My home state was given as the "place of enlistment" in the commissioning roster by a number of men who were originally from other states but had shipped over in the Regular Navy at San Francisco. Their years of service had so homogenized their accents that it was hard to determine places of origin.

In the segregated Navy of wartime, the *Pawnee* seamen, firemen and petty officers were all white except for Signalman J. K. "Papoose" Evans and George Tahbone, American Indians. The government had reason to remember the martial prowess of our native Americans; they were welcome (as enlisted men) in all the armed forces.

Ethnically, the backgrounds were diverse. We had one Greek- and one Armenian-American (Aronis and Aposhian, respectively), but no Jews. There were four Italian-Americans in the commissioning and early 1943 crew: Beli, Laraiso, Narducci, Ortalano. The clearest indication of the failure of the national "melting pot" is that designations by race or nationality are still widely used to distinguish one group of Americans from another.

Several Slavic races were represented: Aristonic (changed to Harris), Bozynski, Figlewicz, Penovich, Primozich.

Irish-American names were common: Brady, Buckley, Day, Driscoll, Higgins, Mahoney, Murphy, O'Donnell, Ragan. Other names indicated Celtic backgrounds: Campbell, Clark, Hughes, McGovern, Walsh.

But most of the eighty-five men of the crew had Anglo-Saxon, Nordic, or Teutonic antecedents: Bell, Byron, Howard, Saxon, Spooner, Swan, Smith, Stone; Englehardt, Erickson, Hansen, Newman; Gerber, Heinrich, Miller, Schmidt, Zahn. "Pappy" Schmidt was the oldest man in the crew at forty and one of the best-liked. The youngest was fifteen; he claimed he had forged the date on his birth certificate. Since he was built like a wrestler and was not at all averse to using his 200 pounds to intimidate smaller seamen, we joked that some judge had given him the choice of enlisting in the Navy or going to reform school.

The *Pawnee* was provided with four officer's servants: two cooks, a steward's mate, and a mess attendant. In the commissioning crew, two were Filipino and two were black (Negro or "colored" in the language of the day). The ratio was soon changed to one Filipino and three blacks when the mess attendant ran amok with a knife, screaming imprecations in Tagalog. He was subdued and sent to the brig in the destroyer tender *Dixie*. Since he had been headed for the crew's quarters, one of the mess-hall humorists asked, "What's he got against us? It's a dumb shit who doesn't know who his enemies are!"

In his journal, George commented that "we almost invariably traveled alone at night and developed quite a fatalistic attitude concerning our chances of being torpedoed or bombed." He was using an editorial "we" to which many members of the crew subscribed, reducing the doctrine of stoic submission to fate to phrases such as "It wasn't our time, that's all," and "When your number comes up, that's it." I preferred Shakespeare's more elegant, "If it be now, 'tis not to come; if it be not to come, it will be now . . . the readiness is all."

But the men of the *Pawnee* read little beyond pulp fiction, comic books, and courses for advancement in rating. Traditionally, men at war have had two escapes from the trenchant reality that other men were trying to kill them: alcohol and sex. In the South Pacific there was little or no liquor; the supply was tightly controlled by the officers, as George's journal demonstrates. The other great escape was largely unavailable, as well. The nurses, as I have pointed out, were off-limits to enlisted men. The only port *Pawnee* visited in 1943 was Noumea, where the French women were sequestered until the sailors and soldiers were safely off the streets, which was well before dark. The one outlet for contact with the opposite sex was the Pink House, which many men of sensitivity disdained because of its demeaning regimentation: stand in line, surrender your I.D. card, pay your five dollars, spend a few minutes with a prostitute probably not of your race, take a full-service prophylaxis before your I.D. was returned.

Without the comforts of liquor and feminine companionship, living sterile and spartan lives, we depended upon mail from home to make our sacrifices tenable. The infrequent mail calls, bringing letters, packages, and periodicals from relatives and friends, were vital to our morale. (I describe a typical mail call on pages 100–108 of *"We Will Stand by You."*) We had allowed ourselves to be reduced to service numbers and ratings, answering to a last name only while required to address anyone with gold braid as "mister," subjected not only to the possibility of sudden death but also the surety of the whims of commanders; we had agreed to this for one reason only: defense of country. The personal letters from that country were the proof that we amounted to something, after all. Back there in town or county, people cared about us as individuals, prayed for our safe return. For that little time we could surmount the regimented present, what Jean Cocteau, the French man of letters, termed "the conspiracy of the plural against the singular." We were of value, defending something of value!

Few crewmen had any clear conception of what the war was about beyond "Remember Pearl Harbor!" We would avenge the unprovoked attack on Pearl Harbor by killing as many Japs as possible before dictating the peace terms in Tokyo. The conflict with Germany was a byproduct, necessary because Hitler had an alliance with Japan and had foolishly declared war on us. The plight of European Jewry was not even considered. We were told little about the concentration camps and nothing about Hitler's campaign to exterminate the Jews. Our purpose was admirably summed up by one crewman who wanted action against the enemy, not to win glory and medals, but so "we can get this shit over with and go home."

The terror that occasionally resulted from our role as seagoing litter-bearers of the Solomons was a fact each man had to confront in his own fashion. In the long intervals between, all had to find ways of dealing with the awful tedium.

With few exceptions everyone smoked cigarettes. "Doc" Ortalano sold them from his Ship's Service cubicle just abaft the mess hall for fifty cents a carton. We sensed but didn't know that they were bad for one's health. After a midwatch and general quarters, during which I would consume more than half a pack of cigarettes and many cups of coffee, I went to breakfast with an upset stomach, a scratchy throat, and the taste of old sweat socks in my mouth, but I didn't even consider quitting. All the film stars smoked, lighting up on all occasions; it gave them something to do with their hands. All the admirals and generals smoked. The scuttlebutt was that Halsey didn't trust anyone who didn't smoke, drink, and chase girls. The president himself smoked; a long cigarette holder was his trademark. The full-color advertisements in the magazines from home (except for *Time* magazine, which was printed in a lightweight overseas edition with no ads) told us that there wasn't "a cough in a carload," and that "I'd walk a mile for a Camel!" Few considered the hidden message in the latter slogan: cigarettes were so highly addictive that a smoker in the grip of his habit would walk a good deal farther than that to get one. Even if we had been advised that cigarettes could cause lung cancer, emphysema, and heart disease, we probably would have shrugged. That possibility was in the future; our need was to relieve the constant tension in the present.

Coffee was the universal Navy stimulant; the large stainless steel urn in the passageway outside the galley was never allowed to run dry. One of the cooks made a fresh supply before turning in to sustain men standing evening and early morning watches. The radioman relieving the watch at 2345 or at 0345 brought a handle-less Navy mug of joe with him. Since he couldn't leave the radio shack on the first super-structure deck—the Fox schedule broadcast from Pearl Harbor ran continuously, twenty-four hours a day—a bridge messenger brought refills.

Even in the steamy heat of the New Hebrides and the Solomons, most of us drank hot coffee in preference to soft drinks. The resulting perspiration, we averred, purged the system of the accumulated poisons from our awful diet of dehydrated eggs and potatoes, canned fruits and vegetables, and "ox meat" or "goat meat" (by the time it got to us you could not tell what animals the Australians and New Zealanders had slaughtered). This dietary cleansing made it necessary to daily take salt tablets from the dispenser located above the mess hall scuttlebutt.

Whenever we were in a port such as Espiritu Santo or Noumea that was largely free from the threat of air attack, we saw movies on the *Pawnee*'s fantail or on a repair ship to which we were moored. Looking at the comparatively few which have survived the decades (many were so bad that not even the Nostalgia channel dares to show them today), it is obvious that the Hollywood moguls produced them with war propaganda uppermost in their minds. They presented an Alice-in-Wonderland world of super-heroism, maudlin sentimental love, and simplistic endings, a world largely devoid of the reality of death (except for the enemy); devoid, too, of ethical or intellectual content.

Several war films we saw displayed the simple heroics of such macho actors as John Wayne (*Flying Tigers*) and Humphrey Bogart (*Action in the North Atlantic*). Aware that Wayne and Bogart had never heard a shot fired in anger, since they fought their battles on Hollywood sound stages, we watched with some skepticism, joking that if only the War Department would send them to the Pacific, they would clean out the Japs in no time. On the other hand, we could only admire handsome Tyrone Power. After starring as an American soldier discovering love and courage with Britisher Joan Fontaine in *This Above All*, he went off to the wars for real (as did Clark Gable and Jimmy Stewart).

When they weren't killing the enemy, the heroes of Hollywood found time for romance; they were usually officers whom women couldn't resist. But the love story prospered even in civilian clothes. In *Strawberry Blonde*, a period piece, James Cagney is enamored of gold digger Rita Hayworth but marries Olivia de Haviland. *Girl Trouble* involves Don Ameche and Joan Bennett in business and love. In another shallow romance, *Powers Girl*, Anne Shirley tries to become a member of the then-famous modeling school. The cynics among us wondered what cozy arrangement between the studio and the firm netted ninety minutes of free advertising. In *Slightly Dangerous*, Lana Turner is a waitress who claims a wealthy father; upward mobility, usually by misrepresentation, was a common theme of these romances.

But the favorite films of servicemen were the lavish musicals, which featured a maximum exposure of flesh by stars such as Betty Grable and

Alice Faye, minimum plots, dialog laced with double entendres, and the swing music of such band leaders as Glenn Miller, Harry James and Benny Goodman. *Alexander's Ragtime Band, Coney Island,* and *Springtime in the Rockies* can still be seen and enjoyed today on cable channels such as AMC.

Many of the films we saw, sitting on hard mess benches behind the officers in their comfortable wardroom chairs, have sunk to a richly deserved oblivion. Examples were *Ranger Bandit,* with Tim Holt in a tall white hat; *What's Buzzin', Cousin?* with Ann Miller, whose dancing skills far exceeded her acting ability and the talent of her screenwriters; and *Pardon My Sarong,* where we expected Dorothy Lamour, a Navy favorite, and got instead the low buffoonery of Abbott and Costello.

Deprived of the carnal reality, some sailors needed more than the occasional film to nourish their fantasy lives. They kept large color photographs of movie stars and other "love goddesses"—American versions of Aphrodite and Venus, the Greek and Roman ideals of erotic love—Scotch-taped inside their locker doors. Betty Grable was a favorite, especially in the famous pose that displayed her trim derriere and "million-dollar legs," allegedly insured for that amount by Lloyd's of London. Two others were Rita Hayworth, nee Cansino, a tall, sultry, once-brunette dancer become red-haired film star; and Carole Landis, a statuesque blonde actress. But the all-time favorite was model Chili Williams, who posed for *Life* magazine in a two-piece polka-dot swimsuit that revealed a hint of a vertical indentation at the crotch. Sex-starved servicemen besieged the publication for copies of the photo.

I thought it foolish to lust after women I didn't have a remote chance of meeting, let alone seducing. I consoled myself with the unpopular observations that Grable seemed a trifle coarse and common, that Hayworth was too tall and didn't look too bright, and that Chili Williams's physical equipment, while impressive, was standard for her sex.

This was all sour grapes, the rationalization of the fox in Aesop's fable that scorned the grapes it couldn't reach. Nonetheless, I swore that the object of my veneration, should I be lucky enough to survive the war, would be a real flesh-and-blood woman who compared favorably with the celluloid and paper images of my shipmates' carnal desire. They said, "Fat chance, Mason!" and went on taping pin-up photos in their lockers and fantasizing how great Grable or Hayworth or Williams would be "in the sack."

(In Sacramento in the 1950s I did find such a woman. She cared for me, but cared more to practice the "conspicuous consumption" of American economist-sociologist Thorstein Veblen, author of *The Theory of the Leisure Class*. In other words, my rival was rich.)

In a war theater where "friendly fire" could pose as great a danger as did the Imperial Japanese Navy, peace of mind might be achieved through a strong religious faith. Alas, few of us possessed such a belief. Three notable exceptions were Yeoman Le Roy Zahn, Motor Machinist's Mate Doyle Saxon, and Steward's Mate A. Head, an ordained minister. (In "*We Will Stand by You*," pp. 88–89, I describe the remarkable, unsolicited burial service Head performed for the dead of *LST-342* at Oloana Bay, earning the respect of the entire crew.)

In the place of an abiding faith, some of us turned to magic: amulets and talismans we hoped would place a shield of protection around us. The Catholics, I felt, were more fortunate in this respect than the Protestants, for they had their rosary beads and St. Christopher's medals as tangible evidences of a caring Divinity. To be sure, I had the King James version of the Bible and *Science and Health*, by Mary Baker Eddy, in weatherproof vest-pocket editions provided by the Christian Science Church. Since I smoked, drank, and otherwise violated the strict tenets of the religion in which I had been raised, I could derive only limited comfort there.

I also kept in my locker the collected works of Shakespeare and the *Rubáiyát of Omar Khayyám*. But the bard of Avon seemed inclined toward fatalism: "We owe God a death. . . . He that dies this year is quit for the next." It was a philosophy perfectly understandable for an Elizabethan society in which life was, in the words of Thomas Hobbes, "solitary, poor, nasty, brutish, and short"—uncomfortably similar to what mine promised to be. Khayyám recommended turning away from religion for a jug of wine and a woman singing at one's side, advice I happily would have taken had I not been deprived of both escapes.

I did have two talismans. One was a heavy silver identification bracelet that I had purchased in San Francisco while serving in the *Pennsylvania*. I wore it most of the time, preferring it to the mundane dogtag; everyone in the Navy had one of those. If it became necessary to identify me, let it be with a piece of jewelry.

The charm in which I placed most confidence was the photo of Bertha Morton, childhood sweetheart and lost love, which I kept in my billfold. It had gone with me through the corrupted waters of Pearl Harbor, through a Blanche Channel swimming with torpedoes aimed at my ship, through many other encounters on the razor's edge. The photo of that lovely, laughing face, half-Cherokee, would go wherever destiny took me, home to the States or full fathoms deep in the trackless Pacific.

We must not leave the South Pacific Theater without an *envoi*. It belongs neither with Michener's fictional war nor with the earnestly real one of Captain George and the crew of the *Pawnee*, but casts the light of ironic commentary on both. I will let Dr. Arthur G. King relate his marvelous true tale of the South Pacific, "Take Her Out and Shoot Her":

One day in 1943 on Espiritu Santo in the New Hebrides, the commanding general of the base stopped at my table when he came into the mess hall for lunch. I was the Surgeon of the command, a member of his staff, and of course stood up as he thundered:

"Do you know an Army nurse named —— ——?"

When I responded affirmatively, he snapped: "Tomorrow at noon you will report to me that she is no longer on the island. That is all."

Right after lunch I consulted the chief of staff, Col. John H. Allen, USA, a close friend of long standing. When I asked him what it was all about, his reply was: "Take her out on the beach, shoot her, bury her, and the Army will never bother you about it."

This startling order and promise of immunity, even though patently hyperbolic, stirred my curiosity. There were only 23 hours left before I had to report to the general the accomplishment of a mission the reason for which I knew nothing.

This nurse was a little older than most of the others, very efficient, and most attractive and sophisticated. Somehow, probably through junior Army and Navy officers, she had met an admiral and charmed him. His headquarters when ashore was on another island (New Caledonia), and she had acted as his hostess whenever he entertained civilian officials and their wives. The Army had cooperated with him by placing her on temporary duty at a dispensary away from her assigned hospital to give her more time and freedom. Then one day she was transferred to Espiritu Santo, where she was reassigned for regular hospital duty. She very quickly had a host of young officers of both Army and Navy at her feet.

On the day of this episode the admiral was scheduled to fly to our island for a conference with the top brass of both services. The mission and the flight were supposed to be ultrasecret because only a few weeks earlier a Japanese admiral had been shot down [Isoroku Yamamoto, killed at Bougainville on 18 April 1943], and it was anticipated that a revenge effort would be made by the Japanese intelligence. No one was supposed to have known of the place, day or time of the conference, and only at the last minute were a few designated officers assembled at the airstrip. There were a half-dozen one- or two-star generals and flag officers, two captains of the Navy and five or six Army colonels including my friend the chief of staff. To insure secrecy no one below that rank was present.

As the Navy plane descended to the runway and taxied to the selected revetment, the officers walked slowly to the plane. It stopped and the admiral descended the short ladder. Suddenly, with perfect timing, there drove into the revetment a jeep out of which stepped the Army nurse. At about the same moment all the high-ranking officers came to a salute which they held awaiting the admiral's return salute.

The admiral, however, distracted by the dramatic arrival of the automobile, turned toward it and did not see the officers. He put his arms around the nurse and kissed her while the officers held their salute. In only a second he recognized the situation, dropped her and returned the salute. She quickly regained the jeep and drove away. . . .

Our commanding general was infuriated by the humiliation of his staff and of the Navy brass in holding a salute while an Army nurse was being kissed. Hence his orders for me to have her off the island within 24 hours and the suggestion of the chief of staff to shoot her. . . .

A telephone call to the hospital had her relieved from duty and held in the office of the chief nurse until my arrival. A thoroughly scared but remarkably poised young woman asked pleadingly: "What are they going to do to me?" I told her what my orders were, but not the added suggestion, and pointed out that the easiest way of getting an individual off the island was as a critically ill patient. Being a nurse she was able very quickly to give me her medical history and the findings of previous examinations. Her only previous hospital admission had been for some obscure gall-bladder crisis, never completely diagnosed.

While she was packing I approached the commanding officer of the hospital and discussed medicine and administrative procedures with him. Of the episode I told him I was completely in the dark, as was everyone else on the island, that it was something very hush-hush, but that I had my orders from the commanding general to see that the girl was evacuated to the States immediately. The hospital C.O. considered himself a man of the world, and with a knowing smirk, nodded: "I think I understand, and of course the true diagnosis has to be kept quiet." He promised me complete cooperation but then startled me with his final remark: "I never thought our general was that good; more power to the old boy."

It was no trick for us to write up a fake history, examination and laboratory report, together with a recommendation for immediate evacuation directly to the United States because of acute, complicated gall-bladder disease. The hospital C.O. signed the necessary medical document but left the administrative details to me. A telephone call to the chief of staff produced mimeographed, signed copies of an order for immediate evacuation to the United States.

The real problem was finding a plane which would depart before noon the next day. I was told that there was one leaving for the United States at 2300 hours that night, but it was full. When it was explained that the patient was a nurse who might die in 48 hours, the dispatcher said he would gladly bump a Marine Corps lieutenant-colonel to make room for her.

The nurse had been forbidden to use any telephone to say good-bye to anyone. Supper trays were brought to the office of the chief nurse who nearly died of unsatisfied curiosity. While waiting till it was time to leave for the airstrip, I felt the full force of the culprit-patient's persuasive personality and sensed her consummate skill. She asked seductively: "Do we really have to go through all this?" and I thought seriously of the advice to take her out and shoot her. In the jeep on the way to the plane she started to cry that she didn't want to leave all her many friends, but I felt it was just technique, and did not even offer her my handkerchief.

At 2200 hours we were at the airstrip right beside the plane, and she had the good sense to pretend she was too sick to walk up the ramp without assistance. As she boarded the plane she had the grace to squeeze my arm and say, "Thank you."

Five minutes later the plane was air-borne and she was indeed off the island. It was with a sense of achievement that when the general came into lunch the next day I was able to stand up, salute and report that the nurse was off the island as directed. He, too, thanked me but asked no questions. No details were ever divulged and the episode was relegated to complete historical obscurity. But it *did* happen just that way.*

*Reprinted with permission from *Vignettes of the South Pacific,* pp. 116–19, with minor excisions and revisions. The identity of the admiral in question, for those who haven't already guessed it: William F. Halsey, commander of all South Pacific forces.

9

Last Hurrah

THE *HOUSTON* TOWAWAY

> Though music oft hath such a charm
> to make bad good, and good provoke to harm.
> —William Shakespeare, *Measure for Measure*

> The ships of the war criminal Halsey have been sunk. . . . You will never see
> your sweethearts and families again.
> —"Tokyo Rose" to CripDiv One

For the crew of the *Pawnee*, the year 1944 began with two unfavorable omens.

The first was the loss of our superb C.O. of the Solomons, Lt. Comdr. Flave George. His replacement was Lt. James S. Lees, a former *Pawnee* executive officer and navigator, a Mustang who was widely disliked in the crew's quarters. In our opinion, he compared unfavorably with George in every way, including shiphandling. On his first time underway in Noumea Harbor, he misjudged the effects of wind and tide and nearly sank *YP-292* while coming alongside. (For the details, see pp. 158–59, *"We Will Stand by You."*)

Even worse, Lees was a man who, as my close friend Don "Flash" Aposhian observed, "Swallowed the book of Navy Regs in the Detention Barracks." He seemed to thrive on this spartan diet; it was the crew that suffered indigestion.

The second loss was nearly as serious for those of us who maintained a belief in the occult powers of amulets and charms. For the first year after her commissioning, *Pawnee* had had a crew member who appeared

186

on no roster, stood no watches, never turned to on ship's work, saluted no officers, ignored all regulations, and was even known to invade the sacrosanct captain's cabin to catch a few winks on his bunk. Despite these lapses in good order and discipline, this unofficial member of the ship's company had the affectionate regard of most of the crew. After our narrow escape from the torpedoes of "PT-boat Kelly" in Blanche Channel she, a female in an all-male world, was considered a good-luck talisman of near-mystic proportions. She was V-6, our mascot.

The short, happy life of V-6, "combat cat," was chronicled by Gunner's Mate Mike Penovich, a plank-owner who served in the *Pawnee* through all our adventures and occasional misadventures in the South and Western Pacific. He writes:

The *Pawnee* was a powerful new salvage and rescue ship which was badly needed in the Solomon Islands. After commissioning, we were ordered to Treasure Island, across the bay from San Francisco, to pick up salvage equipment we needed prior to our departure for the South Pacific.

While returning from liberty one rainy evening a young seaman, Charlie Sellers, happened to pass the T.I. mess hall. Hearing a steady meowing, he found a striped gray kitten huddled against one wall. She was soaking wet and shivering.

As he dried her off with a handkerchief, it occurred to him that the kitten might make a good mascot for the *Pawnee*. But how to get her past the Marine sentry at the gate to the pier? He put her into a pocket of his peacoat, but the kitten continued crying. The best bet, Sellers decided, was to start whistling to cover the mewing.

At the gate the Marine asked him if he knew the two kinds of people who whistle.

"Sure," Sellers replied, remembering his recent boot-camp experiences. "Only damn fools and bosun's mates."

"You're sure no bosun's mate," the sentry replied. "That makes you a damn fool to ride these ships on the ocean. The reason I joined the Marines is simple. I can walk a hell of a lot farther than I can swim."

While the private was chortling at his own humor, Sellers made it through the gate and took the kitten aboard the *Pawnee*. In the forward crew's compartment a number of the young seamen had suggestions about her care. She was given a warm bath in the enlisted men's head on the main deck, dried off with towels and under a hot-air register, and taken to the galley for a bowl of warm milk.

That night she slept in one of the empty bunks. The next morning a cardboard carton was found for a bed, along with a steel spare-parts box.

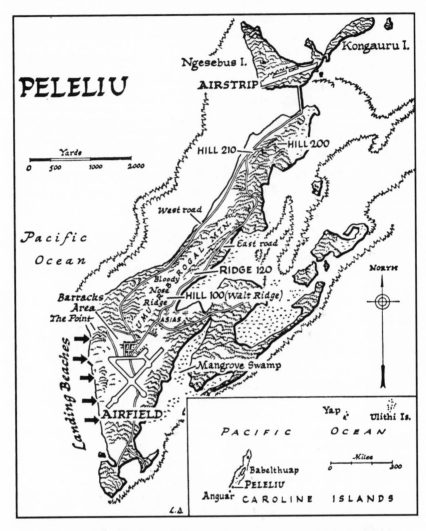

Map of bloody Peleliu, where the unnecessary invasion cost the First Marine Division 3,946 casualties in the first week. Watching the carnage, Mason asked: "Who is controlling the men who control the Pacific Fleet?" (map from E. B. Sledge, *With the Old Breed*)

One of the seamen volunteered to go ashore with a bucket and shovel and find dirt. The bed and "sand box" were stowed alongside the huge towing winch on the fantail, under the break of the boat deck.

The kitten very soon adjusted to shipboard life. She was still too small to jump over the coamings—the raised framework of the water-tight doors between the weather passageways and the mess hall and other main-deck areas—so she would meow until someone lifted her to the other side. Soon learning where the galley was, she sat outside the door and cried until the duty cook opened up and provided food and milk.

When the ship left the States for the South Pacific on 9 December we soon ran out of fresh milk. The cat disliked the powdered skim milk even more than the crew did, refusing to even approach her dish. The only solution was to get her accustomed to canned milk, which she reluctantly did.

Now that she was at least a de facto crew member, she must have a name. Since the seaman who had found her and many others on board were Reserves of the V-6 category, meaning they would serve for the duration of the national emergency plus six months, the name V-6 seemed logical.

V-6 was soon able to jump over the door coamings and to navigate the ladders between decks, so she explored every part of the ship. One day while the captain was ashore, the steward's mate took the opportunity for a field day in his cabin. Not noticing that V-6 had joined him, he locked her in after he finished his work. When Captain Dilworth returned he found V-6 curled up and enjoying a nap on his bunk. The seamen who looked after her fully expected an unwelcome order to get rid of her, but nothing happened. V-6 now had official sanction as our mascot.

As *Pawnee* approached the equator on our long passage to Espiritu Santo in the New Hebrides towing *ARD-5*, a floating dry dock, the steel weather decks became too hot for V-6's sensitive paws. She soon found a way to cool off. When the crew knocked off ship's work at 1700 hours and took their toilet gear to the head, she was waiting for them. Sitting by one of the stall showers, she meowed until a sailor took her into the water with him. She would stay until she was soaking wet, jump out, shake herself vigorously, and join the men in the mess hall, crew compartments, or on the fantail.

On a day of exceptional warmth and humidity, V-6 suddenly started running at top speed from the fantail toward the bow. Someone yelled that she had gone mad in the heat, so everyone got out of her way. After several laps around the main deck, a bosun's mate saw no frothing at the mouth. He threw a towel over her as she skidded around a corner and took her to sick bay. "Doc" Ortalano, our chief pharmacist's mate, examined her and could find nothing wrong. His advice: put her in the shower to cool off.

By the time V-6 was six months old we were spending time at Tulagi Harbor, across "Iron Bottom Sound" from Guadalcanal. The water was so clear you could see the Japanese float planes which were destroyed in our carrier air raids of 4 May 1942. When we held swimming call, V-6 would be handed down to one of the swimmers, where she enjoyed paddling around. One day, however, the shark lookout saw her being carried to sea on the outgoing tide. The whaleboat was called out, and a thoroughly scared cat was scooped from the water.

The seamen decided she must have a life preserver. Two bosun's mates—G. R. ("Stinky") Higgins and C. B. Wilson—fashioned one from pieces of an old life jacket, using a sail needle. She would then be tied into her jacket, with a safety line attached, and lowered over the side to swim with the sailors. When she was brought back on board she would be given a shower to wash all the salt from her fur. V-6 was an exception to the rule that cats don't like water; she was a true sea-going cat!

In one respect V-6 was typical: she didn't like dogs. Taking on fuel for our four diesel engines one day in Purvis Bay, Florida Island, we tied up alongside the *Rail,* a World War I minesweeper which had been converted to an ATO (old ocean tug). The *Rail* had her own mascot, a nondescript mongrel. The dog and V-6, sitting on opposite bitts used in towing, sized each other up. The dog extended a friendly paw. Although she had never seen a dog, she recognized an enemy and began spitting and growling, with arched back. When the unwary dog came closer, she sprang at him with slashing claws, leaving him yelping and bleeding from his tender nose.

On the night of 30 June 1943 we were sent into Blanche Channel to take the crippled transport *McCawley* in tow. I was on the bridge inspecting our starboard 20-mm. gun when I saw a torpedo track approaching the ship. I yelled out, "Torpedo on the starboard bow!" The captain, who was on the flying bridge, responded, "Very well."

As I started down the ladder to the boat deck, I saw a second torpedo cross our stern. Looking over the water, I saw a third one coming at us from amidships. The next thing I saw was the *McCawley*'s bridge engulfed in flame as she went down. It seemed unbelievable that such a large ship could disappear beneath the waves in 33 seconds.

Some of the crew were in the mess hall drinking coffee during the attack; V-6 was among them. (There had been no time to sound general quarters.) Suddenly V-6 jumped into the air, all the hairs on her back standing straight up. She let out a screech and raced down the passageway which led aft to the fantail. Since we were in a darken-ship condition, the door was closed. V-6 scratched at the door, growling loudly, until someone undogged the door and let her out.

Afterward, we decided that she must have heard the torpedo which passed under the ship, probably "kissing the keel." An electrician's mate standing watch at the power panel also heard the torpedo. Our almost miraculous escape from destruction confirmed her value to the crew as a truly lucky mascot.

In November, five months later, she earned another reputation, this time as a "combat cat." We were approaching Empress Augusta Bay in the early morning hours of 17 November with a reinforcement echelon for the Marines at Cape Torokina, Bougainville. We were expecting an air attack, but since we lacked a radar at that time, we had no way of knowing where the enemy planes were.

My gun station was between the two 20-mm. cannons at the aft end of the boat, or 0-1, deck. Adams, a shipfitter from Chicago, mentioned that cats were able to see and hear very well at night. Another sailor suggested that we use V-6 as a possible "early warning system." We kept a large welding machine between the port and starboard guns, which proved an ideal lookout spot for V-6. Adams and I kept an eye on the cat to see which way she was looking.

Suddenly she started looking dead astern and following something coming up on the port quarter. Our phone talker reported "Plane astern!" to the bridge as we watched a Japanese Betty bomber coming in on a low-level attack. The seaman-gunner had never fired his 20-millimeter at night, so I got behind him to help him lead the plane through the ring sights, hoping it would run into a stream of explosive shells when we squeezed the trigger. Unfortunately, the Betty passed out of the range of our guns—but V-6 had spotted it for us. She also spotted another plane which was brought down by one of our escorting destroyers.

[Note: Some of our petty officers scoffed at these early-warning claims for V-6, but Penovich and Adams swore they were the truth. (For a fuller account of this air attack, during which the destroyer-transport *McKean* was sunk, see "*We Will Stand by You*," pp. 140–42.)]

We returned to Purvis Bay in December and again moored to the *Rail*. V-6 and the ATO's mascot sat on the bitts, glaring at each other this time. Very early the next morning we were ordered out on a routine salvage job. It was only after we got under way that we missed V-6; she was nowhere to be found.

We returned a couple of days later, again moored alongside the *Rail*. Very concerned about our mascot, we checked with her sailors. They thought she might have come aboard before we shoved off. When they tied up to the fuel pier, she may have wandered from the *Rail* into the jungle. A couple of sailors scoured the areas where she might have gone but could not find her.

It will never be known if the *Rail*'s mascot, remembering his bleeding nose, chased V-6 off his ship into the jungle, or if she simply decided to conduct her own reconnaissance. She was really missed, for she was a morale booster and a fine mascot.*

For the next eight months *Pawnee* was principally involved in what I have summarized as "a pot-pourri of piddling pursuits." The few highlights were the hurricane of 18 January 1944 at Noumea, where we rescued several ships that had gone aground; a week of R & R in Sydney, long after the one promised to Captain George for our stellar performance in the Solomons; and our participation in the bloodless invasion of Emirau in the St. Matthias Group. In late March, our Task Group 31.2 landed the Fourth Marine Regiment (First Provisional Brigade) on Emirau's Homestead Plantation Beach. This unopposed invasion closed a circle of steel around the enemy stronghold of Rabaul, breaching the formidable barrier of the Bismarck Archipelago and breaking into the Caroline Islands, which guarded the approaches to the Philippines. There followed five months of mopping-up duties around the Solomons, all of which I have described in detail in Chapters Nine through Twelve of *"We Will Stand by You."*

During this period of ennui made nearly unbearable by the petty harassment of the *Pawnee* captain and his executive officer, Lt. H. C. Cramer (whom we soon gave the nickname "Horse Cock" for his loud harangues of the crew at the daily quarters for muster), we had but few outlets. I have commented upon the importance of letters and papers from home and the films we saw in a previous chapter. While few read the books in the ship's library, or the free Armed Services Editions of novels and non-fiction, both contemporary and classical, everyone responded to popular music. It was the principal programming of Armed Forces Radio, which was now operating stations throughout the South Pacific. From the all-wave receiver mounted above the operator's position in the radio shack, the broadcasts were piped to speakers in the crew's quarters, mess hall, and wardroom.

Some of the music was cornball-patriotic, intended mainly for the folks back home: "Remember Pearl Harbor March," "The Japs Don't Have a Chinaman's Chance" (thereby denigrating two Oriental races—one foe, one friend—in one title), and "The Ballad of Roger Young,"

---

*"V-6, Combat Cat," unpublished manuscript by Mike Penovich. Reprinted with permission, with revisions and excisions. Did curiosity kill the cat, some of us wondered, or was it her ancient enemy? (For another vignette of V-6, see *"We Will Stand by You,"* pp. 91–93.)

honoring the Medal of Honor winner who had died charging a Japanese machine-gun nest in the Solomons. When we heard the "Roger Young" lyrics, which included the line, "On the island of New Guinea in the Solomons," we hooted our scorn. Frank Loesser—who also wrote "Praise the Lord and Pass the Ammunition," as well as the equally hokey "They're Either Too Young or Too Old"—hadn't bothered either to read Young's citation or to look at a map: the island was New Georgia, which the crew of the *Pawnee* had good reason to remember.

The music most favored by the men was sentimental and nostalgic, with decidedly sexual implications: "I Had the Craziest Dream," "One for My Baby, and One More for the Road," "You'll Never Know," "You'd Be So Nice to Come Home To," "I'll Never Smile Again," and another prewar favorite with a delicious irony for the world of 1944: "I Don't Want to Set the World on Fire." A perennial favorite, regardless of season, was Bing Crosby singing Irving Berlin's "White Christmas," whose theme line was cleverly parodied as, "I'm dreaming of a white mistress." Only schmaltz which is gloriously bad lends itself to such mimicry.

As the "Dear John" letters began arriving (described on pages 107–8 of *"We Will Stand by You"*), some hit songs assumed a bitter reality not intended in the pristine world of wartime radio, "Where seldom is heard a discouraging word," to borrow a line from "Home on the Range." They included "Don't Sit Under the Apple Tree With Anyone Else but Me," "I'll Walk Alone," "There Will Never Be Another You," "As Time Goes By" (sung by Dooley Wilson in *Casablanca*—the tune expressed an honest sentiment in a dishonest film, Aposhian and I thought), and the truly downbeat and therefore exceptional "Somebody Else Is Taking My Place."

Neither the government nor the Navy could provide any philosophical reason for fighting beyond "Uncle-Sam-needs-you" patriotism, the "Mom-and-apple-pie" appeals of meretricious advertising, and revenge for our early defeats. In the Pacific an added factor was widespread and virulent racial prejudice, typified by Admiral Halsey's famous sign at Tulagi: "KILL JAPS, KILL JAPS. / KILL MORE JAPS. / You will help to kill the yellow / bastards if you do your job well." Consequently, World War II produced no flag-waving music such as the First World War's "Over There." The nearest thing to an Allied song, American and British, was perhaps the rollicking "Beer Barrel Polka" of 1939, where "rolling out the barrel" supposedly put "the blues on the run." If there had been any barrel of beer to roll out, the crew of the *Pawnee* would have been in hearty agreement. In the grim, nonalcoholic South Pacific, we derived what comfort we could from "Bell Bottom Trousers" (especially the unexpurgated version, known to only a few of the "old salts"), and that raucous updating of the Frankie and Johnny legend, "Pistol-Packin' Mama (Lay That Pistol Down)."

In that context I was occasionally asked to recite the bawdy parody of Robert Service's "The Shooting of Dan McGrew," author anonymous, which I had learned from my best friend of the *California*, M. G. Johnson. It began, "A bunch of the boys were whooping it up in one of the Yukon halls, / And the kid who handled the music box was steadily scratching his balls. . . ." and rapidly ascended the scale of obscenity. These recitations were usually for a select group of close friends—Don Aposhian, Dale Gerber, and Al Schleppi—when we assembled in the shaft alley with a can of grapefruit juice and a supply of 180-proof alcohol that Aposhian had managed to liberate from the supplies for his gyrocompass. In the seclusion of the long, narrow passageway housing the propeller shaft, the potent "alky highballs" soon had us telling tall tales of drinking and conquest, of our week in Sydney, of survival at school and work during the Depression, of plans, usually as grandiose as they were vague, for the postwar period. One plan was elaborated upon in loving detail. We would have a glorious postwar reunion at a lodge on Lake Tahoe in the high Sierra. The two essentials for the reunion would be large stocks of good liquor and bad girls.

For a time we forgot the martinet "Jessie" Lees and his designated S.O.B., "Horse Cock" Cramer. Bathed in perspiration in the stifling confines of the shaft alley, we lost ourselves in fine dreams of a past which was better than it really had been, and a future which would be better than we had any right to expect. All too soon the alcohol had been consumed, and we were obliged to weave a tipsy way to our bunks. At the cost of our hangovers, we had accomplished two things: an increase in camaraderie, and an escape for a little while from duty which, under Lees and Cramer, had become scarcely better than sentences at hard labor in a war zone.

In addition to our own sad love ballads, Armed Forces Radio also played the German enemy's sentimental favorite, "Lili Marlene." Beyond the haunting quality of its music and lyrics, so superior to the output of our "Tin Pan Alley," it was a reminder that the theme of love found and lost all too soon in the exigencies of war was a universal one, shared by friend and foe alike (as I myself had learned during the *Paw-nee*'s brief visit to Sydney).

Since many of our crewmen came from farms and small towns, Western music had a special appeal. The 1940 hit "San Antonio Rose," by Bob Wills and His Texas Playboys (a song I had reason to remember from a Seattle hotel room in December of that year), continued to be popular in the South Pacific. Another favorite was 1941's "Tears on My Pillow," sung in the nasal twang of his native Oklahoma by Gene Autrey, the first of the singing cowboys. Other Autrey hits we heard on Armed Forces Radio were "Mexicali Rose" and "South of the Border (Down Mexico Way)."

Increasingly we heard music that was neither ballad nor typically Western. Ernest Tubb, born in the Texas cotton country near Dallas, pioneered what came to be called the "honky-tonk" style of country music. "Walking the Floor Over You," sung in Tubb's deep baritone to the accompaniment of steel guitars, had special significance for service-men, who well understood the down-to-earth lyrics. Two others with resonance for our deprived lives were Tubb's "Have You Ever Been Lonely?" and "I'll Get Along Somehow."

Strangest of all the music we heard, at least to non-Southerners, was that of Roy Acuff, a star of the Nashville institution called the Grand Ole Opry. We shook our heads over "Wabash Cannonball" and "The Great Speckled Bird," sung in a hoarse, emotional style to the accompani-ment of banjo, fiddle, and guitar, and pronounced it "hillbilly" or "Li'l Abner" (after the 15½-year-old hero of the popular comic strip) music. But the Southerners among us, especially those of the Great Smoky Mountains of Tennessee and the Carolinas, grew homesick over Acuff and longed for more.*

Our five-month-long hiatus from the real Pacific War ended in late August, when we joined the attack transports of Task Group 32.3 for the invasion of Peleliu and Angaur in the Palau group of the Caroline Islands. While not the long-awaited return to the Philippines, the

---

*On Acuff's eighty-first birthday in 1984, President Ronald Reagan visited him on the stage of the Grand Ole Opry and praised him as the singer "who brought country music into the mainstream of American life." Armed Forces Radio of World War II certainly deserves some of the credit for the increasing popularity of country and western music in the postwar period. (Los Angeles *Times*, "Reagan Salutes Acuff for 81st Birthday," 14 Sep-tember 1984.)

islands commanded the eastern approaches to the scene of our greatest defeat of the war.

The landing on Peleliu took place on the morning of 15 September. From our position as an inshore screen for the attack transports and dock landing ships, we watched the Marines of the First Division assault the landing beaches, and were shocked at what we saw. I cannot improve on my description in *"We Will Stand by You,"* pages 219–20.

Promptly at 0830 the first wave of tracked LVTs began moving toward the beaches. I could see that it was in trouble immediately. The Japanese emerged from their concealed fortifications in the high denuded ridges, the shell-pocked area behind the landing grounds and a small offshore island to the south and caught the Marines in a murderous cross fire of artillery, mortars and automatic weapons. Great white spouts of shrapnel-laced water erupted among the LVTs. Machine-gun fire flayed the water. Some of the amtracs were hit and burst into flames. I could see tiny figures leaping and falling into the lagoon. Not all of them came up to struggle on toward the dubious shelter of the beach. Soon the entire mile-long landing area was hidden in a thick pall of smoke. . . .

The 1st, 5th and 7th Marine Regiments had now [a few hours later] tied their lines together and held a tenuous beachhead a few hundred yards deep extending to the edge of the airstrip. They were forming up and moving out in company strength to reduce the enemy pillboxes from their blind sides with rifle grenades and flame throwers. From beyond the reef, I could make little order of the confused struggle but I could hear the sharp crack of artillery, the crump of mortar fire and the ceaseless popping of machine guns, like endless strings of firecrackers at this range. Every land breeze brought the musky stench of burning jungle, the acid sting of cordite and another, quite unmistakable smell: putrefaction. Already the dead were beginning to decompose under a remorseless sun which had driven the temperature to 115 degrees Fahrenheit.

"It's a goddam blood bath," I told my friends. "We're towing skids around like a harbor tug, and over there the Marines are getting knocked off like clay pigeons in a shooting gallery."

Aposhian looked as shaken as I felt. "I wish someone would tell me why we landed on this island. Have you seen one Jap aircraft up there? I tell you, this is a criminal waste of good men."

By the time Peleliu and Angaur were secured two months later, the cost had become prohibitive. "Although there still is some confusion as to the exact casualty count," historian Harry A. Gailey writes, "it appears that the 1st Marine Division sustained 6,786 casualties, of which

1,300 were killed in action. Each regiment had slightly over 3,200 men just prior to D-day. The 1st Marine casualties amounted to 53.7%, the 7th to 46.2%, and the 5th to 42.7% of their total authorized personnel. The regimental officer corps had a casualty rate equal to that of the Marine riflemen. In all, 385 officers of the rifle regiments had become casualties. Despite the well-known reluctance of the commanding general [Maj. Gen. William H. Rupertus] to hand out medals, Marines on Peleliu would receive 8 of the 19 Medals of Honor won by the Division in the Pacific." *

General Rupertus had predicted that the Peleliu operation would be completed in four days. On 15 October, a month later, it became necessary to send two regimental combat teams of the Army's Eighty-first Division to relieve the First Marine Division. Their losses were 110 men killed and 717 wounded. On neighboring Angaur, the Eighty-first lost 260 killed and 1,354 wounded.

Aposhian and I and numbers of our shipmates would have been more outraged than we already were had we known that all this bloodletting was unnecessary, that the invasion should have been called off. William Manchester's opinion of the Peleliu operation: "It was a bad battle, fought at a bad place and a bad time, with an enemy garrison that could have been left to wither on the vine without altering the course of the Pacific War in any way."†

Why, then, wasn't the invasion called off by Chester Nimitz, Commander-in-Chief of the Pacific Fleet, popularly known among senior enlisted men as "the great white father"?

Early in September three task groups of Task Force Thirty-eight assaulted Mindanao and the Central Philippines with a series of heavy air attacks. Observing the weakness of the Japanese response even in the Manila area, Admiral Halsey began to question the projected invasions of Yap and the Palaus and the timetable for the Philippine invasion.

"He consulted his staff and decided to 'stick his neck out,'" Gailey writes.

He ordered his chief of staff, Rear Admiral Robert Carney, to send an urgent message to CinCPac [Nimitz], despite his concern that it was

---

*Harry A. Gailey, *Peleliu: 1944* (Annapolis, Md.: The Nautical & Aviation Publishing Company of America, 1983), p. 170.

†William Manchester, *Goodbye, Darkness* (Boston: Little, Brown and Company, 1980), p. 354.

really none of his business and might 'upset a great many applecarts possibly all the way up to Mr. Roosevelt and Mr. Churchill.' The dispatch sent on September 13 recommended three things: (1) that plans for the seizure of Yap and the Palau group be abandoned; (2) that the ground forces designated for these purposes be diverted to General MacArthur for his use in the Philippines; and (3) that the invasion of Leyte be undertaken at the earliest possible date.

Admiral Nimitz reacted quickly to Halsey's suggestions and sent a communication to the Joint Chiefs of Staff then in Quebec for the Octagon Conference between President Roosevelt and Prime Minister Churchill. General MacArthur's opinion was immediately asked for and on the evening before the scheduled Peleliu invasion his reply was received while the Chiefs were attending a formal dinner. A special session was convened in Quebec and within ninety minutes of the receipt of Mac-Arthur's communication, the decision to speed up the Leyte landing by two months was confirmed.

For the Marines approaching Peleliu, points 2 and 3 of Halsey's recommendation meant nothing. . . . Nimitz disagreed with Halsey's suggestion to give up the Palau operation totally and did not include the abandonment of the Angaur and Peleliu phases in his message to the Joint Chiefs. Nimitz never explained fully this decision to overrule Halsey, who believed that whatever the value of the airfields and anchorages, the cost of taking them would be too high.*

The cost proved far too high; the credit for the valor of the Marine First Division far too limited. Peleliu was neglected by the media, Manchester wrote, because "the liberation of France, the Lowlands and the Philippines was more fascinating, and also more successful than this pointless hammering of American flesh on a distant anvil of despair."†

When we heard where the First Marine Division had trained for Peleliu, we had trouble believing that, too. Returning from the successful Cape Gloucester campaign on New Britain, the division badly needed rest from the jungle combat. Instead, the men were shipped to Pavuvu in the Russell Islands. Gailey states:

By all accounts from private soldiers to general officers, hardly a worse site could have been chosen if there was any intention whatever of allowing the Marines to recuperate in decent quarters. Ultimately, Pavuvu proved to be inadequate even for training purposes.

*Gailey, *Peleliu,* pp. 33–34.
†Manchester, *Goodbye, Darkness,* p. 373.

Pavuvu had once been the site of a large Unilever coconut plantation, long since abandoned. It had few roads, no housing or other institutional facilities such as mess halls or recreation buildings, and the Pavuvu rats were everywhere. Before they could train the Marines had to clear training areas of jungle growth and rotting coconut logs. The temperature was uniformly high, as was the humidity. Rainfall during this time of year [summer of 1944] was constant and the mosquitoes and other forms of insect life made Pavuvu a name not remembered with affection by the Marines. These basic facts should have been known to III Corps staff; either they were concealed from the Division or the upper echelon officers had not bothered to reconnoiter the island.*

The only break for the Marines in their preparation for Peleliu was a visit to Pavuvu by Bob Hope and his troupe of entertainers. Some time before, Hope had come to Espiritu Santo, and a large delegation from the *Pawnee* was given special liberty for the event. Aposhian and I decided to go. Dick Garrett, the black officer's cook, one of my sparring partners, asked if he could join us and I agreed, knowing that my buddy would have no objection.

We sat high up in a natural amphitheater above the makeshift stage. According to the scuttlebutt Hope was ill, but faithful to show-business tradition, would go on as scheduled. His troupe consisted of singer Frances Langford, comedian Jerry Collona, musicians, and several scantily clad dancers.

The show was built around Hope's by-then-famous monologues. Freed of the restraints of radio and film censorship, his glib jokes and one-liners were, by the standards of the time, chauvinist, sexist, coarse, and even offensive. The emphasis was upon what servicemen did when they returned to the States, such as plunging into the bathtubs of girl-friends and wives while still wearing their uniforms. Naturally, the large, all-male audience laughed uproariously. We had all heard much worse in our ships and barracks without the benefit of Hope's platoon of gag writers and his keen timing. Starved for diversion as we were, most of us overlooked the vulgarity.

At the opposite pole from Hope's tasteless humor were the sentimental songs by Miss Langford, a favorite of servicemen. Her renditions of such hits as "Stardust" and "I'll Be Seeing You" were greeted with wild applause, whistles, and Rebel yells. Some remembered that the latter song had just been recorded by Tommy Dorsey, with Frank Sinatra as

*Gailey, *Peleliu*, p. 29.

the vocalist. Sinatra was perceived by most sailors and GI's as a skinny little jerk, a 4-F who instead should be wearing a uniform in defense of his country. Miss Langford, on the other hand, was a genuine patriot who in addition to touring with Hope often visited wounded men in Army and Navy hospitals.

I wasn't quite sure why Collona was brought along as "second banana," except possibly to make Hope look good by comparison. He affected an upturned mustachio of the type made popular by RAF fliers. His principal talents appeared to be the salacious leer accompanied by a twirling of the ends of his mustache, and the ability to sing in a tremulous falsetto.

It was the dancers who drew the most absorbed attention from the audience; the few who had brought along binoculars were envied and implored to share the wealth. As with the pin-up photos of Grable, Hayworth, Landis, and Williams, I did not participate in the general enthusiasm. "This is supposed to be good for our morale," I complained. "Show us a lot of female flesh that we can ogle but can't touch."

Garrett smiled thinly. "Ted, now you know what I've been putting up with all my life."

Aposhian and I considered ourselves reasonably free of prejudice. Garrett's remark was a sharp reminder that the world of the enlisted man, where we chafed under the continual reminders of our second-class citizenship, was the world in which our officer's cook had always lived. His skin color forever marked him, to most Americans, as different, inferior, and subject thereby to no end of mean discrimination.

When we heard later that the Marine First Division, which suffered nearly fifty percent casualties at Peleliu, had been entertained by Hope's troupe at Pavuvu, Aposhian and I shook our heads. The young men had been speeded on their way to disability and death with a few songs, a leer, a dance or two by lovely ladies one could admire but not touch, and vulgar monologues by a man who was becoming famous and no doubt rich from ostentatious patriotism. My buddy and I struggled to express our feelings.

Together, we finally did. Our epitaph for the First Division: "Bless the Marines of Peleliu. Before leaving the Russell Islands, they received the last rites from Pope Hope the First."

Following the Peleliu invasion, *Pawnee* and her sister ship *Munsee* were ordered to join Task Unit 30.8.16. It was one of nine or ten fleet oiler units that stood by at sea to fuel the fast carriers of Task Force Thirty-eight. From this forward position, one or both of the ATFs could be quickly dispatched to aid crippled combatants.

The stage was now set for the salvage of the cruisers *Canberra* and *Houston*, perhaps the most famous rescue in the history of this or any navy—and one which assured a proper footnote for insignificant *Pawnee* in the annals of naval warfare. Some crewmen later regretted that our role in this towaway had been accomplished not with one of our two revered skippers, Dilworth and George, but with "Jessie" Lees, especially since the credit for our exploit propelled him toward the captaincy he devoutly desired.*

In the Solomons, *Pawnee*'s contributions had gone largely unnoticed and unsung. Even the promised reward of R & R in Auckland had been postponed in favor of the *Menominee*. While we had been under way up the Slot or Blanche Channel nearly every night for months, our sister ship, under "Black Jack" Genereaux, had been raising the Japanese destroyer *Kikutsuki*, and this impressive but meaningless exploit rated higher with Halsey and his staff than *Pawnee*'s solitary "milk runs" in support of the Third Fleet. But the twin towaway of *Canberra* and *Houston* was accomplished under the close control of admirals ranging up to Commander Third Fleet; the word of our success was passed along and duly noted even by the White House.† To paraphrase a shipmate, Motor Machinist's Mate Cy Hamblen, a former Marine: "It ain't what you do, it's who sees you do it."

On 13 October, while Task Group 38.1 was conducting massive air raids on Formosa, the heavy cruiser USS *Canberra* (named for the Australian cruiser sunk during the disastrous Battle of Savo Island) was torpedoed below the armor belt. Both engine rooms and after fire rooms were flooded; twenty-three men were killed. Rather than scuttle the cruiser, as was the practice earlier in the war, Admiral Halsey decided to

---

*Interestingly, the word was not passed along to Samuel Eliot Morison or to Rear Adm. Worrall Reed Carter, USN (Ret.), author of a well-regarded study of logistics in the Pacific during the war, *Beans, Bullets, and Black Oil* (Washington, D.C.: Government Printing Office, 1952). Both historians falsely credit Lt. H. C. Cramer as the commanding officer. The error arose because Cramer relieved Lees on 24 October, shortly after the towaway.

†Following the successful withdrawal of the crippled ships from Formosa, President Roosevelt sent Halsey a personal message that the admiral broadcast to all hands: "It is with pride that the country has followed your fleet's magnificent sweep into enemy waters. In addition to the gallant fighting of your flyers, we appreciate the endurance and super-seamanship of your forces."

tow her clear, using the heavy cruiser *Wichita*, which was soon relieved by the *Munsee*.

The new light cruiser *Houston* perpetuated the name of the famous heavy cruiser lost in the Battle of Sunda Strait on 1 March 1942. Although operating with Task Group 38.2, she was ordered to take *Canberra's* place as point ship in the northwest sector of the formation. On the evening of 14 October, *Houston* was torpedoed amidships on the starboard side, near Frame 75. All propulsive and steering power was lost, her main engineering compartments flooded, and the ship listed 16 degrees. The damage was so extensive that the *Houston* appeared to be breaking up. The task group commander, Vice Adm. J. S. McCain, detached three destroyers to stand by to pick up survivors.

At about 2030 hours, Capt. William W. Behrens gave the order to abandon ship. The destroyer *Cowell* came alongside to attempt to take off the crew, but in the turbulent seas some men were crushed to death between the two ships. The destroyer was ordered away, and the *Houston's* men abandoned ship in rafts and life jackets, to be picked up by *Cowell* (195 sailors), destroyers *Grayson* (176) and *Boyd* (380, more men than her own roster). All were later transferred to larger ships of the task group.

Thanks to intensive damage-control efforts, the ship's stability improved. Captain Behrens now rescinded his abandon-ship order and requested that the heavy cruiser *Boston* take the *Houston* in tow. By midnight the two ships were under way at 4 knots. But nightfall of 15 October found them still only 200 miles from Japanese-held Formosa, the crippled cruiser leaving an oil slick 50 miles long. The slick, of course, was like an arrow pointing the way for any Japanese pilot or submarine searching for a slow-moving target.

Pawnee was ordered to take over the tow and arrived at daybreak of the sixteenth. Meanwhile, Admiral Halsey's staff on board the battleship *New Jersey* had been monitoring the outlandish claims of Radio Tokyo that land-based planes had destroyed much of the American Third Fleet and that the battered remnants were retiring in defeat. Here was a chance to use the crippled *Canberra* and *Houston* and their escorts to lure out major portions of the Japanese fleet. Halsey gave what soon came to be known as "CripDiv One" close cover from a task group built around light carriers *Cabot* and *Cowpens*, and positioned Task Group 38.3 between the division of cripples and the Japanese Home Fleet. We now acquired another sobriquet: "BaitDiv One," which some modified to

"Streamlined Bait." Monitoring our agonizingly slow progress from the *Pawnee*'s radio shack, I failed to appreciate the humor of the nicknames, particularly since I fully understood the appropriateness of the second one, and its implications for us.

The struggle of the *Houston* against two enemies—the Japanese and the encroaching sea—has been related by Col. John Grider Miller, USMC (Ret.), now managing editor of the U.S. Naval Institute *Proceedings*.* I devoted a long chapter to the towaway in *"We Will Stand by You."* I propose here to view the *Pawnee*'s role from the perspective of the radio shack, using many of the decoded dispatches and visual signals I have obtained. This is not so limiting as the reader might think. As radioman-in-charge, I was shown decodes of some of the messages the radiomen copied. Since I had access to the bridge, I could read the visual signals as they were received; often they were duplicates of the ones put on the fleet-wide Fox schedule.

With some difficulty because of the heavy ground swells, we took the *Houston* in tow from the *Boston* late on the morning of 16 October and began working up speed to $3\frac{1}{2}$ knots. By 1300 hours we were inching up abeam of the *Canberra* at 4 knots. But at 1348, long before we gained our assigned station 2,000 yards on the starboard beam of the *Munsee*, the klaxon sent us to general quarters.

Three planes (of 107 dispatched from Formosa, we later learned) had broken through the combat air patrol of *Cabot* and *Cowpens*. All three were shot down, but one, a Frances torpedo bomber, launched his tin fish at *Houston* in a narrow stern shot.† It struck far aft, at the starboard counter, opening the aircraft hangar to the sea, sending the hatch cover tumbling end over end until it disintegrated in a shower of shrapnel, and igniting the gasoline tanks in the hangar bulkheads. The raging fire quickly engulfed the fantail and spread to the accompanying oil slick. A number of men who had leaped or been blown overboard did not survive.

Houston was again in danger of breaking up and sinking. *Pawnee* was also at risk, since the dead weight of the sinking cruiser might "trip the ship," causing her to capsize before the tow wire could be cut through with an acetylene torch.

---

* *The Battle to Save the* Houston: *October 1944 to March 1945* (Annapolis, Md.: Naval Institute Press, 1985).

†The *Pawnee* fired at the Fran with three .50-caliber machine guns and the bridge 20-mm, scoring some hits. The plane was also hit by the *Houston, Canberra,* and a couple of the destroyers, and they all claimed the kill.

Faced with his most momentous command decision, Captain Lees called the duty signalman, "Papoose" Evans, my shipmate in the *California*, and dictated a visual message for the *Houston:*

WE WILL STAND BY YOU

At the time we gave the message less significance than it deserved. We felt that Lees had only done what the commanding officer of a fleet tug was supposed to do, what it was his clear duty to do. Frank Dilworth or Flave George would certainly have done the same. Writing about the event with the benefit of hindsight, the historians were more enthusiastic:

Samuel Eliot Morison:

Immediately after this second hit on *Houston*, fleet tug *Pawnee* sent her a visual signal that deserves a place among the Navy's historic phrases:—

WE'LL STAND BY YOU!*

Worrall Reed Carter:

In the midst of these disturbing events [the second torpedoing], while Captain Behrens was struggling desperately with one-fourth a crew to keep his ship from sinking, the towing vessel *Pawnee* sent the *Houston* the encouraging message, "We'll hold on," and continued to make the usual 5 knots, in the right direction. This simple message might properly take its place among other immortal words uttered or signaled during the heat of a sea fight—"I have not yet begun to fight!" "Don't give up the ship!"—for here was a relatively small service unit, the fleet tug, giving heart to a crippled cruiser, the little *Pawnee* applauding the courage of the hard-hit big fellow with "We'll hold on!" as much as to say: "You'll make it. We're betting on you!"†

---

* Morison, *History of United States Naval Operations*, Vol. XII, p. 102. Morison altered the original wording slightly, ostensibly for dramatic emphasis. Neither apostrophes nor exclamation points are used in visual signaling with Morse code.

† Carter, *Beans, Bullets, and Black Oil*, p. 228. Note that Carter uses another version of the now-famous message. When I was researching *"We Will Stand by You,"* I discussed the wording with William J. Miller, who as a first-class quartermaster was on *Pawnee*'s bridge at the time, and with Colonel Miller, who was writing *The Battle to Save the* Houston. (Both Jim Evans and Captain Lees were dead.) We all agreed on "We Will Stand by You" ("We'll Stand by You" in Miller's book). I was glad to have an additional verification later from Cleo B. Isom, a radioman who was on the *Houston* bridge when the message was received.

John Grider Miller:

Even after the *Houston* was torpedoed a second time, the skipper of the *Pawnee*, Lieutenant James Lees, was determined not to break the tow if he could possibly avoid it. He wanted Captain Behrens to know this. But he also wanted to know whether Captain Behrens had anything else in mind, such as abandoning ship.

Lee [*sic*] called for Signalman "Papoose" Evans and dictated a short message to him that was sent to the *Houston* by flashing light moments later: WE'LL STAND BY YOU. There was no reply, so Lee assumed that his statement of intent had been agreeable to the *Houston*.

The brief message was more than agreeable. It gave the strongest assurance that any man in combat can give another—that he will risk death rather than abandon his brother-in-arms. For the crew of the *Houston*, the message from the *Pawnee* could not have come at a better time.*

As we made our way toward Ulithi Atoll more than a thousand miles to the southeast at a dogtrot pace, Captain Behrens requested permission from our Task Group commander, Rear Adm. Laurance T. DuBose in light cruiser *Santa Fe*, to remove another three hundred men from the *Houston*, leaving a skeleton crew to continue the intensive damage-control efforts. The heavy seas that had made our approach to *Houston* hazardous, coupled with the severe rolling of the waterlogged cruiser, prevented destroyers from coming alongside; the men had to jump overboard in groups of one hundred and were fished from the sea by the *Ingersoll, Stephen Potter,* and *The Sullivans.*

On board the *Pawnee*, it became apparent that Halsey's bait strategy was luring out strong elements of the Japanese Home Fleet. An urgent message was put on the Fox schedule for decoding and was relayed to us visually by the *Santa Fe:*

TWO ENEMY SURFACE GROUPS X TWO CHARLIE VICTORS [carriers] ONE CHARLIE VICTOR LOVE [light carrier] THREE CHARLIE LOVES [light cruisers] ONE CHARLIE ABLE [heavy cruiser] FOUR DDS [destroyers] SIGHTED APPROXIMATELY TWO HUNDRED MILES NORTH OF YOU X COMTHIRDFLEET SENDS ACTION COM-TASKGROUP THIRTY POINT THREE X TAKE SUITABLE DISPOSI-TION X DO NOT REPEAT NOT DETACH CRUDIV THIRTEEN [Cruiser Division Thirteen] AND ESCORTS TONIGHT X DONT WORRY X MORE LATER

---

*Miller, *Battle to Save the* Houston, pp. 96–97.

Even though Admiral Halsey had, figuratively, patted us on the head and told us everything was under control, I was not entirely assured. His chief of staff, Rear Adm. Robert "Mick" Carney, had been my executive officer and, briefly, acting commanding officer in the *California*. I considered him a man of ruthless ambition, the probable author of the bait strategy, and believed that he would sacrifice the cripples and other ships of Task Group 30.3 for a chance to close with the Japanese Home Fleet.

Admiral DuBose may or may not have shared my feelings, but he took prudent, and ominous, precautions. He quickly devised three battle plans and sent them by visual means to all the ships of his task group:

THIS IS MY BATTLE PLAN ABLE X FOUR DESTROYERS TWO TUGS REMOVE PERSONNEL AND SINK CRIPPLED SHIPS X RETIRE AT BEST SPEED ON REVERSE OF ENEMY BEARING X THREE DESTROYERS WITH CARRIERS [*Cabot* and *Cowpens*] KEEP ABOUT THIRTY MILES REVERSE ENEMY BEARING FROM CRUISER GROUP PROVIDING AIR COVER AND LAUNCHING MAXIMUM STRIKES ON MOST THREATENING ENEMY FORCES X REMAINING CRUISERS AND DESTROYERS JOIN ME TO CONDUCT DELAYING ACTION X COMDESDIV 92 [Commander Destroyer Division 92] ASSIGN DE-STROYERS X PLAN EFFECTIVE WHEN DIRECTED X KNAPP MILLER AND BELL DESIGNATED TO REMAIN WITH CARRIERS X BURNS AND CHANNETTE [probably *Charrette*, DD-581] JOIN CRUISERS

Five minutes later by flashing light:

THIS IS MY PLAN BAKER X SIX DESTROYERS REMOVE PERSON-NEL FROM HOUSTON AND CANBERRA X CONTINUE TOWING X COMDESDIV 92 DESIGNATE DESTROYERS X PLAN EFFECTIVE WHEN DIRECTED

After another five minutes:

THIS IS MY PLAN CHARLIE X SIX DESTROYERS REMOVE PERSON-NEL FROM HOUSTON CANBERRA PAWNEE AND ZUNI [DuBose meant *Munsee*, the ATF towing the *Canberra*] X THEN SINK THESE SHIPS WITH TORPEDOES X CRUISERS FORM ON SANTA FE SCREENED BY DESTROYERS OF TU [Task Unit] 30.3.1 X CARRIERS WITH THEIR DESTROYERS FORM SECOND GROUP X GROUPS RETIRE IN COMPANY AT BEST SPEED EASTWARD X PLAN EFFEC-TIVE WHEN DIRECTED

On board the *Santa Fe* some flag communication officer with real verbal skills, probably a journalist or English professor in civilian life, summarized the three battle plans for a message of urgent priority on the Fox schedule:

C T G 30R3 [Commander Task Group 30.3] BATTLE PLAN EFFECTIVE WHEN ORDERED X PLAN ABLE FOUR DDS [Destroyers] TWO TUGS REMOVE PERSONNEL SINK CRIPPLES RETIRE REVERSE ENEMY BEARING X PLAN BAKER SIX DDS REMOVE PERSONNEL CRIPPLES CONTINUE TOWING X PLAN CHARLIE X SIX DDS REMOVE PERSONNEL CRIPPLES AND TUGS THEN SINK THOSE SHIPS

It was with a sinking feeling that I read these messages, especially Plan Charlie. For a few moments I was standing on the quarterdeck of the burning *California* at Pearl Harbor, preparing to abandon ship in black smoke so dense I could scarcely see. All around me shipmates were plunging into the oily water, which was now afire along the fantail, and striking out for Ford Island. With the abandon-ship order, we were no longer a disciplined crew but rather a mass of individualists intent upon survival. At such desperate times, leadership must be exercised by the few to prevent the mass from becoming a mob.

In the kind of seas we would probably encounter if we abandoned *Pawnee*, casualties were certain to result. The *Houston* had lost a number of men because they panicked and suffered the awful fates of being crushed between their ship and the rescuing destroyer during the first abandon ship, or burned to death in the flaming water following the second torpedoing. I was not overly concerned for myself if Plan Charlie was ordered, for I was a good swimmer and in excellent physical condition from my program of exercise and boxing. But some of my shipmates did not swim well, and many were certainly out of shape. It would be my responsibility and that of other leading petty officers, such as Cy Hamblen, Don Aposhian, and Bill Miller, to maintain some order while we were in the water awaiting rescue.

All that afternoon and evening we moved across the eastern approaches to Luzon Strait at 4 knots, anxiously awaiting the urgent messages that would tell us the Japanese striking force was closing and to prepare for one of Admiral DuBose's battle plans (Baker, I hoped). During the daylight hours land-based planes from Formosa continued to threaten CripDiv One, but fighter planes from our two escorting carriers drove them off or shot them down.

In a commendable attempt to make light of conditions on board the *Houston*, the captain sent a visual message to flagship *Santa Fe:*

OFFICERS AND MEN NOW ABOARD ARE BATHING FROM BUCK-
ETS. SLEEPING ON THE DECK AND USING OVER THE SIDE SANI-
TARY FACILITIES. EATING FROM CANS. IN VIEW OF THESE CON-
DITIONS IMPRACTICAL TO BERTH ANY PASSENGERS.*

Actually, conditions were much worse than that.

The *Houston* was rolling ponderously in beam seas. All four engine rooms and both fire rooms were flooded to the overhead. Many hatches and doors were warped and leaking. Worse, her main longitudinal beams had been buckled by the impact of the first torpedo. If they gave way, the ship was certain to break up or capsize. On the positive side, bucket brigades and submersible pumps were keeping the flooding in check while damage-control personnel worked feverishly by battle lantern and flashlight to shore up weakened bulkheads and sagging decks. For most of the 16th, topside crewmen had been lightening ship, casting overboard everything which could be pried loose. Before the air attack, the starboard catapult and its damaged seaplane had been jettisoned. They were being followed by A.A. directors, winches, davits, searchlights, ready lockers of now-use-less 5-inch ammunition, even the radio gear and coding machines.

Assuming we could fend off the pursuing ships, planes and I-boats, the *Houston* would need very good luck and weather to stay afloat. On our bridge, a signalman kept his long glass trained on the cruiser, as much to detect any signs of foundering as to copy her blinker-gun signals. "Pappy" Schmidt and our shipfitters stood a continuous watch at the acetylene torch [near the towline], which would be used only if *Houston* threatened to take *Pawnee* to the bottom with her.†

When I got off watch at 2345 of that very long 16 October, I went to the bridge and read a dispatch from *Santa Fe* a signalman had copied two hours before:

---

*This message was among a number passed on to me for my research years later by Cleo B. Isom and Kermit A. Lamm, both radiomen in the *Houston*. While all the dispatches were on official message-blank forms, this one, untypically, had been retyped, using periods instead of the standard "X" of Navy dispatches, and was undated. I have no doubt, however, of its verity.

† *"We Will Stand by You,"* pp. 247–48. *Pawnee* had inadvertently contributed to *Houston*'s lighten-ship exercise. When we came alongside to pass the messenger line across, her starboard anchor fouled on our port bulwark, sheared from its chain, and fell into the sea, but not before taking eight feet of our bulwark and gouging out a foot-square section of the main deck. The anchor weighed 1,300 pounds.

IN UNFORTUNATE EVENT HOUSTON IS LOST PLAN IS FOR YOU TO TANDEM TOW [*Canberra* with] MUNSEE X MUNSEE NOW READY TO PASS YOU 100 FATHOMS TWO INCH WIRE BENT TO HIS [*sic*] ANCHOR

Early on the morning of the seventeenth I was on the fantail with a mug of coffee. Since we hadn't been at general quarters during the night, I knew the *Houston* was still with us, but I took heart from the seeing. The seas were moderating under a 10,000-foot overcast, but our charge was still rolling uneasily in the continuing ground swell. A mile off our port beam the *Munsee* and *Canberra* kept station. Visiting Flash Aposhian in his gyro-compass room, where he was standing watch and watch, I saw that our heading remained 130 true and gyro, although the *Houston*, I told him, was "staggering around back there like a boot seaman on his first liberty." We were making 106 rpm on all four engines, about 4.3 knots.

With no Armed Forces Radio station within our reception area, my contribution to the ship's morale was to tune in Tokyo Rose. Between the ballads aimed at reminding us unhappily of home, such as "You Always Hurt the One You Love," "Long Ago and Far Away," and "I'm in the Mood for Love," she gave us the war news as Radio Tokyo saw it. Most of the Third Fleet commanded by the war criminal, Admiral William F. Halsey, had been sunk; we, the retreating remnants, would soon go to the bottom, too. We would never return to our loved ones, she told us with saccharine regret in a soft, Americanized voice without a trace of an accent. We knew she was lying, but we also knew that we were the bait in Halsey's trap. Since he had achieved fame by issuing orders such as "ATTACK REPEAT ATTACK," we were aware that guile was not the trademark of his strategic thinking. Would he and his chief of staff be outwitted by some clever chess player in a Japanese admiral's uniform?

We were reminded of the price of failure when we half-masted our colors for funeral services on the *Santa Fe*. Watching the brief but always-solemn ceremony through binoculars from 4,000 yards, Aposhian and I prayed that we would never be sewn into canvas shrouds and weighted down with shell casings, an ultimate irony, to become food for the voracious predators of the deep. One of the great tragedies of war, we decided, is that it killed young men before they had a chance to accomplish anything, often even before they could enjoy a close relationship with a woman. Speaking with the cynicism war engenders, we agreed that most of us would not amount to anything, anyway: we had come from the anonymous multitude, and to anonymity we would return. The awful sin was that we were being denied the chance even for such modest goals as marriage and children; denied the chance to which everyone was entitled: to challenge the odds and possibly achieve something of value for society. Even if failure resulted, it would be the fair measure of a deficiency of the individual, not, as in war, the unaccountable failure of entire nations.

Across the horizon the Combat Air Patrol of our escorting carriers shot down several planes trying to finish off our cripples and kept the other "sea eagles" at bay. The dozen ships of our inner screen formed a rotating circle around us, steaming at 15 knots in a clockwise formation. The Navy called it "Disposition 3-V," an A.A. formation. After some discussion, Bill Miller and I decided it could more colorfully be described as "the merry-go-round formation." As the threat of air attack diminished, the task group shifted to cruising disposition 3-R, with cruisers *Santa Fe, Mobile,* and *Birmingham* zigzagging independently on either beam and astern of the towing group, and the nine destroyers (*Boyd, Caperton, Cogswell, Cowell, Grayson, Ingersoll, Knapp, Stephen Potter,* and *The Sullivans*) ranging ahead on assigned patrolling stations.

In the early morning of 18 October we discovered that all three cruisers and four of the destroyers had vanished during the night. I soon discovered that there was no cause for alarm; in fact, we had reason for elation. By radio and flashing light, we had copied a long operational-priority dispatch from our task-group commander shortly after midnight:

SUMMARY X JAP FLEET RETIRED AFTER SIGHTING HALSEY X TWO TASK FORCES HIT LUZON TODAY AND THURSDAY OTHERS COVER US X CRUDIV 13 AND DESDIV 100 DETACHED LAST NIGHT X COMCRUDIV 10 [in *Boston*] NOW IN CHARGE X HALSEY WILL NOT FURTHER REDUCE OUR OUTFIT UNTIL NINETEENTH OR TWENTI-ETH OCTOBER X LOCATION CRUDIV 5 NOT KNOWN TO ME X CINCPOA [Nimitz, now Commander-in-Chief, Pacific Ocean Areas] STATES WE RAISED HELL AND MENTIONED TORPEDOES DAM-AGED TWO MEDIUM SIZED SHIPS

As he left the command of CripDiv One, also known as BaitDiv One, Admiral DuBose sent all hands a congratulatory message. The gracious thank-you added to the regard in which he was held by those of the

Pawnee crew who had been able to follow the course of our withdrawal from Formosa. His performance, we thought, had been outstanding; his willingness to share information with all the men of his task group made him a rarity among flag officers.

I WANT TO THANK ALL HANDS FOR THE SPLENDID JOB AND WELL DONE TO OUR PILOTS AND THE PERSONNEL OF OUR INJURED FRIENDS AND TO MUNSEE AND PAWNEE FOR GETTING US OUT OF THE DANGER AREA

The next day Admiral Halsey added his compliments, relayed through Admiral L. J. Wiltse, Commander of Cruiser Division Ten in the *Boston:*

FOLLOWING RECEIVED BY CTG 30.3 FROM 3RD FLEET QUOTE YOUR CHEERFUL COURAGE SKILL AND DETERMINATION THROUGH A TOUGH SPOT HAS [*sic*] BEEN A CREDIT TO YOU AND YOUR COMMAND X WELL DONE AND KEEP GOING X HALSEY

Since this dispatch seemingly gave Admiral Wiltse of our outer screen most of the credit for our safe retirement from Formosa, and contained a grammatical error as well, I shrugged. The midshipmen at the Naval Academy should be required to spend more time at the English language and less time at close-order drill, I told my buddies. More to our liking was a later message from Bull Halsey:

FOR SKILL AND GUTS THE SAFE RETIREMENT OF THE DAMAGED CANBERRA AND HOUSTON FROM THE SHADOW OF FORMOSA COAST UNDER HEAVY AIR ATTACK WILL BECOME A NAVY TRA-DITION X TO ALL HANDS WHO CONTRIBUTED TO THE JOB WELL DONE X HALSEY

We also took pride in Admiral Wiltse's endorsement to Captain Lees's action report of 16 October. He wrote: "Commander Cruiser Division TEN notes with pleasure and admiration the valiant efforts made by PAWNEE to defend the crippled tow."

At 1000 hours on 20 October, the Central Philippines Attack Force of 700 ships began landing the first assault waves of some 132,000 troops on the beaches of Leyte Island.

"People of the Philippines, *I* have returned," proclaimed Gen. Douglas MacArthur. Listening to the "Voice of America" broadcast over the ship's loudspeakers, the crew of the *Pawnee* proclaimed in turn that the detested "Dugout Doug" was an egomaniac who had, as usual, forgotten all the sailors, GIs and Marines who had got him there. Our turn to cheer came when we sighted our relief ship *Zuni*, accompanied by the destroyer-minesweeper *Trever* and the merchant rescue tug *Watch Hill*.

The next day our sister ship *Zuni* took over the tow of the *Houston*, and the *Watch Hill* relieved the *Munsee*. As we departed for Peleliu, we sent a final message to our special light cruiser by flashing light:

GOOD LUCK AND SMOOTH SAILING

"WELL DONE PAWNEE" was *Houston*'s official response. Unofficially, a number of sailors on the weather decks gave us a good-bye salute. After a tow of some 1,500 miles, the *Houston* arrived at Ulithi Atoll on Navy Day, 27 October 1944.

An association which lasted less than a week at sea endures to this day ashore. When the USS *Houston* Association was founded in 1977 with twenty-seven members, a special detachment was created for the *Pawnee*, a generous gesture that indicates the type of leadership which has made this association so successful. Currently, about 500 former *Houston* sailors,* 22 crewmen from the *Pawnee*, and 14 men from other ships, mostly CripDiv One, are on the roster. Friendships are renewed each year at the reunions.

Ship associations and other military reunion groups are not without their critics. Typical are the comments of columnist Otis Pike, a former congressman:

"Perhaps we celebrate military victories too much. For too many Americans, World War II was the greatest adventure of their lives and they spend the rest of their lives gathering in organizations that reinforce their belief in their own heroism. This is not a peculiarly American institution; all peoples in all lands do the same.

"If we did not so glorify war[s], we might be less eager to fight them."†

I do not think it is love of war that brings the *Houston* and *Pawnee* sailors to the reunions. Heads nodded in agreement when, in a talk

---

*This number includes about 125 sailors from the heavy cruiser (CA-30) which was sunk early in the war. The original *Houston*'s last stand is recounted by Capt. W. G. Winslow, USN (Ret.), in *The Ghost That Died at Sunda Strait*, one of the Bluejacket trade paperback books from the Naval Institute Press.

†"U.S. should keep D-Day in its place," *Oregonian*, 5 June 1994.

before another reunion of World War II veterans, I said: "Anyone who glorifies war either has never been shot at, or is a damn fool."

What brings the old sailors together is remembrance of the comradeship they knew, of their participation in great events that tested their valor, events that have entered the historical record. We live in a society which has a very short attention span. Our government, like all governments, is concerned with the present, not the past; its favors are bestowed upon those who can bring pressure upon it. The contributions of the men who fought World War II have largely been forgotten.

But the old sailors of the ship associations have not forgotten. For a few days every year, or every other year, they can gather together, wearing caps and jackets emblazoned with the names of their ships—reminders to each other, if not to the country, that once they were special men.

The motto of the Guadalcanal Campaign Veterans has a particular significance here:

"It isn't the cost of belonging—it's the price you paid to be eligible."

10

The Civilian Navy

For each age is a dream that is dying,
Or one that is coming to birth.

—Arthur W. E. O'Shaughnessy

I sat in the observation-lounge car of the Streamliner City of San Francisco, a bourbon and Seven-Up beside me, on a late March day in 1945. Outside my window, glittering in brilliant sunshine, were the snowy escarpments of the Sierra Nevada, my own "range of lights," as the three-unit diesel labored up the steep grade, pulling its coaches and Pullman cars. Occasionally we passed through a long snow shed, a reminder that the snows of winter were measured here in feet, not inches. Just ahead was Donner Pass, elevation 7,089 feet, named for the Donner Party that had been stranded there in 1846 and had resorted to the unthinkable to survive.

Even as I wondered what I would have done if faced with starvation, I gave thanks that I had survived my own ordeals: the attack on Pearl Harbor, followed by twenty-six months in the South and Western Pacific, where the war had been and was being fought with a savagery these civilians in the lounge car would not believe.

Following the rescue of the *Houston*, the *Pawnee* had engaged in routine operations around the Palau Islands and Ulithi Atoll until ordered to Pearl Harbor for a yard overhaul. On 12 February I was transferred to the receiving station, for further transfer to the Naval Training School (Pre-Radio Materiel) Herzl Junior College in Chicago, with 30 days' leave and travel time.

Returning to San Diego from Pearl Harbor in a British "Jeep" carrier I jestingly named HMS *Pinafore*, I had spent my leave as men back from the wars usually did. I renewed old acquaintances and made a few new ones in my hometown of Placerville; visited my parents and foster-parents, finding with no surprise that time and war had not reduced the distance between us; spent a good deal of time in Sacramento with dark-haired, green-eyed Betty Baker, back from boarding school and living with her mother and stepfather, Cora and Perry Baker. I had been infatuated with Betty since I met her in 1941 in Placerville at Mac's Jumbo Fountain to the jukebox music of "The Nearness of You," and her words from Poe, "All that we see or seem / Is but a dream within a dream."

When it was time to depart for Chicago, I decided to enjoy the luxury of a Pullman berth, even if only an upper, for the forty-eight-hour trip. I brought along plenty of cash for the dining and bar cars and stuffed several books, including *Great Modern Reading,* an anthology of short stories and poems selected by Somerset Maugham, into my canvas carryall. Not expecting to make friends with any civilians, I was pleasantly surprised when I did.

During my month's leave in California, I had learned that most of the citizens were caught up not only in the war fever but also in the feverish pursuit of "the Yankee dollar" (as it was called in a hit song of 1944, "Rum and Coca-Cola"). Nearly everything was rationed or officially unavailable—and, as in Sydney, everything was available, for a price, on the black market. The quality of service and civility had declined as sharply as had the quantity of goods. Any criticism was likely to be met with the all-purpose rebuttal: "Hey, don't you know there's a war on?" (To which I occasionally responded: "Where are your campaign ribbons, Mac?") Some civilians, to be sure, wished to be friendly to the men in uniform. But their questions about the progress of the war against Japan and Germany were inanely repetitive. Next would come the mention of the brother, son, nephew, or neighbor who was serving in the Navy/Army/Air Force/Marines/Coast Guard. Such attempts at solidarity left me yawning, for I knew that most of these civilians in uniform would never see any action.

In the restrooms of the restaurants, taverns, and cocktail lounges I found, along with the lewd drawings, propositions, and phone numbers, the epigram, "Kilroy was here." It would have pleased me if all the Kilroy clan were shipped to the Pacific, where their services were needed as we began the assaults on the approaches to Japan's home islands.

But the civilian who occupied the lower berth of my Pullman, with whom I was having drinks in the observation car at the rear of the train, was different. For one thing, he asked intelligent questions. For another, he was familiar with most of the books I had read as a youth or in the Pacific. He was a Canadian, therefore an ally, and a dentist. Because of his interest in books, I was willing to overlook his profession. I still remembered, would always remember, my last visit to a dentist. In the summer of 1943, a filling became dislodged as I was chewing on a piece of Australian beef of the consistency of an old inner tube. On Banika Island in the Russells, alongside the Marine fighter strip, a Navy dentist had practiced his healing arts in the open air under the coconut trees. Using a foot-powered drill, he took what seemed an entire afternoon to prepare the tooth for a new filling. The weak injection of Novocaine did little to allay my exquisite pain. The dentist smiled and hummed tunelessly all through the ordeal. I was reminded of the Marquis de Sade, the French author whose name is the source of the noun "sadism."

The discussion of literature with my Canadian seatmate extended over many pleasant hours, several meals in the crowded dining car, and a number of drinks in the chrome-and-red-leather comfort of the observation lounge as the train hurried across the sagebrush desolation of Nevada's Great Basin. At Ogden, Utah, we reached the terminus of the SP's Central Pacific Line, 780 miles from Oakland. Our train rode the Union Pacific tracks as far as Council Bluffs, Iowa, where the Chicago and North Western took us on to the "windy city."

I didn't care who claimed the trains or the tracks. I was thoroughly enjoying the travel time. Like my leave, it was an interlude of comparative freedom from regulations and intrusive discipline. Only an occasional Shore Patrolman—a first-class boatswain's mate according to his rating badge, but a boot judging by the way he wore his shapeless white hat—passed down the aisle to remind me that I was still wearing Navy blues, even if mine were tailor-made. Since I was now in the territory of the civilian Navy, I was also wearing the campaign ribbons and battle stars to which I was entitled: American Defense with Fleet clasp; American Campaign; Asiatic-Pacific Campaign with one silver and three bronze stars—seven for the *Pawnee*'s war, one for Pearl Harbor.

I had been pleased to discover that the dentist, whom I shall call Robert, was a mutual admirer of Maugham. I had read several of the British author's novels and his autobiographical *The Summing Up*, not only for pleasure but also to increase my vocabulary. I kept a small spiral-bound notebook and a Webster's *Collegiate Dictionary* on the mess-hall table where I did most of my reading. When I found a word I didn't understand (which was often enough, for Maugham had an extensive vocabulary), I wrote it down, looked it up in the dictionary, and copied the definition. Then I looked for a chance to use the word in conversation, often to the good-natured bewilderment of the radio gang and my close friends Aposhian, Gerber, and Schleppi.

I was particularly impressed by one remark in *Summing Up* and had written it down for memorization. After meeting many famous men, he wrote: "I could not discover in the eminent statesmen I met [in English houses] any marked capacity. I concluded, perhaps rashly, that no great degree of intelligence was needed to rule a nation. Since then I have known in various countries a good many politicians who have attained high office. I have continued to be puzzled by what seemed to me the mediocrity of their minds."*

Robert and I were inclined to agree with Maugham's assessment, citing as a conspicuous example the policy of demanding "unconditional surrender" of the Axis powers. We wondered if Roosevelt and Churchill had taken leave of their senses, for the policy ensured the continuation of the war by Germany and Japan past any possible hope of victory and at a cost of innumerable casualties.

Crossing another mountain range, the Rockies, our conversation turned from the writings of Ernest Hemingway, John Steinbeck, Jack London, and H. G. Wells, and the plays of George Bernard Shaw (which I hadn't yet read) to the movies. It occurred to me, for the first time, that few of the films I had enjoyed in peacetime were shown in the Pacific, where the fare was largely escapism and war propaganda. Prewar favorites included *Dark Victory*, starring Bette Davis; *Romeo and Juliet* (despite the advanced years of Leslie Howard and Norma Shearer); *The Charge of the Light Brigade* and *They Died with Their Boots On* (in both of which, I confessed, I was more impressed with the décolletage of Olivia De-Haviland than with Errol Flynn's derring-do in leading his men to certain death); and *Beau Geste*, Hollywood's version of the fine P. C. Wren novel I had read as a teenager. Smiling, Robert pointed out that some government agency was probably censoring the films that went to the

---

*W. Somerset Maugham, *The Summing Up* (New York: The Literary Guild of America, 1938), p. 3.

servicemen. The ones I had mentioned were too highbrow or too
graphic in their depiction of the cruelties and murderous blunders of
officers such as Gen. George Armstrong Custer to be suitable for view-
ing by naive young men who had been sent out to die, if necessary, for
their country.

He asked if I had seen *Four Feathers*, a British film about a young
officer who receives the white feathers of cowardice and must redeem
himself by his valor in saving fellow officers in the Sudan. It was another film I hadn't seen; cowardice was dealt with in a most gingerly
fashion in the ones sent to the war theaters. The "universal" ship crew
or infantry platoon of Hollywood mythology usually included among
its mixture of races and types (except for blacks) one enlisted man who
was terrified of dying. He needed counseling and, if necessary, firm discipline by a gruff but kindly chief, sergeant, or officer to restore him to
virtue. In the climatic battle, the chastened fellow at last died gloriously,
with little blood or pain, to save his comrades.

When conversation palled, I spent hours at the windows of Pullman
or lounge car drinking coffee and watching the scenery unroll. I had
never before been east of Reno; no amount of reading in novels or
American history had quite prepared me for the vastness of the country
I had been defending. It seemed impossible that settlers in covered wag-
ons pulled by teams of horses or oxen could have crossed these rivers,
mountain ranges, and deserts, all in the face of opposition not only from
nature but also from hostile Indians whose lands they were invading.
Every mile the pioneers gained in their westward migration had been
paid for with the bones of their men, women, and children.

On the facade of one of the state government buildings in Sacramento was the inscription, "Bring me men to match my mountains."
The men who had crossed the plains, the Rockies, the Great Basin, and
the Sierra Nevada to reach the promised land hardly were giants; by and
large, they were the dispossessed, failures in the east. But they had
brought a spirit as indomitable as that which had sustained Capt. Flave
George and the crew of the *Pawnee* on the nightly "milk runs" up the
Slot and Blanche Channel, at the time among the most dangerous
waterways in the world. From my experiences at Pearl Harbor and in
the South Pacific, I had learned that the best fighting men, like those
dauntless pioneers, came from poverty-stricken or broken homes. In-
heriting little, they had little to lose.

On the afternoon of 29 March we came into the terminal of the Chicago and North Western on Clinton Street, near the intersection of the North and South Branches of the Chicago River. Robert and I took a cab to the downtown Loop area, where we parted, I to find a room at the YMCA, he to visit friends before going on to Canada. I gathered that he would have liked to continue our travel friendship by mail, but I knew that the radio school would make too many demands on my time. Robert was a fine companion, but what time I could steal for writing must be used to keep up my correspondence with friends far closer to my heart: the three other members of the "four musketeers." Aposhian was attending gyrocompass school on the East Coast; Gerber was being treated at the Oakland Naval Hospital for a perforated ulcer; Schleppi was still with the *Pawnee* somewhere in the Western Pacific. I had no doubt that my friendships with these staunch comrades would last beyond the war that had brought us together and far into the peace.

Since I didn't have to report to Herzl until 0800 the next morning, I had my uniform pressed and went out on the town. In a Loop bar I met a fellow radioman first from the Pacific Fleet, also ordered to Herzl, whom I shall call Carl. We soon discovered that the natives were friendly, and demonstrated it in a most welcome way: they insisted on buying us drinks. The young ladies were friendly, too, and let us insist on buying them drinks. While the Loop area was dirty and noisy from the roar of the elevated trains, the atmosphere was more congenial and certainly more patriotic than that of blasé California.

Schleppi's one-word description of Chicago had been "Caponeville," but the populace included Germans, Scandinavians, Irish, Jews, Poles, Czechs, Lithuanians, Croats, Greeks, Chinese, and blacks, as well as Italians. To be sure, the city was noted for corruption (Cook County, with its seat in Chicago, was known as "Crook County"), for ward-heeling politicians on the take, for gangsters and unsolved murders. The locals seemed rather proud of this, afflictions to be stoically endured, as they did the climate. On this blustery March evening, Carl and I were carrying peacoats; some of the drinkers scorned coats for shirts with the sleeves rolled up.

During the evening we met several other radiomen. We were surprised to learn that the Navy had taken over a huge pier extending five-eighths of a mile into Lake Michigan and converted it, first into training schools for machinist's mates and then into an advanced radio materiel school. If—and the petty officers emphasized the caveat—we got through pre-radio screening at Herzl and then through one of the several primary radio schools in the country, we could request Navy Pier, Treasure Island, or Bellevue for the advanced training.

One of the radiomen, an instructor, told us an amusing tale about Navy Pier that perfectly illustrated the Chicago ambience. With the growing importance of electronic warfare, BuShips decided to establish a third radio materiel school (RMS) that would turn out a class of radio technicians every week, instead of every month as Bellevue and T.I. were doing. Consequently, the Navy Pier schools for machinist's and aviation machinist's mates were moved, and the radio school at Treasure Island was given the task of providing executives and instructors for the new RMS.

Lt. Merrill M. Holt, a Mustang, was sent to Navy Pier to evaluate the situation. To his astonishment he found forty-three lieutenant commanders attached to the two mech schools. Those officers were executives from NBC Radio, the stockyards, and meat-processing plants such as Armour. Commissioned as light commanders with neither Navy background nor sea duty, they commuted to the pier daily from their homes in the suburbs, just as if they were still civilians.

Lieutenant Holt took action. Through channels he started shipping them out to Pearl Harbor. Since the new school was under BuShips and the old ones were controlled by the Ninth Naval District, it took a while for the light commanders to organize their resistance. Holt got rid of half of them before he, in turn, was shipped out.

The radioman who told us the story spread his hands in a gesture of resignation. "Only in Chicago!" he said.*

The next morning Carl and I, nursing mild hangovers, threw our seabags into a cab. Herzl City Junior College—named for Theodor Herzl, a Hungarian Jew (1860–1904) who was the founder of modern Zionism—was located on the near South Side, in the center of the Jewish district.

---

*Verified by letter from Leroy Nelson of 24 May 1994, and by phone call from Earl Marshall on 17 October 1994. After enlisting in the Navy, both men were graduates of pre-radio and primary and secondary radio materiel schools. As radio technicians first class, both became instructors: Nelson at Treasure Island and Navy Pier, Marshall at Navy Pier. As a member of the Naval Reserve, Nelson was recalled during Korea, serving in the flag complement of the *Princeton* as a CPO. Both men used their Navy technical training as bridges to long, successful careers as radio engineers in civilian life.

I got the impression that the drab, gray South Side was very old. Since the city had been nearly destroyed in the great fire of 1871, it wasn't old even by American standards. It just looked that way.

The college and its campus (if it could be dignified by that term) occupied the entire 3700 block of Douglas Avenue. The venerable three-story red-brick building had been recently painted, no doubt by the Navy. The grounds had been adorned with many flower beds, another Navy make-work project, I guessed. Behind the building was a paved playground-parade area and a softball field of crushed rock.

Arriving at the first-floor executive offices well before 0800, our first surprise was that the nearby mess hall was empty; there would be no breakfast, not even a cup of joe. The second one came from the junior officer who examined our papers and checked them against a list. The next session of the school wasn't scheduled until late April, he informed us. Consequently, our orders had been modified. We were to report the following morning to the primary radio school at Dearborn.

"Dearborn?" I asked. "Isn't that where Henry Ford makes his cars?"

"Exactly," the JO replied. "Mr. Ford built a radio school at his River Rouge plant and donated it to the Navy. You will take the New York Central to Detroit this afternoon. Here are your new orders and travel chits."

"Sir, what about our pre-radio?" Carl asked.

"You'll get that at Dearborn before the three months of primary. That school is for you men from the fleet."

We had been told the previous evening that at least 40 percent of the fleet radiomen regularly were "bilged out" from Herzl and from Wright Junior College in the city. They had to compete with whiz kids who had at least pre-college engineering and ham radio backgrounds and who had passed a preliminary screening test. Dearborn couldn't possibly be that bad, we reasoned.

The next morning a friendly civilian picked us up at a streetcar stop on Detroit's Michigan Avenue and deposited us at the main gate of the radio materiel school on Schaefer Road in Dearborn. The extensive, landscaped grounds, which occupied a meander of the River Rouge, were a great improvement on Herzl. Across the road was the huge, integrated plant of the Ford industrial empire; we could see the tall stacks of the open-hearth furnaces of a steel mill and the docks at which the iron-ore freighters from the Great Lakes tied up.

The school was comprised of eight gleaming-white barracks in the classic H-configuration, an administration building, mess hall with adjoining ship's service and gedunk stand, sick bay, and large recreation building. Our attention focused first on the mess hall, where this time we were served a cafeteria-style breakfast. It was standard Navy chow, no better and no worse than was served at other shore stations, but superior to any ship. Still, the atmosphere here, so near a plant belching fire and smoke, so far from any ocean, disturbed me. As Carl remarked, reading my thoughts: "By God, we're a hell of a long way from the real Navy."

Our two-story barracks, though, met with our approval. It employed hardwood throughout, not the soft pine of most wartime construction. The bunks were single rather than double- or triple-high; spacious tables and benches for writing and study were provided. The heads were tiled, with all-modern plumbing. The barracks at Dearborn were Lincolns, not Fords.

Why did old Henry Ford have such a fondness for radiomen? we wondered. We soon found out that he didn't; his concerns were of a more practical nature. A year before Pearl Harbor, on 6 December 1940, ground was broken on a naval facility designed for the training of machinist's mates. Ford Motor Company paid for the school, leasing it to the Navy for one dollar a year. When the production of automobiles resumed after the war, the company would need well-trained ma-chinists.

Present at Dearborn to accept the facility from Henry Ford Sr. on 15 January 1941 were Rear Adm. Chester W. Nimitz, then chief of the Bureau of Navigation, and Rear Adm. John Downes, Commandant of the Ninth Naval District and Commanding Officer of the Great Lakes Naval Training Station.

I was shown a photo of Ford and Nimitz taken at the inauguration ceremonies. Ford, then seventy-seven, was one of the richest and most powerful men in America. In a little less than a year, Nimitz would reach the pinnacle of his naval career: promotion to full admiral as Commander-in-Chief, Pacific Fleet.*

My class of some five hundred now began a four-month course of instruction more concentrated than I would ever endure in college. Anyone who hadn't studied basic mathematics, algebra, trigonometry,

---

*Much information about the Dearborn school facility was provided by the Research Center of the Henry Ford Museum & Greenfield Village, Dearborn. In December 1944 the school for machinist's mates was converted to a radio materiel school. The radio school was in operation from January through December 1945.

and logarithms (as I had for a college preparatory course in high school) could not have passed the first examination.

We started with an Annapolis textbook: *Refresher Course in Fundamental Mathematics for Basic Technical Training*, published by the U.S. Naval Institute. All too soon came Cooke's *Mathematics for Electricians and Radiomen*, which covered trig and complex algebra, Dawes's *Fundamentals of A.C.* and his *Fundamentals of D.C.*, and Terman's *Fundamentals of Radio Engineering*.

We were also informed that we must invest in a slide rule and quickly learn to use it: our survival in that pre-computer era depended upon it. We had our choice of the Cooke radio slide rule or a log log duplex decitrig rule from Kueffel & Esser. Since Nelson M. Cooke, who designed the rule and wrote the math text we used, was the most renowned chief radio electrician in the Navy, practically running Bellevue, we naturally chose his slide rule. The cost of each was ten dollars.

Our instructors were mostly first class radiomen, obviously Reserves since they had neither hash marks nor campaign ribbons. What they did have, often, were Bronx accents, having been teachers of math, physics, and electronics at high schools and junior colleges in the New York area. In the opinion of the radiomen from the fleet, they were mere civilians in uniform who had found a good way to serve their country in safety. As I scribbled notes during the dry lectures, I sometimes wished I could have one of these patriots in a radio gang in the forward area.

Whether in class or at evening studies of math, trig, logarithms, vector algebra, and the theories of the mad dance of the atoms, I often wondered what the hell I was doing here. I cared little for this highly theoretical material. I could diagram an English sentence, but the complexities of circuit diagrams, where everything was reduced to symbols, was a different order of abstraction.

Then why not give up and flunk out? If I failed any of the monthly exams, I would be shipped off to new construction and a good chance of facing the kamikazes at Okinawa, where a massive U.S. invasion force had landed on 1 April. By 6–7 April some 350 suicide planes had attacked the ships off the beachhead, inflicting major damage according to the censored news reports—which meant it was much worse than that. The attacks continued, providing motivation for me to continue my studies. I needed a little more time before I was ready to again face the enemy and the petty chickenshit of officers such as Lees and Cramer.

Not all the fleet radiomen shared my feelings. Idling in the barracks one evening while I pored over the Annapolis refresher course and Cooke's math, one Regular with hashmarks said in disgusted tones:

"Look, I've handled plenty of hot circuits in the Sopac. I can send 25 wpm with my fist, and 35, 40 with my bug [speed key]. But I can't get a handle on this goddam algebra and Ohm's Law crap. What do they think I am—Einstein?"

Grinning, I asked: "What are you going to do about it?"

"Plenty. I'm gonna have me a helluva vacation. The first exam's in about two weeks. When I flunk, it'll take 'em another two, three weeks to ship me out. Then I'll have maybe two, three months while I wait for my ship. With any luck we'll have cleaned out the kamikazes before I get there."

That is exactly what he did. I was reminded of several senior firsts in the *California* before the war. Occasionally Chief Reeves would send one of these superlative operators to Bellevue radio materiel school at the Naval Research Laboratory in Anacostia, in those days a requisite for making chief or thin-stripe warrant. After reporting in, the designated students were given an extensive entrance exam. Nearly half the class would fail and be sent back to their former duty stations. While a few of our senior firsts went on to make chief or warrant, it was not unusual for one to report back to the *California* radio gang, still first class but well rested from the extended vacation the chief had given him. It is a commentary on the severe requirements at Bellevue that at least two who "bilged out" there were commissioned during the war. As would be expected, they were excellent communication officers.

Nothing better illustrates the dichotomy between radio operators and technicians (later electronic technicians) than an incident in the reminiscences of William Nameny. In the late 1930s he joined the Naval Reserves in Northern Indiana as third-class radioman because he had an FCC amateur (ham) license. By the time he volunteered for active duty in November 1940, he had taken the required exams and advanced to radioman first. He joined the crew of the old gunboat *Sacramento,* which was being returned to service; she arrived at Pearl Harbor "in the late summer or early fall of 1941; our primary assignment was to patrol the coast of Oahu from Diamond Head to Koko Head." Ambitious to make chief, Nameny passed a screening exam in math and was transferred off the gunboat exactly one month before the Japanese attack, scheduled for Bellevue and rapid promotion from student to instructor, from first class to warrant radio electrician and a commission. He writes:

I took the transport USS *Wharton* to San Francisco and once on board reported to the radio shack for assignment because those who didn't ended up swabbing decks or polishing brass.

There was one particular old-timer radioman first whose sole job was to copy fast press for the ship's newspaper. He never seemed to be in any uniform other than undress whites without the jumper. He would sit at the receiver, a mimeograph master rolled into his mill, and copy press at a speed where I was unable to recognize more than an occasional "the" or "and." As he finished each master he would rip it out and leisurely roll in another master while the code was coming in at an undecipherable rate. With no indication of panic, he would proceed to catch up on what had been sent. A striker would run the finished master down to the mimeograph room and stand by for the next one; so as fast as the news came in it was being processed.

He had a cigarette drooping from his lips, the smoke curling around his eyes. When he finished one cigarette he would casually reach over to a pack, fish out a cigarette, reach for his lighter and with no hint of hurry light up, take a puff or two, and then proceed to catch up with his copy.

I would have thought that the bustle and talk that went on in the radio shack might have distracted him, but he was fully aware of the trend of the conversation and occasionally would break in with a comment of his own. I had never before seen such casual competence in any radio operator; until then I had mistakenly thought I was a fair operator.*

As if the math and radio physics weren't enough, the "hands-on" side of the curriculum added to my burden. The laboratory was fully equipped, from drawing boards and tools for cutting and shaping metal to the latest in signal generators, cathode ray oscilloscopes, crystal oscil-

---

*William F. Nameny, letter to author, 19 September 1994. Like Leroy Nelson and Earl Marshall, previously cited, Nameny went on to an outstanding career in electronics, specializing in technical education. He had an interesting comment on the difference between the warrant and commissioned ranks:

"While I was a warrant [at Treasure Island] I used to regularly have young trainees come to me with their problems, and they felt perfectly comfortable discussing all sorts of family, marital and other problems with me. If there was anything I could do to help or to give them counsel, I would. However, after I received my commission all that ceased, although I was the same person that I was before. As Nelson M. Cooke had indicated to me [when Nameny was a student at Bellevue], there was something special about being a warrant."

lators, and frequency meters. We learned the use of this test equipment in "scoping out" radio receivers, along with translation of those baffling circuit diagrams, parts identification, and application of the soldering iron.

The only chance to relax in a schedule which began at 0800 and continued to 1700 hours, except for a dinner break, came in the audio-visual classes of slide presentations and 16-mm. films. I considered them largely a waste of time, since it was too dark to make notes or read a textbook. I did not learn from staring at a screen but from reading, followed, if possible, by doing.

At the end of each month of instruction, the students assembled in the recreation building and were seated at classroom-type desks. To eliminate any possibility of cheating, the examinations came from the Bureau of Navigation in sealed envelopes. The seals were ceremoniously broken by an officer in front of the class and distributed. At a signal we began, slide rules in hand, racing the clock for two hours. Those who flunked this ordeal—which a Catholic classmate labeled "an inquisition by Torquemada"—were soon on their way to new construction. The most dreaded assignments from the detailers, next to ammunition carriers, were destroyers, destroyer escorts, and destroyer minesweepers, ship types which were taking fearsome punishment on radar picket duty off Okinawa.

Even for those who passed the written exams, another trial remained. Each radioman was given a chunk of metal and a bewildering array of parts and wires. From that, he had to build an eight-tube superheterodyne AM receiver. If it failed to work, the hapless student was bilged out on the spot.

Using a template, the chassis was shaped and cut to accommodate the receiver. With a circuit diagram as a guide, the variable condensers, oscillator and demodulator circuits, vacuum tubes, resistors and condensers, filters, and speaker were assembled, using small tools and a soldering iron. But for the generous help of a classmate, a radio technician and former ham who whistled his way through this assignment, I would have failed. More than once he saw that I had misread the abstruse diagram and wired a lead to ground.

Finally my set was as ready as it ever would be. While I wiped sweaty palms on my dungarees and my benefactor beamed his confidence, the instructor turned on the power supply. We were rewarded by a warm-up hum and then the glorious sound of music from a Detroit radio station.

The instructor tuned across the dial. More stations came in.

"Got a little static there," he observed. "You need to brush up on your soldering. Okay, you pass. You can disassemble your set."

I had been at the school less than two weeks when I decided to visit a Dearborn cocktail lounge where, I had been told, the locals did indeed "roll out the barrel," using the beer to chase their schnapps. An occasional liberty was necessary to relieve the stress of long classroom days and evenings with books and slide rule.

I was waiting at the roofed shelter outside Gate 12 when a car stopped. The middle-aged driver looked somber; his wife was crying.

"Have you heard the news?" he asked.

I shook my head. The radio in my barracks, as usual, was turned off.

"Our president is dead." Roosevelt had passed away of a cerebral hemorrhage in Warm Springs, Georgia.

Everywhere I went that day, people were huddled around radios on the streets and in the stores, or were conducting wakes in the bars.

Dearborn was a working-class city of ethnic minorities, largely drawn from Eastern and Southern Europe. They regarded FDR as the man who saved the country from collapse, renewed their pride and dignity, restored their jobs. While I could not disagree, I did not fully share their sorrow. The president, in my opinion, was a sick man who increasingly had delegated his enormous wartime powers to the military chiefs of staff and to the industrialists who were producing the means of fighting a many-fronted war.

We were sustaining what I considered unacceptable casualties in our Pacific island-hopping campaign, and doubtless in Europe as well. Neither the president nor his top civilian deputies seemed to care. In concert with Churchill and Soviet dictator Joseph Stalin—and with a bare nod of recognition to Gen. Charles De Gaulle, the arrogant, stiff-necked supreme commander of the Free French armed forces, and to Chinese President Chiang Kai-shek (known irreverently to enlisted men as "Chancre Jack")—Roosevelt's failing energies had been devoted to negotiating the shape of the postwar world. I feared he had forgotten the common people who had four times elected him to his high office, the very ones who were now mourning his loss.

I recalled two relevant quotations from my readings while serving in the *Pawnee*. The brilliant Thomas Jefferson, one of my idols, wrote: "Offices are as acceptable here as elsewhere, and whenever a man has cast a longing eye on them, a rottenness begins in his conduct." The higher the office, the greater the harm. "Power tends to corrupt," Lord Acton wrote; "absolute power corrupts absolutely." I thought it would take a while for relatively unknown Harry Truman to become corrupted by his power as commander-in-chief of the armed forces of the most powerful nation in the world. I could not have known just how short that time would be.

On 7 May, less than a month after the death of Roosevelt, Gen. Alfred Jodl, the German chief of staff, signed his country's unconditional surrender documents at the Rheims headquarters of Gen. Dwight D. Eisenhower, Supreme Commander, Allied Expeditionary Force. The announcement of V-E Day on 8 May set off wild celebrations by huge crowds in New York, London, and Moscow.

The reaction in our barracks was more restrained. Hitler and Mussolini were dead, but the Japanese militarists were still in full control. Hideki Tojo, the bellicose, bullet-headed general who became premier in 1941, had reminded a shipmate of Pooh-Bah, Lord High Everything Else, in *The Mikado*. As architect with Admiral Yamamoto of the Pearl Harbor attack, he had proved anything but funny. He had resigned in 1944, however, over the loss of Saipan, and was replaced by another general, Kuniaki Koiso. We had no doubt that he and his fellow samurai, true to their Bushido code, would go down fighting, taking hundreds of thousands, if not millions, of their countrymen with them, and countless Americans as well.

Regardless of our misgivings, perhaps because of them, Carl and I decided a celebration was in order. In a dimly lit basement-level night club on the outskirts of Dearborn, which was well and favorably known in the radio school as "the passion pit," we met two young ladies of Slavic heritage I shall name Erika and Stella. After a few drinks they invited us to the home they shared in West Dearborn. We had progressed to necking in their living room when we were startled by a loud rat-a-tat and an even louder male voice.

"O my God!" Stella exclaimed, breaking away from Carl. "It's my husband—and he's got a gun. I thought he was driving his damn bus."

The knocks continued. "I know you're in there with two sailors," the man shouted. "Open up!"

Bus drivers and streetcar conductors were a surly lot at best, I had observed. What an ultimate irony if Carl and I had survived more than three years of war only to be gunned down by some jealous bus jockey.

"Battle stations," I told Carl. "You stand behind the door. I'll take this side. When he's leaning on it, jerk it open. I'll cold-cock him before he can use his gun—I hope. Back me up."

Meanwhile, Stella created a diversion. Racing to the front bedroom, she took a suitcase and pitched it through a window, which she hastily relocked.

"Take that and get out!" she screamed. "I never want to see you again."

The knocking ceased. "I'll be waiting for you sailors," the husband shouted, a final despairing threat. When we checked a little later, the suitcase was missing. Carl and I hadn't finished celebrating V-E Day. We decided to stay a while.

"How was I supposed to know?" Carl said later. "She wasn't wearing a ring."

"She used us to make a final break with her husband," I observed. "She had his suitcase all packed, and took a chance he might use his gun on us. The most dangerous campaign of all began in the Garden, when Eve outsmarted poor dumb Adam. It never ends."

At the end of July we survivors of pre-radio and three months of primary assembled for the final exam, which would determine our fate. I thought I had done poorly. But many others, even more perplexed than I at difficult subject matter that had to be digested so quickly, did worse. When the results were posted, I could hardly believe that I had finished 61st in a class of 189, just within the top third of a group that had originally numbered around 500.

Now we survivors were asked to list first and second choices of secondary schools. I selected Treasure Island in my home state. (Not all Westerners did; the T.I. base was well known for boot-camp regimentation.) Many Midwesterners chose Navy Pier, while those from the East Coast favored Bellevue. A final option, favored by the aviation-oriented, was Corpus Christi. My alternate selection was Bellevue; I had never been in the nation's capital, and I wanted to meet CRE Nelson Cooke, whose text and slide rule I carefully stowed in my sea bag.

Before leaving Dearborn, the entire graduating class was given a final overnight liberty. Although it was muggy midsummer, we wore dress blues with campaign ribbons and battle stars, mainly to distinguish our-selves from the civilian Navy. Someone suggested we were entitled to a special award for surviving the River Rouge's radio school: a slide rule rampant on a blood-red shield sprinkled with perspiration and tears.

Some sailors went to the "passion pit" and other Dearborn night-spots. Carl and I joined a small party at the upscale Book-Cadillac Hotel, located at the corner of Michigan Avenue and Washington Boulevard. The hotel's spacious garden-court lounge was a favored place to meet young ladies of the better class, along with occasional members of the demimonde. A classmate who was an ardent baseball fan described it as the best location in Detroit for "sharpening your batting average against the curve ball." He and I had attended a couple of big-league games in Tiger Stadium, where the right-field bleachers were free to servicemen. When the Detroit right fielder charged a ground-ball single and let it go through his legs to the wall for a triple, I could see that the draft had greatly diluted the talent pool; that sort of fielding error was a no-no even at the high-school level. Except for the pitching, the caliber of play was little better than in the Pacific Coast League, the top minor, which I had followed in the San Francisco *Chronicle*'s "green sheet" until I went into the Navy.

At the Book-Cadillac Carl was joined by his bride of a week. Ironi-cally, we had met her and a blonde companion here at this lounge a couple of months before. We double-dated two or three times, I with the brunette Carl was to marry. She and I quickly realized we did not like each other. Beneath a flashy facade, I found her shallow and coldly ambitious, while she obviously thought I was too Bohemian. I quoted poetry, dined at Russian and French restaurants, and had mentioned seeing a film version of Leoncavallo's opera *I, Pagliacci* at a Detroit art theater. By mutual agreement I dropped out, and Carl took over. On this last evening I could see that my presence made the bride uncom-fortable. I excused myself and went to the phone. Not long before I had met an eighteen-year-old Polish girl who gave me a ride to Detroit from Gate 12. Her blonde good looks and figure reminded me more than a little of Yvonne "Pat" Leckie in Sydney. Stephanie thought that poetry and *Pagliacci* were "dreamy." She picked me up at the entrance to the Book-Cadillac, and we drove to a lover's lane. Back at the barracks, I thought it a good thing I was leaving Dearborn very soon. Stephanie was altogether too attractive.

Later that morning the radiomen boarded a train for Chicago, where I transferred to a troop train for Oakland on the tracks of the Atchison, Topeka & Santa Fe. Carl had opted for Navy Pier. We parted with regret; we had shared some fine adventures. I thought his impulsive, liquor-laced marriage a mistake, but said nothing. Such wartime liaisons were common enough. We men coming back from war were more vulnerable than most to that powerful allure which has not changed from the time of "the old Adam."

The Santa Fe line was justly renowned for its all-passenger Chief, which made the nearly 2,000-mile run from Chicago to Los Angeles in forty hours. The only resemblances between the Chief and the train I was riding were that both carried no freight, only people, mail, and baggage, and were pulled by steam locomotives. Our troop train consisted of fourteen or fifteen sleepers, a baggage car, and another that had been converted to a galley; it served chow that reminded me of the *Pawnee*'s in the South Pacific.

The car in which I found myself with a couple of dozen other radiomen was of ancient vintage. It must have been slumbering in the weeds of some lonely siding since the end of the First World War, to be resurrected when the railroads recalled all their rolling stock for another war. Wheel flanges grinding, the car swayed and creaked arthritically on every curve. Since it had no air conditioning, the only relief from the stifling heat of the Midwest and Southwest was to open all the windows. I thought of the American Legion's "Forty et Eight" honor society, which a Ford workman, a Legionnaire, had told me about one evening in a Dearborn beer garden. The name was derived from the boxcars used in France during World War I; they accommodated forty men or eight horses.

But radiomen from the fleet are a resourceful lot. We shifted into T-shirts and dungarees. Someone provided a large galvanized-iron wash tub, which we filled with ice and beer. At every stop along the way—and there were many, for we had a low priority and were often held up in towns or shunted onto sidings while fast freights or passenger trains thundered past—we dispatched a working party to replenish our stocks. The elderly porter shook his gray head over the antics of "you young gentlemens" but did not report us to the Shore Patrol or his conductor; he even provided ice on occasion. To show our appreciation, we took up a collection for a generous tip.

All the way to Kansas City we had stowaways in our car: two Navy wives. The niggardly allowance for dependents permitted few frills in an enlisted man's marriage; here was a chance to save substantially on transportation. Obligingly, our porter made up two of the lower berths with extra pillows. Chuckling, he noted that the Army put two in a lower berth and one in an upper, but the Navy regulation called for one to a berth.

We enjoyed crisp white linens on our berths, but discovered in the mornings that our hair was so stiff from accumulated cinders and soot that it was difficult to force a comb through. Unable to take showers, we resorted to what we called "the Marine bath": wash cloth and soap in a basin of hot water. All we lacked to become real "ground-pounders," we grumbled, were helmets.

As I had on the trip east, I spent many hours at a window while the train labored toward California, often with a second "helper" engine on the grades and mountain ranges. We passed through cities and towns I had never seen before, and doubted I would see again:

Topeka; Amarillo; Albuquerque; Gonzales (near the top of the Continental Divide, at what I considered a modest elevation of 7,248 feet); Gallup in Navajo country (where we had dinner at Fred Harvey's El Navajo restaurant, admired the native blankets and jewelry, and bought souvenirs); Seligman, Arizona, turning our wristwatches back an hour for Pacific War Time. We crossed the Colorado River into Needles (a town I thought aptly named for its prickly heat), sweated through the Mojave Desert into Bakersfield, and rattled on up the San Joaquin Valley to Oakland. Our trip, with so much time spent "in the hole," in railroad terminology, had taken four days. We were transferred to buses for the short trip across half the eight-mile span of the San Francisco–Oakland Bay Bridge to Treasure Island. We reported to the secondary radio materiel school on 7 August.

As one of the commissioning crew of the *Pawnee*, I had taken a bus from Treasure Island's Barracks "E" to Alameda on 7 November 1942. Now, as we approached from the Bay Bridge ramp, I could see many changes over the past two years and nine months.

"Look at this mess," a Dearborn classmate said. "If the Navy built ships the way they do shore stations, they'd all sink when they're launched."

I agreed. Some of the original buildings from the Golden Gate International Exposition of 1939–40 were still standing, transformed into nondescript barracks, offices, and a mess hall. At least forty-five or fifty jerry-built structures, mostly of the H- or U-configuration, cluttered the island. At the north end, replacing the fighter airstrip of 1942, were an athletic field, the headquarters of the Armed Guard, and an ammunition-storage area. The only structure of any distinction was the scimitar-shaped administration building at the entrance, and the Navy had inherited it from the exposition.

"Temporary wartime construction," I said.

"Yeah," the other radioman replied. "That's the excuse for everything that's done in wartime. How much you want to bet that most of these eyesores are still here forty, fifty years from now?"

I didn't accept the wager. I wasn't sure that *we* would be around that long.

Ship's Service No. 1 was still in Barracks "I," very near the pedestal where the statue of Pacifica, ironically a symbol of peace among the nations bordering the Pacific Ocean, had once stood. Sailors could buy gedunks, hamburgers and milkshakes, toilet articles, wristwatches, rings, and other gift items. They could also buy, no questions asked, campaign ribbons and battle stars they might not have earned. To avoid identification with these heroes of the home front, I took mine off.

Much in evidence around ship's service, the mess hall, and elsewhere were German and Italian prisoners of war. They were housed on the San Francisco side of the island, near the bachelor officers' quarters. The scuttlebutt was that they were treated better than the American enlisted men. Walking around the island, I could understand the resentment. The atmosphere was cold and regimented, with many SPs and MPs in evidence.

The brig at the north end was filled with malefactors, confined mostly for petty offenses. Armed marines moved them everywhere at double time. The POWs, on the other hand, marched at regular time, the Germans making a special effort, by the smartness of their drill, to show up the lackadaisical Yanks.

Eugene Hildeman, a student at the radio materiel school when I arrived, reported on this rivalry:

There were many German POWs on T.I. who worked in the mess halls and performed other services. They usually marched around the base under the supervision of one or two armed guards. When we students would march from one class to another near them, they would laugh at

us because we were so sloppy in formation. Most of us were more interested in knob twirling than in military protocol.*

The radio materiel school occupied nine wooden buildings in the
center of the island, conveniently near the huge mess hall and bakery
(the former "foods and beverages palace" of the exposition). Six were
barracks, the standard two-story H-type; the other three were devoted
to classrooms, laboratories, and administration. The lab that housed the
ultra-secret radar gear could be identified by the cluster of antennas
protruding from its roof.

"Secondary school was conducted considerably different [sic] from
primary," Hildeman notes. "Much of the equipment was confidential,
and security measures around our classrooms were of a much higher
level. Some of the classrooms were surrounded by barbed-wire fences,
with guards at the entrances. . . .

"Most of our books were customized in notebook form. Many of
them were classified confidential and could not be removed from the
classroom. In addition, they were kept in a vault and had to be checked
out for each class and for evening study. We also used the equipment
maintenance manuals."†

I was assigned a bunk and locker on the first deck of one of the barracks. Most of my bunkmates were seamen, fresh-faced kids who had

---

*Letter to author, 31 July 1994. Hildeman had enlisted in the USNR from Alameda High
School in January 1945 and passed the Eddy screening test while in boot camp. He attended
pre-radio at Wright Junior College in suburban Chicago and primary RMS at the Del Monte
Hotel in Monterey, California. He was graduated from secondary school at T.I. with Class
97 as a radio technician third class, and was discharged from Mare Island in July 1946.

"My Navy technical education served me very well in civilian life," Hildeman comments. "It also provided me with a very enjoyable hobby. I easily obtained both my commercial and amateur FCC radio licenses. I was employed by Pacific Telephone (now Pacific Bell) as a technician and later as management. I retired as a district manager in
December 1983."

†Hildeman adds an amusing incident:

"About one month before my class graduated, Japan surrendered. . . . The Navy
decided to survey our intentions. Since most of us were USNR, they told us that if we
would sign over to the regular Navy, they would let us finish school and receive our RT
rate. Otherwise, we would be returned to regular duty as Seamen first class.

"To make the survey, they lined up all the students in the school and had us walk by
WAVE yeomen seated in chairs. If we were willing to ship over we should say 'yes' as we
passed the WAVE. Otherwise, we should say 'no.' These were the most attractive young
WAVES I had ever seen, and I don't think they ever had this many young men say 'no' to
them before or after this exercise. In any case, [the Navy] decided that students in the
classes with a short time to finish could do so regardless of their intentions."

taken math and engineering courses in high school or junior college; some were ham operators. All had passed the tough Eddy screening test and had been graduated from pre-radio and primary schools. None had ever been to sea.

At the first opportunity I called Dale Gerber at Oak Knoll Hospital and arranged to meet him in San Francisco. On the way to the reunion, I saw the screaming newspaper headlines at a kiosk on Market Street. We had just detonated a second nuclear device over the Japanese city of Nagasaki, nearly destroying it. The first bomb had been unleashed over Hiroshima on 6 August, and had been announced by President Truman the same day our troop train arrived in Oakland. Weary from the four-day trip and concerned with finding a shower and a decent meal, I had not read a newspaper and ignored the near-hysterical radio reports.

Now I bought a copy of the *Chronicle* and read it with increasing dismay. My stomach reacted as if I were still in the Solomon Islands. A weapon of unimaginable power which harnessed the atom, the basic energy of the universe, had devastated two Japanese cities, killing tens, perhaps hundreds of thousands, of children, women, and men. "What the hell have you people done?" I muttered aloud.

When I met Gerber at a nearby bar, I showed him the paper.

"A goddam super-bomb!" he exclaimed. "How do you figure it, buddy?"

"Ever see the old *Frankenstein* film?"

"Yeah, saw it when I was drivin' a hack in Salt Lake City."

"The mad Doctor F. was trying to play God, create life. What our mad scientists have done is Anti-God. They've found a way to destroy life— all life. Now no one is safe."

Gerber took a pragmatic view, pointing out that the bombs would shorten the war. "We're gonna be civilians soon!"

"Yeah, by slaughtering women and children. Why didn't this Pendergast politician arrange a demonstration for the Japs, drop a bomb offshore where it wouldn't kill the kids?"

My *Pawnee* shipmate believed that the A-bomb would save many American lives by canceling the planned invasion of Japan. But I thought of the price. From now on, the entire world was on standby for Armageddon. I hoped devoutly that all those responsible for unleashing this measureless horror upon our planet would have bad dreams.

"Forget your ulcer, buddy," I said. "Let's have another drink. Hell, let's have several drinks."

Shortly after my San Francisco liberty, I was called into the office of our barracks commander, a slick-arm chief boatswain's mate. I was sure he had no sea duty. He had been, I guessed, involved in high school or junior college athletics. His manner was that of a football coach motivating a member of his squad to greater efforts for good old Siwash.

"I've been looking at your record, Mason," he said. "We're glad to have you aboard. With your war record, you should be an inspiration for our younger students. I would like to make you my leading petty officer."

I had been expecting something like this. Before the bombs, I might have accepted. Some men prefer to give orders, most men to receive them.

"Chief, I've been a leading petty officer," I said. "Let me tell you how it is in the fleet. My superior put me in charge of the radio gang in my last ship. He spent all his time brown-nosing on the bridge. He made warrant and was shipped back to the States. I kept on running the radio gang. When an opening for OCS came along, I was passed over as too valuable to the ship. I'm sorry, but I must decline your offer."

The chief frowned; he was not accustomed to rejection. "I'm sorry to hear that, Mason. Your refusal to accept responsibility just might affect your status in this school."

I smiled at the veiled threat. "The only thing that might affect my status in this school, chief, is if I can't keep up with these whiz kids in the classroom."

Every morning the students were mustered in front of the barracks and marched to class. The morning after my refusal, the chief called me out of the formation. "Since you're a senior petty officer, Mason, I want you to take over the marching detail."

I had forgotten what little I had learned of close-order drill at San Diego Naval Training Station. But the best defense, when dealing with small-bore bureaucrats, is a good offense.

"Chief, do you think I marched my radiomen around the decks of my ship? I haven't marched since boot camp in 1940, repeat 1940." I turned to the class.

"Men," I said, "I'm not able to march. I have shrapnel in one knee from the attack on Pearl Harbor, where my ship was sunk."

The seamen were looking at me with a new respect. "I defer to your present squad leader; he's doing fine."

We marched to class. I brought up the rear, affecting a slight limp.

The instructor in my first class, a thin-stripe warrant radio electrician, gave a sobering outline of the curriculum:

Month 1: A review of basic electronics; power supplies.

Month 2: Communications receivers.

Month 3: Communications transmitters, antennas, and transmission lines.

Month 4: Sonar.

Month 5: Search radar.

Month 6: Fire-control radar; IFF; electronic countermeasures; special applications.

Month 7: Two weeks of instruction in new equipment and applications.

The young seamen seemed eager to tackle this daunting material. I felt the kind of anxiety my *Pawnee* skipper knew in the Solomons. By only the most intense study, plus a measure of luck, would I be able to navigate these reef- and shoal-strewn waters.

On Tuesday, 14 August 1945, President Truman announced the good news we had been expecting since the bombing of Hiroshima and Nagasaki and Russia's entry into the Asian war by attacking Japanese armies in Manchuria and Korea. Japan had surrendered, but not quite unconditionally: Hirohito must remain on the imperial throne. Truman agreed. It was a foolish concession, many sailors thought, considering the emperor as great a war criminal as the militarists whose puppet he was.

The announcement that the war was over unleashed a riotous two-day celebration across the country. Gerber and I joined in, drinking many a toast to victory, the "four musketeers," our great good fortune in surviving the Pacific war, peace, freedom for the many after long regimentation—and, of course, the girls of Salt Lake City, Sacramento, Sydney, and other places.

With my hangover came the realization that the national emergency which had kept me in the Navy since the summer of 1941 was over. The Army already had a point system for early discharge in place; the Navy would be obliged to follow soon. No matter what system was devised, I would qualify for a quick honorable discharge. I had enlisted in the Naval Communication Reserve in June 1939; volunteered for a year's active duty with the fleet in July 1940; was at Pearl Harbor when the

Japanese attacked in December 1941; had served in Pacific war theaters in the *Pennsylvania* and *Pawnee* for more than three years, returning to the States on 22 February 1945; had earned eight battle stars and a Philippine Republic Presidential Unit Citation.

The Navy recommended me for reenlistment. Should I accept? If I made it through secondary RMS—a large if—I would certainly be promoted to chief, possibly warrant. I knew I was not likely to be commissioned, short of another war. Like many children of adoption, I was deficient in respect for an authority that I had so often seen misused.

There was another factor, a probative one. I realized that I would never be more than a second-rate electronic technician. Quite simply, I lacked the innate aptitude required. If I went to college, where I could utilize my small talents for language and literature, I had a chance to be a first-rate journalist or teacher.

On 6 September, four days after the surrender documents were signed on board the battleship *Missouri* (chosen by the president to honor his home state), I left the RMS barracks to board a bus for Camp Shoemaker and my honorable discharge. A few of the seamen and the slick-arm chief bosun's mate were there to see me off.

"If I run across any of you guys some day," I said with a grin, "I'll buy you a beer and tell you about the real Navy."

But what was the "real Navy"? Certainly it was the Navy I would write of later in three memoirs, and it was much more than that.

It was a Navy of rigid hierarchical structure, of officers and enlisted men, segregated forever in an ancient class system of gentlemen and gobs, with the warrant officers, former "bluejackets," somewhere between.

It was a Navy capable of the most appalling blunders: Admiral Kimmel and his subordinates at Pearl Harbor; all three admirals—Turner, Fletcher (by his absence), Crutchley of the Royal Navy—involved in the crushing defeat at Savo Island; Wright at Tassafaronga. And it was a Navy capable of brilliant victories: Admirals Spruance and Fletcher at Midway; Commanders Moosbrugger and Burke in the Solomons; Spruance again in the Philippine Sea.

It was a Navy capable of the most resolute self-sacrifice: Admirals Callaghan and Scott and all the officers and men lost off Guadalcanal on "Bloody Friday the Thirteenth of November 1942"; the suicidal torpedo attacks of destroyers and destroyer escorts during the battle off

Samar in the Philippines when Admiral Halsey failed to properly cover his Leyte invasion forces.

It was a Navy capable, too, of the most flagrant examples of bias and discrimination: the prosecution of the civilian master of the SS *President Coolidge* to cover naval blunders; the RHIP policy of liquor for officers in the South Pacific, nothing for the enlisted men; the courts-martial of fifty black sailors for mutiny when they refused to resume loading ammunition following the Port Chicago disaster of June 1944.

It was a Navy capable of almost unbelievable heroism: Thomas J. Reeves, Robert Scott, Donald K. Ross at Pearl Harbor, to name but three holders of the Medal of Honor. It was also capable of permitting some officers, in pursuit of glory and career enhancement, to usurp credit earned by the valor of subordinates.

And it was a Navy where the sharing of hardships, of danger, and of second-class citizenship forged comradeship of a very high order. The friendships one made, as I well know, could and often did endure to the death and beyond.

It was a Navy part of me hated, and part of me loved.

Damn, I would miss it.

11

In Closing

I often show visitors my study, a comfortable room whose picture window affords a view of Devil's Lake, a half-mile from the Pacific Ocean on Oregon's central coast. I have made it a refuge that reflects my background and interests, with many books, a few paintings, art objects, framed awards and plaques, and other memorabilia. What guests will not find are photos of me with prominent men; the few I have are put away in my photo files. Here I was influenced by W. Somerset Maugham, who wrote in *The Summing Up:* "I have always wondered at the passion many people have to meet the celebrated. The prestige you acquire by being able to tell your friends that you know famous men proves only that you yourself are of small account."

After a recent visitor ignored everything of substance in the room to pick up two .50-caliber machine-gun shells that had been converted to cigarette lighters during World War II, I took a closer look around my sanctuary. I was surprised to see that most of its contents were devoted to *the* war. It has become a cliché that war is the defining experience in the lives of most veterans, but it is true, nonetheless. On a wall of my study I see the plaque I was given when *"We Will Stand by You"* won the John Lyman award for American Naval History. Above it is a certificate, also from the North American Society for Oceanic History, testifying that *Battleship Sailor* was awarded first honorable mention in the same competition eight years before. That plaque and that piece of parchment represent more than a decade of research, writing, rewriting, and dealing with publishers—and that does not include the additional years that have been devoted to this, my third naval memoir.

I sometimes think I must be mildly deranged to have spent so much of my time and energy on books which, while they have been praised by critics and readers, have provided such a modest financial return. I would have done better, in a material way, if I had been writing commercial bilge. Why didn't I, then?

During the war, one of the few books I found space for in my cramped shipboard locker was the *Rubáiyát of Omar Khayyám,* which so perfectly expressed the philosophy of many men at war. Two lines which advised seizing the present moment at the expense of the uncertain future exclaimed: "Ah, take the Cash, and let the Credit go, / Nor heed the rumble of a distant Drum!" Those who live to write naval memoirs must reverse the sentiments, aware always of that drumbeat's sure increase in volume.

The name on the title page, then, must be one of the great, if intangible, rewards of writing war memoirs. Some years ago an attorney of my acquaintance, aware of the media attention I was receiving for *Battleship Sailor,* leafed through the book and offered his critique: "You've been on a big ego trip!" "That may be," I agreed, "but my ego trip has put me into the Library of Congress. Where has yours put you?"

But that is only one reason for taking the credit over the cash. Four shelves of one tall bookcase in my study are devoted to naval literature, with many pocket books stored elsewhere. They are devoted almost entirely to the essentially elitist perspectives of the decision-makers, and the historians and journalists who come to praise them. Where, I asked, were the stories of the white hats, the enlisted men who did the fighting and dying to such scant recognition? Histories that ignore or slight their contributions are not complete histories. I found but a few books written from the white hat's perspective, and the bulk of those were self-published to as little recognition as the authors and their messmates had received from the naval historians. (And it must be admitted that these volumes often fail to meet professional standards.) This convinced me that writing my own memoirs would be a worthy project. That the Naval Institute Press, located in that citadel of the military establishment, the Naval Academy at Annapolis, has now published all three of my books is a source of wonder to some, and of deep satisfaction to the author.

It is another truism that, for a writer to write well, he must bring a near-total commitment to his work. A glance around my study illustrates the extent of my involvement. Dominating one wall (and, indeed, the room) is the 24- by 36-inch painting of the *Pawnee* under torpedo attack in Blanche Channel, the one which appeared on the dust jacket of *"We Will Stand by You."* Hanging nearby is the commission pennant that flew from the staff at the top of the mainmast on that unforgettable 30 June

1943, a gift from Mary George, the widow of the ship's then-command-ing officer. The signatures of some *Pawnee* officers are still faintly legible.

On another wall are two photos in black and white of my ship, the *California*, burning and sinking during that other event that is branded into my memory, the attack on Pearl Harbor. A framed display of my medals and campaign ribbons might be considered a second ego-trip, but I do not so regard it. After I gave the keynote address at Pearl Harbor on 7 December 1990, I signed copies of my two naval memoirs. On the table before me, beside the books to be signed, was my Pearl Harbor Survivors garrison cap, with three rows of campaign ribbons. A lad of thirteen or fourteen paused in front of the cap and ran his fingers lov-ingly across the brightly colored ribbons. He who was just entering puberty sensed what they symbolized: recognition that I had passed a test of manhood.

There are other mementos of rites of passage in my study. A diorama to scale of *Pawnee* towing *Houston* to safety from the waters of Formosa, a gift from my staunch *California* shipmate, Robert H. "Rebel" Boulton. A paperweight from the *New Jersey,* sent by a chief gunner's mate from the "Jersey" as a thank-you for signing his copy of my battleship mem-oir. An old white hat. An Acme beer can, an exact replica of ones from which I drank at the Pearl Harbor Sub Base in 1941. A figurine of an "Old Salt," a ship's logbook in hand. A nautical clock. A certificate of membership in The Society of Wireless Pioneers. I don't want to feel that old, a grizzled survivor from the days of Morse code, the hand key, and the Fox schedule, but that is what I have become. My consolation is that it is better to be a pioneer than not to be one.

Another indication of the echoing drumroll of time is on display atop a cabinet: my elderly Underwood manual typewriter, purchased in the mid-1950s, a near-duplicate of the ones I found in Navy radio shacks (except that the latter had all-cap keys). I used it to pound out the numerous drafts of *Battleship Sailor.* When I started *"We Will Stand by You,"* I advanced with some reluctance to a Smith-Corona electric; it served, but it will never occupy a place of honor in my study. Bowing to the inevitable, *Rendezvous with Destiny* was written and rewritten on a computer. These advances in technology have made the physical act of writing easier (and much more expensive); they have contributed little or nothing to its quality.

Not everything in my study relates directly to the Navy. I have a framed wall certificate of my lifetime membership in Phi Kappa Phi, the national scholastic honor society. That award would not have been possible, of course, but for my six years in the service, five of them on active duty. I have other keepsakes, my most prized one a statuette in alabaster of the famous sculpture "Boy with Thorn." My great-uncle, the Rev. Lyman R. Bayard, acquired it in Rome on a trip to the Holy Land in the 1920s. Most important of all are the photos on my desk of my wife, Rita, who has provided the balance and stability that are the requisites for any sustained achievement, even so modest a one as mine.

I have maintained a rather extensive correspondence with old sailors, and a few young ones. Many are vehement in their condemnation of American society today, and the Navy which it supports, a Navy which now enlists women for shipboard duty, and even homosexuals. They are convinced that such developments indicate a country in a severe ethical and moral decline, one that will leave us, at some time in the near future, in mortal danger which we will lack the means and the will to survive.

Consider this vivid word-picture of a society about to fall:

There is no one, any more, in whom enlightening goodness prevails; no real wise man, no saint, no one uttering truth and standing by his sacred word. . . . Old people, destitute of the true wisdom of old age, try to behave like the young, and the young lack the candor of youth. The social classes have lost their distinguishing, dignifying virtues; teachers, princes, tradespeople and servants sprawl alike in a general vulgarity. The will to rise to supreme heights has failed; the bonds of sympathy and love have dissolved; narrow egotism rules. Indistinguishable ninnies conglomerate to form a sticky, unpalatable dough. When this calamity has befallen the once harmoniously ordered City of Man, the substance of the world organism has deteriorated beyond salvage, and the universe is ripe for dissolution.

This description of a perishing society could have been drawn from our newspaper and television coverage of the decades since the end of World War II. In fact, it appears in the *Matsya Purana*, a classic of the Hindu religion, which dates the decline to at least three thousand years ago.*

*The quotation is taken from Nancy Wilson Ross, *Three Ways of Asian Wisdom* (New York: Simon and Schuster, 1966), p. 66.

Rather more recently, the Roman Empire appeared to reach an apogee of corruption during the reigns of Augustus, Tiberius, Caligula, Claudius, and Nero (27 B.C.–A.D. 68), as luridly depicted in the British television series *I, Claudius*. Many citizens of that era doubtless predicted that the empire would soon fall from the weight of its moral depravity. Instead, it endured for another three hundred years.

Still, the words of Thomas Jefferson, our illustrious third president, author of the Declaration of Independence, are cautionary. In his *Notes on the State of Virginia*, he wrote: "Indeed, I tremble for my country when I reflect that God is just."